W9-CTT-187

Table of Contents

Chapter 1: Introduction

Chapter 2: Theoretical Perspectives of Physical Literacy in Children

Chapter 3: Children with Disabilities / Inclusion

Chapter 4: Balance and Stability Skills

Chapter 5: Locomotor Skills

Chapter 6: Manipulative Skills in Games

Chapter 7: Planning and Assessment Strategies

CHAPTER 1: *Introduction*

PURPOSE OF THIS BOOK

The *Educator's Guide to Teaching Fundamental Movement Skills* book has been designed as a resource for post secondary students who are in the discipline of physical education, kinesiology, recreation and leisure, and education. Teachers, leaders, and coaches may also use the resource and adapt the activity ideas to suit each particular situation. The book pertains to pre-adolescent children who are in the Active Start, FUNdamentals, and Learning to Train stages of the Long-Term Athlete Development (LTAD) program. This book is designed to provide the following:

- A description of the mature movement pattern for the fundamental motor skills;
- Specific tips to help the teacher develop these motor skills in their students;
- A number of activities that utilize motor skills;
- Targets movement educators of pre-adolescent children;
- Builds on foundational loco-motor, stability, and manipulative skills that have been developed in the Active Start and FUNdamentals stages;
- Emphasizes more advanced (specialized) elaborations and combinations of movement skills that can be applied or transferred to a variety of sport, recreational, or active living settings such as dance, gymnastics, games, track and field, fitness and outdoor adventures;
- Broadens its focus beyond skill development by integrating developmentally appropriate knowledge and understanding (e.g., skill cues and characteristics, tactical decision-making) with emotional (e.g., self-control), motivational (e.g., perceived competence), social (e.g., life skill such as respect) and spiritual (e.g., meaning joy) outcomes; and,
- Transitions to more sport-specific qualities.
- Provide adaptations for children with physical and developmental disabilities.

The resource aims to assist with planning and delivering quality learning experiences that support the development of fundamental and specialized skills.

The activities in this book are intended to supplement physical education lessons. There has not been content included that would act as a lead-up to these activities in a lesson with a full progression. Teachers still need to design learning experiences (e.g. lesson plans) that develop the motor skills included in the provincial/territorial physical education curriculum documents and the Long-Term Athlete Development model. The list of equipment associated with each activity is only a suggestion and alternative equipment may be substituted. It is also recommended that participants be allowed some choice in the types of equipment they use for the activities. For example, some students may find it easier to strike, field, catch, and throw a tennis ball than a baseball. Creativity and choice adds fun to the learning of specialized skills and creates a movement experience where every student feels successful.

A DEFINITION OF PHYSICAL LITERACY

A main outcome of this resource is the development of physical literacy among children. Physical and Health Education Canada (PHE Canada) defines physical literacy as:

Individuals who are physically literate move with competence in a wide variety of physical activities that benefit the development of the whole person.

- Individuals – celebrates the unique abilities and characteristics of each individual
- Competence – able to perform skills in ways that are optimally proficient for themselves
- Wide Variety of Physical Activities – exposed to a wide variety of physical activities to develop a repertoire of skills
- Whole Person – physical development (e.g., fitness, skill development), cognitive development (e.g., thinking, understanding, problem-solving skills), social skills (e.g., positive peer interactions, communication, teamwork, cooperation)

This definition is more holistic than the more sport-based definition provided by sport-based organizations such as the Canadian Sport Centre which defines physical literacy as: "...the development of fundamental movement skills and fundamental sport skills that permit a child to move confidently and with control, in a wide range of physical activity, rhythmic (dance) and sport situations."

Educational notions of physical literacy should reflect the *balanced emphasis* placed on youngster's physical, social, mental, emotional, motivational, and spiritual development. For example, according to the definition of PHE Canada, *physically literate individuals consistently develop the motivation and ability to understand, communicate, apply, and analyze different forms of movement. They are able to demonstrate a variety of movements confidently, competently, creatively and strategically across a wide range of health-related physical activities. These skills enable individuals to make healthy, active choices throughout their life span that are both beneficial to, and respectful of, their whole self, others, and their environment.* This resource will help all movement educators foster equal and equitable access to the development of the skills, knowledge, and attitudes needed to become physically literate.

THE IMPORTANCE OF MOVEMENT

The movement experience that children engage in should be meaningful to them, allowing the experience to enhance their learning and understanding. As children evolve into adults, movement plays a pivotal role in the acts of life. Movement can be viewed as a means of communication, that is expressed through actions rather than words (Department of Education and Science, 1972). Therefore the engagement and exposure to a variety of different movement forms (dance, games, gymnastics and fitness) and experiences is critical in developing a child's language of movement or physical literacy. As a child begins to engage in movement he or she should do so at a developmentally appropriate level and at a level of progression. The beginning stage would be to learn basic movement and the development of fundamental movement skills. **Fundamental movement skills** are the foundation or building blocks of movement; they provide individuals with the understanding and skills to be able to advance to more complex and sport-specific skills. These foundational motor skills are critical in individuals developing a passion for engagement in physical education, physical activity and sport. If they have not been worked on and matured later participation may be difficult and displeasing. Rates of child and youth participation in movement experiences like physical activity and sport tend to be higher when participants:

- Value and enjoy their experiences;
- Choose, rather than are forced to, participate;
- Have supportive and active parents and siblings;
- Are capable performers and, perhaps more importantly, perceive themselves so;
- Are accepted by their peers;
- Exhibit intrinsically oriented goals;
- Do not experience chronic anxiety from performance pressure; and,
- Have instructors who teach using a democratic style that foster feelings of autonomy, competence and support.

The fundamental movement skills can be characterized into three types of categories: stability and balance, locomotion, and manipulation skills. **Stability and balance** focus upon the creation of equilibrium so that the body stays steady. **Locomotion** skills refers to the ways in which the body travels across an area for running, galloping and skipping. Finally, **manipulation** refers to the controlling of an object. Object manipulation can be executed with and without the use of an implement. An example with an implement would be hockey where the stick is used to manipulate the puck as opposed to soccer where the manipulation is done with the use of the feet.

PHE Canada
Physical & Health Education Canada

MATURATIONAL DIFFERENCES IN CHILDREN AND YOUTH

There is wide variability in physical maturation levels of children and youth. Haywood and Getchell (2001) note that development is influenced both by nature (e.g., heredity) and nurture (e.g., environment, training), and is related to, but not determined by, age. For example, age of onset of puberty can vary by several years. Early maturing boys tend to be stronger and taller than later maturing boys. This provides them with performance advantages in sport earlier in later childhood and early adolescence. However, late maturing boys tend to catch-up in late adolescence and may surpass the physical capabilities of their early-maturing peers. In girls, the trend tends to be reversed. Their early maturation is associated with being heavier than in late adolescence so girls maturing later may have performance advantages in skills related to vertical jump. Another important developmental factor to consider when teaching or coaching children and youth is the differences between sexes that typically exist. For example, girls on average are more physically mature than males (by approximately one year in early childhood and two years at puberty).

A DEVELOPMENTAL APPROACH TO MOTOR SKILL DEVELOPMENT

The teaching tips in this book are based on a developmental approach to teaching children. **The developmental approach considers that although children are the same chronological age (e.g., most grade one students are six years old) there will be a wide range of development in terms of their abilities to perform the motor skills** outlined in this handbook. These developmental differences are a result of the variation among individuals and their behaviours and opportunities. It is critical that teachers and coaches understand and adopt the developmental approach, since they are usually teaching and coaching children of the same age group, many of whom vary tremendously in their ability to perform specific motor skills.

Another principle of the developmental approach to teaching/coaching is that all motor skills develop according to a predictable sequence: from movement that is immature, to movement that assumes the look of the mature pattern. Learners of motor skills tend to progress through three phases (Fitts & Posner, 1976). First, they enter the early stage, a relatively short "cognitive" phase in which they focus their attention on critical cues about the entire skill to mentally picture the skill and how it should be performed. Since the focus is on understanding, skill improvement may be slow, and contribute to a higher risk of burn out or giving up. In the second (intermediate or "associative") phase, the learner is able to utilize the kinesthetic "feeling" of the skill established in the first phase as they apply more focused effort on improving and refining the actual performance of the skill. Eventually, proficient movers or mature movers are mechanically efficient, can often coordinate several skills, apply the skills to highly variable settings, make more strategic and rapid decisions, better detect and correct errors, and have more knowledge about the skill (Doyle, 2001).

Most youth aged 8 to 14 are in a transitional period of motor development in which they refine their motor and perceptual-motor abilities, fitness status, and fundamental movements and apply them to more elaborate combinations of fundamental movements and specialized movement settings in sports and recreational activities. For some motor skills (e.g., over arm throwing) researchers have identified specific stages of development. For other motor skills (e.g. log roll) research has not provided the documentation to identify specific stages of development so the authors have utilized common knowledge of these

motor skills to identify stages of development. In this handbook, the motor skills described fall into both categories as most fundamental skills have extensive research documenting the stages of development. However, there is less extensive documentation for the steps of development for some skills such as the log roll and dodging.

FUNDAMENTAL TO SPECIALIZED SKILLS (READINESS AND MATURE MOVERS)

It is also important for teachers to realize that just because a child or youth is in a less mature stage of development, it does not mean that their movement pattern is wrong. With practice, and in conditions that are developmentally appropriate, the child or youth will develop more mature movement patterns. Of course, some remediation of the perceptual-motor and more basic fundamental movements may be necessary. However, the key is for teachers and coaches to identify the practice conditions and activities that will support this maturation. Cote and Hay (2002) cite studies reporting that children tend to drop out of sport because of "interest in other activities, lack of fun, lack of playing time, too little success, loss of motivation, dislike of the coach, overemphasis on competition and performance, and hard physical training". They add that play and enjoyment are critical components of a child's early sport experience and that the emphasis should be on "deliberate play" (developmentally purposeful) not "early specialization" or "intense training." As participants opt for increasingly specialized sporting challenges, they can experience more "deliberate practice" which is more structured, informative, and challenging. It is important to guard against specializing youngsters too early in sport settings. The American Academy of Pediatrics (Cote & Hay, 2002) recommends against participation in organized sports for those under six years of age or specializing in one sport prior to age fourteen.

LONG-TERM ATHLETE DEVELOPMENT MODEL

The Long-Term Athlete Development (LTAD) Model is a seven-stage model that provides a general framework of athlete development. Part of the Canadian Sport for Life, the Long-Term Athlete Development framework aims to embed developmentally appropriate structures within the sport, recreation, and education systems. The model acknowledges that physical education, school sports, competitive sports, and recreational activities are interdependent.

The first three stages of the model- Active Start, FUNdamentals, and Learning to Train- focus on developing children's physical literacy and movement skills. Stages four to six- Training to Train, Training to Compete, and Training to Win- focus on developing excellence. Lastly, stage seven- Active for Life- encourages lifelong physical activity. The focus of this book is stage one (Active Start), stage two (FUNdamentals), stage three (Learn to train) with a movement to stage seven (Active for Life).

Physical Literacy for Life
A Model for Physical Education

Individuals who are physically literate move with competence in a wide variety of physical activities that benefit the development of the whole person (Physical and Health Education Canada, 2010).

ACTIVE FOR LIFE

active leisure *fitness* *recreational activities*
therapeutic activities *competitive training and sport*
activities of daily living

MOVEMENT APPLICATIONS
(e.g., Increased Adaptations, Options, Voluntary Play, Protocols, and Transferability)

FUNDAMENTALS
(e.g., Perceptual-Motor Ability and Motor Abilities;
Free Play and Guided Play; Transport, Stability and
Object-Control Skills; Combinations, Elaborations, and Applications)

ACTIVE START
(e.g., Motor Abilities, Perceptual-Motor Ability, Rhythm,
Free Play and Guided Play, and Creative Exploration)

MATURE INTERMEDIATE EARLY

COGNITION

Knowledge
(e.g., of what, how, when, and why)

Beliefs, Values, and Morals
(e.g., commitment, self-confidence)

Decision-Making
(e.g., overcoming challenges)

Self-Regulated and Aware
(e.g., ongoing management)

Healthy Living

Motivation
(e.g., enjoyment, self-confidence)

MOVEMENT

Fundamental Movements

Movement Combinations

Cooperative Activities

Games
(Target, Striking/Fielding,
Net/Wall, Territorial)

Dance

Educational Gymnastics

Alternative Activities
(e.g., hiking, swimming, yoga, martial arts,
curling, skiing, spin cycling, jogging)

AFFECT

Social Well-being
(e.g., empathy and cooperation
with others)

Emotional Well-being
(e.g., self-control, resilience,
managing stress)

Spiritual Well-being
(e.g., sense of purpose,
personal accomplishment)

Environmental Health
(e.g., active transportation,
connection to nature)

Culturally Responsive

PHE Canada
Physical & Health Education Canada

Figure 1

An Explanation of Physical Literacy for Life: A Model for Physical Education

This evolving and dynamic model (Figure 1) of physical literacy for life is intended for use by educators to provide a visual summary in order that physical literacy will be promoted at various levels of dissemination. The model reflects the "what" of physical literacy, (general concepts) according to Physical and Health Education Canada's definition of physical literacy, and does not reflect "how" to deliver physical literacy (pedagogy).

The Physical Literacy for Life model emphasizes life-long development of physical literacy with active for life as the central aim. Physical Literacy stems from three pillars or dimensions of a physically literate person: cognitive, motor (movement), and affect (social, emotional, spiritual) while also linking to health and nature (the environment). Movement takes the central position and has enjoyable play as a central theme. It is bordered by the cognitive and affective dimensions all of which integrate continuously throughout the life-span. The wide variation in maturation and development by age and the lack of credible cut-off age-points for various characteristics of such warrants the use of developmental clusters (early, intermediate, and mature) rather than age or grade levels. The circular arrows between the phases and dimensions reflect the ongoing recursive and spiralling nature of the interactions between each.

RESOURCE ORGANIZATION

In Chapter Two the literature concerning teaching and organizational strategies will be discussed, focusing on physical literacy, physical activity, fundamental movement skills, and stages of development. Chapter Three discusses the importance of inclusion and provides strategies to facilitate inclusion in physical education. The fundamental movement skills of stability and balance will then be explored in Chapter Four, providing characteristics and cues on various skills. There are also activities outlined and teaching tips to help develop the various skills and to provide extra guidance for children experiencing difficulties. Chapter Five presents the fundamental movement skills of locomotion. The chapter provides characteristics and cues on various ways to travel as well as activities and teaching tips to assist in the development of skills. Subsequently, Chapter Six examines manipulative skills presenting in a similar format as chapters three and four, characteristics and cues of the skills, activities, and teaching tips to guide skill development. Finally, Chapter Seven provides an explanation and exemplars of assessment and evaluation strategies that could be used to assess the readiness and mature movement patterns of students.

In addition to the general content for teaching fundamental motor skills to children with typical development, where possible, content has been added for most skills with adaptations and teaching strategies for children with physical disabilities and children with developmental and/or behavioural disabilities.

CHAPTER 2:
Theoretical Perspectives of Physical Literacy in Children

A significant amount of attention is being given to the concept of physical literacy in Canada. The term is helpful in the shift from specific sports skill development toward fundamental movement skills in both coaching development and community recreation. It is also becoming a key component in the evolution of physical education curriculum for practitioners, teachers, and researchers.

Since there has been a move away from physical education specialist teachers in the public education system, there has been less emphasis on physical education pedagogy or the way in which we teach. Politics dictate course of action in education and any alteration in course will be dependent on changing the attitude of decision makers. Advocates of physical education and physical activity have an opportunity to mobilize with the emergence of physical literacy. This politically shrewd term has the potential to help enhance the profile and importance of quality daily physical education in schools.

This chapter explores the relationship of physical literacy to the acquisition of fundamental movement skills in every child's development. The meaning, significance, and philosophical rationale of physical literacy and its role in undergraduate education are also discussed.

PHYSICAL LITERACY

The matriarch of physical literacy, Margaret Whitehead, from the United Kingdom, is largely responsible for the development of the philosophical groundwork and rationale of the concept. Her work is primarily based on her holistic perspective of people: one where the body and mind are not considered separate (Whitehead, 2001). Whitehead believes that there are different dimensions to each individual and that anything that happens to a single element affects the whole person. This belief stems from (and is aligned with) the philosophers such as Sartre (1943) and Merleau-Ponty (1962) who suggest that we are the result of the interactions we have with our surroundings and that we are, by nature, 'beings of the world'.

Whitehead's (2007) short definition of physical literacy includes four key elements (p. 282):

1. Physical literacy can be described as the ability and motivation to capitalize on our motile potential to make a significant contribution to the quality of life. As humans we all exhibit this potential; however, its specific expression will be particular to the culture in which we live and the motile capacities with which we are endowed.

2. An individual who is physically literate moves with poise, economy, and confidence in a wide variety of physically challenging situations. Furthermore, the individual is perceptive in 'reading' all aspects of the physical environment, anticipating movement needs or possibilities, and responding appropriately to these with intelligence and imagination.

3. A physically literate individual has a well-established sense of self as embodied in the world. This, together with an articulate interaction with the environment, engenders positive self-esteem and self-confidence. Furthermore, sensitivity to, and awareness of, our embodied capacities leads to fluent self-expression through non-verbal communication, and to perceptive and empathetic interaction with others.

4. The individual has the ability to identify and articulate the essential qualities that influence the effectiveness of his/her own movement performance, and has an understanding of the principles of embodied health, with respect to basic aspects such as exercise, sleep, and nutrition.

Physical literacy is a capacity that everyone can achieve within their own sphere of being (Whitehead, 2007). She argues that no matter how limited an individual's capacities, such as in respect of those with embodied impairment, any increase in physical literacy will have a marked effect on quality of life. Motile capacities such as agility, balance, coordination, flexibility, speed, strength, power, rhythm, spatial awareness, and endurance are embodied capabilities that are unique to each individual and are related to one's ability to move with poise, economy, and confidence (Whitehead, 2005). These abilities serve as an indicator of how important fundamental movement skills (FMS) are when aspiring to achieve physical literacy. The fourth key element of Whitehead's physical literacy definition reinforces the importance of a holistic perspective and guides physical educators in their effort to help children develop a positive attitude about physical activity and healthy lifestyle choices.

One element missing in Whitehead's earlier definition of physical literacy was any reference to the social and cultural contexts in which we learn and use movement. It did not recognize how certain repertoires of being (including movement) are socially constructed in relation to gender, class, and race, and how some forms of movement have relevance for particular social and cultural contexts (Wright &Burrows, 2006). Whitehead's (2010) book, *Physical literacy: Through the lifecourse,* acknowledges the unique challenges and opportunities in varying demographics and cultures. She believes that human beings are all capable of developing and enhancing physical literacy and the distinctive world in which individuals live will foster a particular deployment of their embodied capability (Whitehead, 2010).

A CANADIAN PERSPECTIVE OF PHYSICAL LITERACY

The proposed definition of Physical Literacy for Canadian physical educators is intended to bridge the gap between sport and Physical Education. The Physical and Health Education Canada (PHE Canada) abbreviated definition is: "Individuals who are physically literate move with competence in a wide variety of physical activities that benefit the development of the whole person" (Mandigo, Francis, Lodewyk & Lopez, 2009, p. 28). Three key elements of the PHE Canada's definition state that physicaly literate individuals:

1. consistently develop the motivation and ability to understand, communicate, apply, and analyze different forms of movement;

2. are able to demonstrate a variety of movements confidently, competently, creatively, and strategically across a wide range of health-related physical activities; and,

3. possess the knowledge and skills to make healthy, active choices that are both beneficial to, and respectful of, their whole self, others, and their environment.

The flexibility intended in the educational description allows for personalized proficiency during the process of skill acquisition. It also addresses the development of the whole child from the perspective of the physical, cognitive, social, and affective domains (Mandigo et al., 2009). There are many other similar and relevant definitions, such as the Canadian Sport for Life (CS4L) version which reads: "Physical literacy is defined as the development of fundamental movement skills and fundamental sport skills that permit a child to move confidently and with control, in a wide range of physical activities, rhythmic (dance) and sport situations" (Higgs, Balyi, Way, Cardinal, Norris, & Bluechardt, 2008, p. 5). Not only should children be exposed to a wide variety of activities but also those activities should take place in a variety of settings. Physical literacy relies on the development of confidence and physical competence which should be experienced in the following environments:

On the ground – Any solid surface such as gym floors, grass, sand or cement. The majority of games, dancing, and sports take place on this type of surface.

Off the ground – Maintaining an awareness of where one is situated in the air is a difficult accomplishment that requires practice. Participating at a young age in airborne activities such as jumping on the trampoline, diving, or gymnastics skills will help increase an individual's responsiveness when off their feet for whatever reason.

In an aquatic environment – Being physically active in swimming pools, lakes, rivers, and/or oceans is not only advantageous from a perspective of physical literacy, but can also save lives. Every child should learn to swim and by extension, learn to move comfortably without fear in or on the water. Activities such as paddling, rowing, surfing, sailing, and water skiing require a certain degree of water confidence before a person can begin to master the more complex tasks of dynamic balance and stability in and on water. Other water sports such as snorkeling, SCUBA diving, water polo, diving and synchronized swimming all rely on swimming in one way or another.

In a winter environment – Many Canadians spend a good deal of time in snowy or icy environments. In order to fully capitalize on the opportunity to be active in the winter, balancing on snow and ice is a necessity. Snowshoeing and skating at a young age translate into confidence on a snowboard or on downhill and cross-country skis.

While other scholars have published definitions of physical literacy (Kentel & Dobson, 2007; Killingbeck, Bowler, Golding, & Gammon, 2007; UK Sports, 2002), they may be narrower and may not address the breadth of concept as it was originally intended.

PHYSICAL LITERACY IN SCHOOL

The most important objective in any physical education program is to instil a positive attitude about health and physical activity in every student. Unfortunately, over 12 years of physical education classes not every student's experience of physical education is personally rewarding and filled with the joy of movement. A quality physical education program coupled with a balanced lifestyle at home offers a world of active opportunities in much the same way that learning to read and write do. Language literacy and numeracy are two core measures of success in any school district; equally important is the pursuit of physical literacy that stems from having an enriching experience in K-12 physical education.

Physical literacy promotes the idea that each individual has their own potential physical ability and physical education should be focusing on providing opportunities and learning experiences for individuals to discover their own potential. Essentially, to become physically literate, a child needs to be able to perform basic movement competencies (within their own physical capacity), apply these in a variety of situations and activities, understand how they can learn further, and have the internal motivation to do so independently. (Haydn-Davies, 2005, p. 46)

The fight against the increasing prevalence of overweight children is a shared responsibility in which schools, families, and communities play an important role. Establishing a habit of making healthy choices and engaging in daily physical activity throughout a lifetime certainly helps in this struggle for children. Mastery of fundamental movement skills has been shown to be an important factor in preventing unhealthy weight gain among children and youth (Okely, Booth & Chey, 2004). However, the development of those basic skills is dependent on the ability of a physical educator, leader, or coach to balance major considerations. Aside from environmental limitations, the two biggest constraints to motor learning are the difficulty of the task and the skill level of the learner (Okely et al., 2004; Hay & Cote, 1998). Csikszentmihalyi (1990) suggests that 'flow' exists when challenge and ability are in balance in the learning situation. This equilibrium is an important aspect in the development of an intrinsic motivation to participate in physical activity, as well as a task which is meaningful to the student (Wall and Murray, 1994).

A quality daily physical education experience during the elementary school years is the foundation upon which children establish competency in basic movement patterns (Siedentop, 2001). A trained teaching specialist is a key component to the success of any school physical education program (Wall, Rudisill, Goodway & Parish, 2004). A teacher who possesses sound content knowledge (what to teach) coupled with competency in psychomotor methodology (how to teach) can influence children in a positive manner (Lacy & Douglas, 2003). A passionate and knowledgeable elementary school teacher with a well designed physical education program, which offers diverse and age appropriate activities in a nurturing environment, provides children with the opportunity to discover their fundamental movement skills potential. "The focus on physical literacy in physical education is to enable children to develop motor skills and apply these to various contexts in order to develop understanding of the physical self in space, time, and direction" (Marsden & Weston, 2007, p. 384) . This optimal setting would use a variety of instructional strategies and innovative equipment to ensure children have the opportunity to explore and experiment without risk. Studies that have investigated similar experiences that occur outside the school setting have also been shown to enhance the development of basic motor skills (Raudsepp & Pall, 2006). The strong connection between childhood motor skill development and physical activity confidence and success throughout a lifetime requires that physical education teachers instruct with that goal in mind. Patterson, Anderson & Klavora (1997, p. 6) write that it is important for the teacher to:

- Teach with an emphasis on building movement confidence and competence.
- Begin as early as preschool.
- Emphasize individual progress.
- Emphasize qualitative rather than quantitative performance.
- Relate physical skills to play opportunities and other activities outside of class time.
- Make real connections between fundamental skills and participation in a variety of culturally valued sport, recreation, and leisure activities.
- Weave physical skill development into the fabric of daily school life.

"Developmentally appropriate physical education" is a term used to suggest that a child-centered-or learner centered-approach to movement experiences provides the best opportunity to explore individual movement potential (Sanders & Stork, 2001). Penney and Chandler (2000) point out that even though motor development is the primary contribution of physical education, knowledge, skills and understanding of body awareness, and enjoyment and expression are all related to the holistic development of children. Therefore, the multi-disciplinary nature of physical development requires consideration of the social and psychological elements when planning and teaching children's physical activities (Penney & Chandler, 2000). Killingbeck, Bowler, Golding & Gammon, (2007 p. 22) describes the link of physical literacy in secondary education to the following physical competencies:

1. The ability to read and respond efficiently and effectively to the environment and to others in interaction.
2. The ability to use the body as an instrument of expression and/or communication.
3. The ability to articulate and/or demonstrate knowledge skills and understanding of health.

These authors suggest that each of these competencies take place in diverse areas of activity or movement forms: athletics, dance, games, and outdoor/adventurous activities (Killingbeck et al., 2007); while other curricula define movement forms as games, gymnastics, dance, fitness, and outdoor activities. Each of these areas contributes to the foundation of motor learning in distinctive ways. For example, gymnastics and dance are grounded in the building blocks of agility, balance, and coordination. Children also learn to run, jump, throw, and catch in games activities. These basics serve as the underpinning for more complex sport skills that are mastered as a child develops into adolescence. Research from New South Wales found that acquisition of fundamental movement skills is significantly associated with participation in organized sports but not in unstructured physical activity among adolescents (Okely, Booth & Patterson, 2001). Unfortunately, there is no consensus in the literature on the method that should be used to assess fundamental movement skills in children (Fisher, Reilly, Kelly, Montgomery, Williamson, Paton, et al.,2005; Hay & Cote, 1998).

THE ASSIMILATION OF PHYSICAL LITERACY, PHYSICAL ACTIVITY, AND FUNDAMENTAL MOVEMENT SKILLS

A relationship exists between fundamental movement skills and childhood obesity levels (Okely et al., 2004; Okely et al., 2001). The foundational skills of walking, running, jumping, climbing, skipping, catching, and throwing are essential to master during early childhood. They provide a sound basis upon which all refined sports skills are based. It is essential that young children have the opportunities to practice and master these vital skills as early as possible (Sheehan & Katz, 2010). The ages between three and nine represent a critical time for children to learn the motor skills associated with physical literacy (Pangrazi, Chomokos & Massoney, 1981). If a child has not been introduced to a particular movement activity or missed out on the opportunity to develop a basic skill, it is more difficult to establish mature patterns of movement as each year passes (McClenaghan, 1978). Early success in movement improvement is crucial to subsequent skill achievement and can impact the participatory levels of children in health-related physical activities and could eventually affect their choice of leisure activities as an adult (McKenzie, 2004). A childhood experience that does not include a successful initiation and subsequent mastery of foundational skills could result in a lack of interest in physical activity and contribute negatively to the trend of overweight children who have no interest in sports or exercise (van Beurden, 2003; Eckert, 1987). Regrettably, only limited research has examined the relationship between fundamental movement skills and physical activity (Fisher et al., 2005; Okely et al., 2001; Okely et al., 2004).

The blending of fundamental movement skills and more specific skills that permit a child to move confidently and with control in a wide range of rhythmic and sport activities is the premise of the Canadian Sport for Life (CS4L) definition of physical literacy (Higgs et al.,2008). There are, however, many interpretations of fundamental movement skills and what exactly they are (Fisher et al., 2005; Hands, 2002; Hart, 2005; Knowles, 2000). The parental guide for developing physical literacy, created by Canadian Sport for Life as part of Canada's Long Term Athlete Development Plan (LTAD), places a heavy emphasis on the acquisition of fundamental movement skills during the optimal years of readiness prior to puberty (Higgs et al., 2008). Agility, balance, laterality, and coordination are arguably at the core of all movement, and are considered by many as the necessities. Beyond those essentials, one might suggest that running, jumping, and throwing are the subsequent skills to focus on.

The period of time that is most critical to the development of basic motor skills is the primary school years (Gabbard, 2008). A variety of robust physical experiences are essential for a child that is exploring and experimenting with their physical potential. Regular opportunities for dynamic physical activities are necessary to ensure proper growth and development in the following areas:

- Skeletal bone tissue – length and width;
- Skeletal muscle tissue; and,
- Neurological connections related to movement patterns and skills (Malina, Bouchard & Bar-Or, 2004).

During the early phases of natural movement and unstructured play, the behaviour of children and their level of physical activity are significantly related to motor proficiency (Butcher & Eaton, 1989). These authors also suggest that there is a relationship between high energy gross motor activities and running proficiency and another between fine motor choices (with low activity levels) and visual motor control and balance (Raudsepp & Pall, 2006).

FOSTERING NATURAL MOVEMENT WITH CHILDREN

Intentional free flowing movement is an important component in the quest for physical literacy. The ongoing mastery of dexterous movement patterns is a vital source of motivation for learning. Children who learn competency and confidence by having success with the basic skills such as crawling, climbing, walking, or pedaling are inevitably more likely to run, jump, and throw with proficiency. Moving naturally reflects a certain style or manner according to the laws of the body (Streicher, 1970). It is not simply a combination of movements or skills that have been choreographed by a coach or teacher; it is the unstructured and skilful movement often displayed by children who first enter into school. Their ability to move freely about their space without regard for mechanical or choreographed movement is the essence of natural movement.

Parents and early childcare providers play a critical role in influencing the youngest of children to engage in unstructured or deliberate physical activity. Modeling natural movements and basic skills for young child will provide an environment rich in opportunities for normal physical development. Children learn valuable life lessons while participating in physical activity, including the ability to cope with success and failure, resolving conflicts with others, and concepts of sharing. All of these attributes are natural for children to experience in an active setting. Exploring and risk-taking in a safe environment is essential to a child's growth and development.

As the initial psychomotor and social-emotional abilities are forming, unstructured and naturally occurring experiences should be encouraged. Game play should be creative and constantly evolving with rules and objectives in a continuous state of flux. When the needs of the children change, so should the setting, equipment, and whatever else is necessary to encourage exploration and experimentation. If physical literacy is to be learned by acquiring fundamental movement skills, it should be done so as part of natural play. Children should perceive movement as an ability to express themselves free from the limitations of their daily routine. Constructing opportunities for infants and toddlers to move over, through, and around obstacles promotes creative body expressions and encourages problem solving. Working safely with objects of varying size and texture will enable a child to start developing eye-hand coordination and a multitude of other fundamental movement skills. Parents and child care providers should seek out quality opportunities for children to be creative, expressive, and functional in their movement.

LABAN'S MOVEMENT ANALYSIS TO FACILITATE MOVEMENT UNDERSTANDING

Rudolf Laban (1879-1958) was a pioneer in the study of human movement and creative modern dance (Laban, 1971). The application of Laban's movement analysis has influenced physical literacy by establishing the importance of educating children about movement in support of their holistic development. The analysis and understanding of movement principles theorized by Laban are transferable to all observable human motion and applicable to every aspect of physical education, sports, dance, and play.

With an understanding of Laban's principles and an acceptance of freer forms of activity, the concept of *movement education* was introduced by teachers as a means of enabling students to master motor skills by understanding the movement principles in them. Strategic questioning (based on Laban's principles) is still an essential component of helping children learn about their movement potential. It is also an integral part of the teaching games for understanding (TGfU) pedagogy and the similar guided discovery pedagogy used in creative dance and educational gymnastic teaching. Elementary physical education teachers often ask children about how their bodies are moving in relation to the space, others, and the equipment. This technique of student engagement can produce a mastery of the skill which results in a feeling of achievement and the ability to tackle more sophisticated tasks.

Regardless of the specific task, many experts have agreed that all movement can be divided into three categories: locomotive, non-locomotive (stability), and manipulative skills. As well, movement can be expressive or functional. Expressive movement is where the body is used as a mechanism to transmit thoughts, feelings, or moods. Functional movement is intended to complete a task or specific skill related to a known outcome (e.g. scoring a goal or shooting a basket). Laban describes these as the 'body aspect'; which is the first of four components in Laban's movement framework (Langton, 2007). Table 1 describes the key aspects of this framework.

ASPECT	FOCUS	STUDENT OUTCOMES
Body	What is the body doing? • body shape • body parts • locomotion • balance	Students understand and utilize locomotor (travelling), non-locomotor (balancing or hanging in a body shape), and manipulative skills (stressing a body part) to improve the quality of the movement.
Space	Where is the body moving? • directions • levels • pathways • planes • extensions	Students understand and utilize personal and general space, directions, pathways, levels, planes, and extensions appropriately to improve the quality of the movement.
Effort Quality	How the body is moving? • time (fast/slow) • weight (heavy/light) • space (straight/flexible) • flow (ongoing/interrupted)	Students understand and utilize time, weight, flow, and space appropriately to improve the quality of the movement.
Relationship	To what or whom is the body relating when it moves?	Students understand and utilize awareness and skill in how the mover relates to other individuals, groups, apparatuses, and objects.

Table 1: Four Aspects of Laban's Movement Framework - Adapted from Langton (2007)

The understanding of body awareness, space awareness, effort quality, and relationships is essential in establishing a solid foundation of movement on which children can build. The awareness of one's body is focused primarily on *what* the body is doing. This includes the basic actions of the body (bend, stretch, curl etc.), actions with the body parts (such as supporting the body, sending and receiving objects etc.), the activities of the body (locomotor, non-locomotor and manipulation), and shapes the body can make (Laban, 1971).

Space awareness is about *where* the body is moving relative to the personal space and the broader space shared by others. An opportunity for natural movement exists when children are asked to travel at different levels, in varying directions. Moving far away from a spot and then close to that spot with limited guidance helps broaden space awareness in children. Clarifying the plane in which one moves is helpful when diagnosing difficulties encountered in skill acquisition. For example, children often hit down instead of across or parallel to the ground when swinging a baseball bat.

Children are capable of performing similar tasks in very distinct, yet skilful, ways. Functional or expressive motion is an example of *how* the body is moving and is described by Laban (1971), as effort quality. The effort quality of movement is the way we use our body. The time factor is essentially concerned with speed in motion and the amount of time used in a movement action. For example, the ability of a child to accelerate and decelerate is an important element to master for safety in motion and later for strategy in games. Being light on your feet or being very strong and firm is an indication of how the element of weight is managed by a child. Laban (1971) states the conscious control of energy produces different intensities of strength and lightness in movement. The theoretical elements of weight efficiency and flow are consistent with, and related to, Whitehead's (2007) description of a physically literate individual who moves with poise, economy, and confidence in a wide variety of physically challenging situations. Providing opportunities to help children discover the way movements flow together could be a vital factor in enhancing natural skilled movement. Laban (1971) notes that the 'flow' can be bound or free; the former is restricted, broken up, undecided, and stoppable whereas the latter is enduring, flowing, smooth, and unstoppable.

It is the interaction with others and objects that help define the relationship aspect of Laban's (1971) analysis. This category is concerned with *what* relationships are occurring as movement proceeds. Relationships occur with oneself, with objects, individuals and groups to and with each other, relationships with equipment, apparatus, rules and boundaries (Laban, 1971).

Laban saw a natural harmony in bodily actions where the body is seen as an instrument of the individual's personality. Acknowledgement and understanding of the innate movement instinct and control of rhythm, shape, and form are important for efficiency in movement (Laban, 1971). The four motion factors of time, weight, space, and flow are considered essential to an understanding of both functional and expressive movement (Laban, 1971). Providing natural movement opportunities for young children to explore their bodily actions, their environment, and for the development of relationships with objects, equipment, and other children are important principles to consider when learning how to teach physical education.

STAGES OF DEVELOPMENT AND OPTIMAL READINESS

It is increasingly clear that physical literacy needs to be promoted and explicitly supported for every child in Canada. All children have the capacity to achieve their own personalized level of physical literacy, but not all of them will master the fundamental movement skills in the same order or at the same age. Each individual has his or her own distinctive timetable since the pace and level of physical maturation is individually determined (Brady, 2004). Children learn fundamental movement skills in a progressive pattern according to a series of identifiable stages. Movement education focuses on gross and fine motor functioning which leads to the consideration of multiple stages through which the learner progresses toward the acquisition of maturity in fundamental movement patterns (Maude, 2001). The variety and quality of early skill learning experiences and the freedom allowed each child to experiment and explore may influence that individual child's chance for acquiring skills earlier or later in comparison to other children.

Predictable stages of development are common but there are also periods of ideal readiness when children are physically, emotionally, and cognitively prepared to learn motor skills. Motor learning specialists describe the sequential nature of change from the time a skill first emerges to the time it reaches its most mechanically efficient form of development (Haywood & Getchell, 1995; Payne & Isaacs, 2002).

Magill and Anderson (1996) are responsible for a multidimensional perspective on child development with elements that consider motivation, maturation and prerequisite skills. This model has been used as a tool to help determine the optimal readiness of an athlete learning a sport. Another model created by Canadian Sport for Life (CS4L) was introduced in a physical literacy guide for parents (see Figure 2) (Higgs et al., 2008). The Canadian Sport for Life (CS4L) diagram uses thirteen fundamental movement skills (in three categories) and identifies when a child will normally acquire this ability and the ideal time to teach the skill. This model uses chronological age which provides an imprecise guideline for each fundamental movement skill. Although normal development of these skills is age-related, it is not at all age-dependent (Gallahue, 1989; Gallahue & Donnelly, 2003).

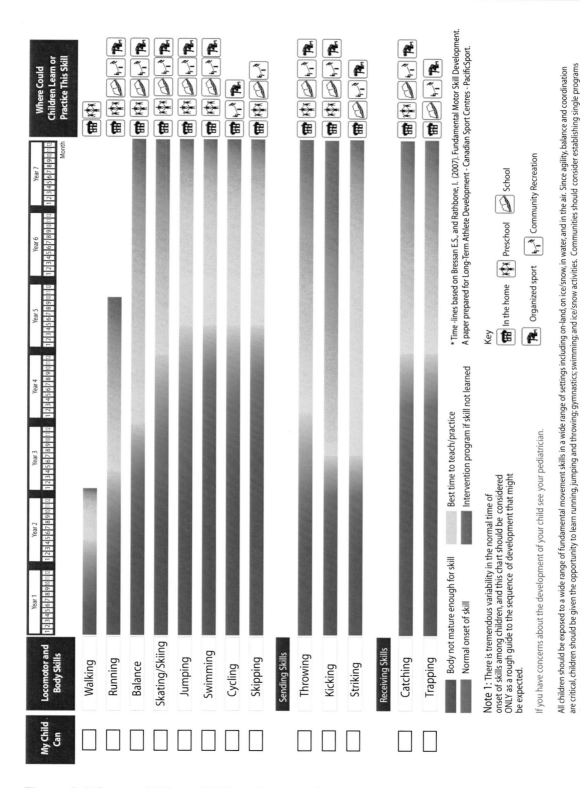

Figure 2: When and Where Children Learn and Practice Fundamental Movement Skills

During early childhood, basic skills are acquired by gradually integrating a series of more complex single body actions into a coordinated and refined movement style. To become physically literate, children need to incorporate these skill combinations into fluid movement patterns that translate into more complex sports skills. Eventually the movement patterns become second nature as the child's competency and confidence increases. Early success in movement improvement is vital to subsequent skill achievement.

There is typically a pattern of developmental progressions that each child passes through as they learn a new skill. Recognizing the phase of advancement is important for a parent, coach, or teacher. Children should not be expected to throw like an adult when they are learning the skill. Instead, each child should be encouraged to work through subsequent phases of development as their body matures and becomes stronger and more capable. For example, early attempts to throw involve inefficient use of the arms only. With experience, the throw eventually becomes a highly complex movement pattern combining efficient use of the whole body in a naturally flowing and biomechanically sound action. Mastery of the basic overhand throw leads to multitude of sports skills such as serving a tennis ball, clearing a badminton shuttle, and spiking in volleyball (Thomas & French, 1985). Refining a simple overhand throw and other fundamental movement skills as a child ages can increase the likelihood of participation in physical activity throughout their lifetime (Raudsepp & Paasuke, 1995). It is also evident that the acquisition of basic movement patterns and skills will strengthen a child's readiness for organized sports (van Beurden, 2003). The Coaching Association of Canada breaks down the process of 'learning to throw' into four distinct stages (National Coaching Certification Program, 2009):

1. Emerging – Throwing from the elbow with almost no shoulder action. There is very little body or foot movement.

2. Early Developing – The shoulder, elbow and wrist are used as the arm is taken up and to the side. There is some shifting of the body weight while the leg on the throwing side moves slightly with the toss.

3. Late Developing – Distinctive step forward with the same foot as the throwing side. Increased use of the shoulder, arm and wrist. More use of the trunk, but little or no twisting.

4. Mature Throw – Full rotation and power generation from the trunk by stepping forward with the opposite leg. Shoulders, arms and hands are properly utilized in harmony with the rest of the body. The body weight shifts from back to front with good follow-through.

Most of these fundamental movement skills will follow a similar sequence of development; however, in some cases the developing stage is not broken out into 'early' and 'late' since the differences can be too subtle (Gallahue & Donnelly, 2003). A child arrives at each stage in their own distinct way and with their own unique timing. As they master each stage they start to develop a 'tool box' of essential skills that will help them cross the proficiency barrier into successful sport and recreational participation (Seefeldt, 1980).

Early skill proficiency is related to the concept of differentiated developmental rates in that there is relatively no connection between a child's initial successes and later performance (Sage, 1984). Early maturing children who excel initially in sports are often expected to perform well later on, but since athletic performance involves multiple factors, any effort to forecast future success is likely to be ineffective (Matsudo, 1996). Transference of skills from earlier experiences can often result in initial success in sports at a higher level, but this advantage diminishes as proficiency increases and specificity is accentuated (Schmidt,

1991). Parents and teachers need to be cognizant of the maturational range that exists within a group of children who are the same chronological age. Early and late maturing children should be provided with learning activities that are appropriate for their individual needs and that respect the variability of growth and development.

Growth and maturation are often used in conjunction with the term 'development' and although they are closely related, both must be viewed as dynamic. Growth focuses on size attained at a given point in time, whereas maturation focuses on progress (rate) toward adult size and maturity (Malina, 2004). Malina describes development as the acquisition and refinement of behaviours expected by society which includes both motor and social competencies. The ultimate intention is to assist each child in progressing through these stages with confidence and a positive attitude toward physical activity and personal health. The greatest emphasis should be on movement skill acquisition during the preschool and early elementary grades (Colvin et al., 2000).   Emphasis should always be placed on learning basic skills in a non-competitive environment (Brady, 2004). Creating balance in a child's life by having them cultivate relationships in a variety of settings will reduce burn-out (Gould, 1996). To increase the likelihood of developmental success, children should experience as many different physical activities as they can (McPherson & Brown, 1988). Early specialization in sports may actually limit a child's ability to learn a wide variety of skills that are important for an active lifestyle into adulthood (Wall & Cote, 2007; Rowland, 1998). The message for professionals who teach or coach elementary-age children is clear: teach an assortment of basic skills in multiple environments to maximize the potential of each child.

CHAPTER 3: *Children with Disabilities / Inclusion*

BEST PRACTICES FOR INCLUSION

Inclusion is a topic that has been debated for decades. To date there is no consensus as to what is the best practice. The United Nations Convention on the Rights of Persons with Disabilities was adopted in December 2006 (United Nations, 2007) and this marked a significant paradigm shift in attitudes and approaches to persons with a disability. *Article 30* includes specific reference to cultural life, leisure, recreation and sport for persons with a disability. Specific instructions are given to encourage and promote the participation, to the fullest extent possible, of persons with a disability in sporting activities (at all levels) to ensure that persons with disabilities have an opportunity to participate on an equal and equitable basis. Defining inclusion has also gone through a variety of iterations. Presently, inclusion implies more than merely integrating children with challenges into the same physical space as their non-disabled classmates. Full inclusion means that the child with a disability participates in the least restrictive environment. This is an environment where social opportunities to interact with other children are equal to other children, and the child participates in the same activities as their able-bodied peers to the fullest extent possible.

According to authors at the *Centre for Inclusive Education*, located in the Faculty of Education at the University of Western Ontario, inclusion can be achieved with a supportive environment, positive relationships, feelings of competence, and opportunities to participate (Centre for Inclusive Education, 2008). With that, teachers or coaches can have an impact by simply encouraging a more inclusive culture; facilitating social interactions between and among students with and without disability; finding areas of strength where children with a disability can flourish; and, providing opportunities to learn those activities that are valued by other children. It is difficult to provide perfect learning opportunities for every student in every environment and this is the case regardless of disability. The key is that every effort is made in the attempt.

ICONS

for children with physical disabilities

for children with developmental and/or behavioural disabilities

PHE Canada
Physical & Health Education Canada

Overview of the Disabilities and Associated Behavioural Considerations Included in This Resource

Over their careers, teachers, coaches and leaders may encounter children with numerous developmental and behavioural disabilities in the physical activity setting. Each child will be different and unique in his or her own way — even those children with the same formal diagnosis.

Children that use wheelchairs (manual and/or electric) often do so as the result of an acquired spinal cord injury or a congenital condition affecting neuro-motor control.

Spinal Cord Injuries

For spinal cord injuries, paralysis is determined by the extent of damage to the spinal cord at a particular level. Generally, the higher the level of injury on the spinal cord the more severe the injury and the less muscle activation available.

Spina Bifida

Spina Bifida is caused by a neural tube defect that takes place early in pregnancy and results in the developing vertebrae not fully closing and thus exposing the spinal cord at birth. The most common location of the malformation is the lumbar and sacral areas of the spinal cord. The lumbar nerves control the muscles in the hip, leg, knee and foot, and help to keep the body erect. The sacral nerves control some of the muscles in the feet, bowel, and urinary bladder. Some degree of impairment can be expected in these areas, resulting in varying degrees of paralysis, absence of skin sensation, and poor or absent bowel and/or bladder control as well as curvature of the spine (scoliosis).

Muscular Dystrophy

Muscular Dystrophy is the name given to a group of genetically caused neuromuscular disorders with a progressive wasting of muscles that control body movement. Duchenne Muscular Dystrophy is the most common. Age at onset is usually two to six years; symptoms include general muscle weakness and wasting. This muscle weakness affects the pelvis, upper arms, and upper legs; and eventually involves all voluntary muscles. As the muscle tissue deteriorates, it is replaced by fatty connective tissue. As with most disabilities the spectrum of ability level for each individual will vary depending on a number of factors.

Cerebral Palsy (may or may not use a wheelchair or mobility aids)

Cerebral Palsy (CP) is an umbrella term encompassing a group of neuro-motor disorders affecting body movement and muscle coordination. CP is caused by damage to the motor control centers of the developing brain and can occur during pregnancy and childbirth or after birth up to about age three. It is a non-progressive disorder, meaning the damage to the brain does not worsen, but secondary orthopedic difficulties are common. There is an enormous range of disability within the general heading of CP from very minimal to extremely severe.

- Spastic hemiplegia occurs when one side is affected. Typically, people that have spastic hemiplegia are the most ambulatory, although they are often prescribed ankle-foot orthoses.
- Spastic diplegia is where both the lower extremities are affected with little to no upper-body spasticity.
- Spastic quadriplegia is where all four limbs are affected. People with spastic quadriplegia are the least likely to be able to walk, or if they can, to want to walk.

Children with Amputations (may or may not use a mobility aid or wheelchair)

Amputation is the removal of a body extremity by trauma or surgery. Reasons for amputations range from circulatory disorders, cancer, trauma and infection among others. Two issues for the teacher and coach to be aware of include whether the loss of limb was congenital or acquired and the type of prosthetic. Lastly teachers and coaches will need to be aware of issues pertaining to skin care of where the prosthetic meets the remaining limb.

Children with a Visual Impairment

Visual impairment is a condition of lacking visual perception due to physiological or neurological factors. Vision loss can be caused by a number of conditions present at birth or acquired later in life such as infections, environmental factors or trauma. Within the general description of visual impairment are several levels or ranges including total blindness (a complete lack of form and visual light perception) to having vision recorded as 20/200. For a person to be defined as "blind" their vision must be 20/200 or less or their range must be 20° across or less.

Deaf Children

According to the International Committee of Sports for the Deaf, "Deaf" is defined as a hearing loss of at least 55 dB in the better ear. Some deaf students may be able to read lips or use hearing aids while others will be able to communicate using sign language. Deafness is the one realm where "person first terminology – i.e. person with a disability versus the disabled person is not promoted. People who are deaf do not consider the deafness to be a disability but instead a unique cultural distinction.

Autism Spectrum Disorder (ASD)

Autism spectrum disorder (ASD) is a complex developmental disorder that generally presents in early childhood and is defined by marked delays and impairments in social reciprocity, expressive and receptive communication, and imaginative play as well as restricted range and repertoire of interests and activities. It is often, but not always, associated with intellectual disabilities (American Psychiatric Association, 2000).

With this disorder, the term *spectrum* refers to a continuum of severity or developmental impairment. Each individual child is unique — no one person with an ASD diagnosis responds or behaves exactly like another with the same diagnosis. Children and adults with ASD usually have particular communication and social characteristics in common, but the conditions cover a wide spectrum, with individual differences in (1) number and particular kinds of symptoms; (2) severity, from mild to severe; (3) age of onset; (4) levels of functioning; and (5) challenges with social interactions.

When speaking of ASD, most people are referring to the three most common pervasive developmental disorders (PDDs):

- *Autistic disorder* (AD) (also called autism and classic autism): Autism occurs in approximately 20 of every 10,000 Canadians. Cognitive impairments, deficits in verbal and non-verbal communication, deficits in social understanding, unusual behaviours and restricted activities are hallmarks of autism.
- *Pervasive developmental disorder not otherwise specified* (PDD-NOS) (also called atypical autism). A child is likely to receive a PDD-NOS diagnosis when there are severe and pervasive impairments in some areas, such as reciprocal social interaction (e.g., being very socially awkward), or restricted activities and interests (e.g., fixations on topics, objects or words), *but the strict criteria for autistic disorder are not met*. In other words, these

children are "autistic" in many ways (e.g., in the way they behave or in the way they interact socially), but they do not meet the exact clinical diagnostic criteria for autism.

- *Asperger syndrome* (AS) (also called Asperger disorder) occurs in approximately 5 of every 10,000 Canadians. Although there is considerable debate as to whether Asperger syndrome is a unique disorder or whether those who exhibit the characteristics associated with AS just represent the highest functioning individuals with autistic disorder, this diagnosis is commonly encountered within the school system.

Down Syndrome (DS)

Down syndrome, a genetic condition that is identified before or soon after birth, carries with it the certainty of developmental delays. DS occurs approximately 1.36 times in every 1,000 live births (CDC, 2006).

People with DS experience intellectual disabilities ranging from moderate to severe. Children with DS also experience significant delays in the onset of early motor milestones and display qualitative differences in movement patterns when compared with children with typical development (TD) (Block, 1991; Palisano et al., 2001). Most children with DS eventually learn a basic repertoire of motor skills; however, they seem to fall further behind their peers as they get older (Block, 1991; Menear, 2007). Jobling and Virji-Babul (2004) discuss how children with DS may have difficulty keeping up with their peers. They may fall more often and be unsure about running, climbing, jumping and playing games that require balance and coordination; consequently, they may avoid these types of activities. Poor motor skills can impact various aspects of the lives of children with DS including school, vocational work, community, overall motor performance and physical activity participation.

Atlantoaxial instability is increased mobility at the first and second cervical vertebrae (atlantoaxial joint) and affects approximately 15% of children with DS. Clearance by a doctor is necessary for all activities involving rolling, diving, tumbling.

Attention Deficit Hyperactivity Disorder (ADHD)

Attention deficit hyperactivity disorder (ADHD) is a highly complex neurobehavioural disorder that results in a combination of developmental problems, with important medical, educational and social implications (Cantwell, 1996). Some of the symptoms and behaviours that characterize a child with ADHD include, *but are not limited to*, the following: (1) often fails to pay attention to detail or makes careless mistakes, (2) often has difficulty sustaining attention, (3) often does not listen, (4) often does not follow through on instruction and fails to finish tasks, (5) often fidgets, (6) often runs about or climbs excessively in inappropriate situations, (7) often talks excessively, (8) often interrupts or intrudes on others (American Psychiatric Association, 2000). Children with ADHD are at risk for low levels of physical fitness, poor motor skills and negative attitudes towards physical activity, and so it is important that they participate and learn fully in physical education.

Developmental Coordination Disorder (DCD)

The hallmark of DCD is the inability to perform culturally normative motor skills with acceptable proficiency for one's age and intellectual ability, and this is unrelated to any other known neurological motor impairment (American Psychiatric Association, 2000. Children with DCD have difficulty learning new skills, even with practice, and are likely to avoid physical activity to prevent negative experiences in active play, physical education and recreational and competitive sport (Bouffard et al., 1996; Missiuna et al., 2008). These children are not likely to have an official diagnosis unless the awkwardness is so severe they have been referred by a medical professional for therapy. Children like these are present in

most physical education classes and early community recreation teams. They will likely self-select out of physical activity when they are older.

Teachers and coaches should be aware that "bad behaviour" may in fact be a tactic these children use to receive a time out. In other words, a time out is exactly what the child wants. Upon reflection on the motor skills of their "class clown," teachers and coaches may realize that often such children may not be very skilled in the motor domain. It is important that teachers and coaches engage these children because they may actually need the most help in developing their fundamental motor skills.

Intellectual Disability (ID)

The spectrum of intellectual ability is vast. The more severe the intellectual disability, the more challenging it can be for teachers and coaches to provide instruction at the child's individual ability level.

The reason a child has an intellectual disability may not be as clear as a diagnosis of ASD or DS. There are hundreds of disorders and conditions, both congenital and acquired that may result in decreased cognitive functioning. It is beyond the scope of this resource to provide a description of these disorders, as many are quite rare. However, fetal alcohol syndrome (FAS) is a condition that is being more commonly diagnosed. Most of the features of FAS are variable, and they may or may not be present in a given child. The most common and consistent features involve the child's growth, performance, intelligence, head and face, skeleton and heart. FAS can result in diminished early growth, symptoms of hyperactivity, impaired fine motor skills, poor hand-eye coordination and delayed cognitive development.

Fragile X is a genetic disorder that primarily affects boys and is characterized by a long face, prominent ears, hyperextensible finger joints, double-jointed thumbs, flat feet and low muscle tone. Prader-Willi syndrome is quite rare, but children with Prader-Willi syndrome present with speech delays, poor physical fitness, excessive weight gain, delays in motor development, and intellectual disabilities in childhood. Other children may have an acquired brain injury that has resulted in an intellectual disability.

Since most children in Canada who have disabilities have both physical and intellectual deficits (Kowalchuk & Crompton, 2009), many of the topics discussed in this resource are applicable to children with various physical disabilities. For example, children with cerebral palsy or spina bifida often have intellectual disabilities as well as their physical disability. The implication for a coach or teacher is to tailor the lesson to the ability level of the individual children.

Six Tips for Inclusion

Celebrate your success.
- Tell someone, take photographs, share with parents.

Avoid looking for issues.
- Identify what worked well, and apply what you learned to other activities.
- Ignore perceived barriers, and eliminate real barriers where possible.

Involve the participant.
- Ask the participant how he or she would like to be involved.
- Share problem solving with members of the group.

Provide opportunities for participants to shine.
- Permit participants to demonstrate accomplishments, such as proficiency in wheelchair basketball or swimming.

Use instructional support.
- Facilitate your instruction by involving support personnel in planning and implementation.

Foster equal relationships.
- Use a needed rather than needy framework for establishing social and instructional relationships among participants.

(Goodwin, Gustafson, & Hamilton, 2006)

Teachers and instructors should always strive to include a participant with a disability as much as possible in the activity. The level of participation should be based on the match between the participant's skill level and the complexity of the task. Sometimes the child's participation will differ from that of his or her classmates — the important thing is to not have children with disabilities sitting on the sidelines doing nothing. There can be a range of participation in any given activity.

Range of Participation

Full participation. The participant participates in the activity with no modification. For example, a participant with high-functioning autism fully participates in a game of basketball.

Modified active. The participant participates in the activity with modifications made to the equipment, rules, distances or complexity of the skill. For example, a game of soccer is played on a reduced-size field to include a participant with Down syndrome.

Active parallel. The participant participates in the activity but at his or her own skill level. For example, a participant with multiple developmental disabilities works on water orientation skills with an adult educational assistant while the rest of the group receives instruction from the pool staff.

Adaptations

Children with a disability within an inclusive setting may require a number of modifications or adaptations. Try, however, to remain as true to the original activity as possible while at the same time allowing participants to challenge themselves and make progress, without compromising the integrity of the education of the able-bodied children in the group.

There are five basic ways to adapt or modify any activity for a participant with a disability. They include (1) task/curriculum, (2) equipment, (3) environment, (4) instructions and (5) rules. Options for any of these are unlimited and are constrained only by your imagination.

TASK/CURRICULUM: Based on the child's individualized education plan (IEP), it may not be appropriate for all aspects of the physical education curriculum or activity session to be achieved in a given school year/season. The curriculum and/or tasks should be adapted to the unique needs of each child. It is important to individualize the task difficulty when working with children with disabilities.

EQUIPMENT: Objects can vary in size, shape, colour, weight and texture; the nature of the child's disability will influence the final choice. For example, some children with ASD will have either colour preferences or aversions; therefore a teacher or instructor can select a ball that is the child's favourite colour. Additionally, adapted balls with textures, patterns and even sounds can be great for children with ASD.

ENVIRONMENT: The environment can be changed by decreasing distances or removing obstacles and distractions. For example, when a child with ADHD is participating in a physical education class where the gymnasium is split into two classes, it would be best to draw the curtain or the movable wall to separate the two sides and decrease distractions.

INSTRUCTIONS: Instructions can be modified to incorporate visual, tactile and verbal cues. In addition, the teacher or instructor can be positioned in a way that facilitates greater understanding for the learner. For example, for a child with a severe cognitive impairment, verbal, visual and tactile cues may be necessary when teaching a specific motor skill (see the continuum of prompts section). Many children with autism spectrum disorders (and other children with intellectual disabilities) may use a picture exchange communication system, where storyboards are created using picture symbols, or "pic-syms," to communicate. Teachers and instructors can use the symbols to illustrate to a child with ASD what the schedule of activities is going to be. Following are a few examples of pic-syms that can be used in physical education class. Work with the child's special education teacher or coach to create a number of relevant pic-syms.

playground

lineup

bike

RULES: Rule adaptations can include partner assistance for the child with a disability, flexible time limits and rule changes pertaining to the game itself. For example, a child with an intellectual disability may be allowed to take up to three steps without dribbling during a basketball game with peers. Be sure to explain the rules and modifications to *all* the participants in the class to facilitate fair participation by all.

The most inclusive environment is one where the learner can participate fully by employing the most appropriate adaptations given the context and the participant's individual strengths and weaknesses.

Specific examples for each motor learning skill are provided throughout this document, but for other general ideas on ways to adapt your lessons, we recommend the following resources: Block's *A Teacher's Guide to Including Students With Disabilities in General Physical Education, Second Edition,* and Lieberman and Houston-Wilson's *Strategies for Inclusion: A Handbook for Physical Educators.*

Use of Peer Tutors

Peer tutors can be very useful, especially when resources for educational assistants are scarce. Children with disabilities benefit from smaller ratios of teacher/instructor to learners, and having another child work with them helps accomplish this optimal ratio. Peer tutoring increases socialization among all participants and promotes leadership. An added benefit is that the tutors often learn the skills even better by helping another child learn them.

Generally, peer tutor programs are very successful. Peer tutors can be used spontaneously in a lesson, or a school can develop a formal peer tutoring system. When setting up a formal peer tutoring program, it is recommended that parents/guardians be notified. Peer tutors are selected by the teacher or coach and trained to work with a child with a disability in his or her group or in a younger group. Tutors can have an established and formal role, or different children can play the role in different groups. In some contexts, older children with disabilities can be peer tutors for younger children with disabilities. The role of the peer tutor will be determined by the needs of the child with a disability, but generally the tutor will need to be empathetic, encouraging and able to provide feedback and leadership to a child with a disability. This model can be very beneficial to all the participants. See *Strategies for Inclusion* for a more in-depth discussion of peer tutoring programs (Lieberman & Houston-Wilson, 2002).

Behaviour Management Techniques

As a teacher or coach, it is critical that your expectations for behaviour are clearly communicated and consistently enforced and rewarded in your classroom or coaching environment. Set your expectations appropriately for each child, and if behaviour management is embedded in every lesson, then your efforts will be rewarded with hard work and persistence.

Many off-task behaviours have a purpose or may be a form of communication; although the child may not be able to articulate his or her feelings or needs, careful and detailed examinations of the antecedents, functions and consequences of the behaviour can reveal its purpose. When working with children with varying levels of developmental and behavioural disabilities, the safety of *all* the children in the class is always the most important priority. Although we advocate the most active participation possible by all children regardless of ability, over the course of your teaching or coaching career there will be occasions when the behaviour of the child having the "tantrum" or "episode" will endanger him or her or other children in the class. In these instances, it is appropriate to remove the child from the class to provide a safe environment for working through the behaviour and returning to a stable state. It is critically important that an educational assistant or other trained staff person who is familiar with the needs and behaviours of the child be with him or her at all times (i.e., don't leave the child having a behavioural episode unattended for the rest of the class).

Like most of us, children with developmental and behavioural disabilities thrive on routine and structure. The use of a pictorial schedule or storyboard has already been described for children with ASD. However, many children will benefit from a written or pictorial schedule. Being able to anticipate what is next and having "fair warning" that a task or activity will change can go a long way in preventing some challenging behaviours. If possible, a schedule on the gymnasium wall is helpful, but if it is just one child, a piece of paper with the lesson's schedule is often enough to prepare the child for the day's lesson. Additionally, keeping a similar structure to your lessons can be beneficial at a macro level. For example, if you always do a warm-up, then teacher instructions, then individual work on a skill (through stations or otherwise) and then a game situation, this routine structure will help a child with behavioural challenges transition from one activity to another. He or she won't necessarily know what skill or what game, but the structure of the lessons is consistent over time.

Basic Behaviour Management Techniques

Prevention is the best policy.
- Know what tends to set your participant "off" in terms of behaviour.
- Teach positive behaviours.
- Use consistent structure in every session (e.g., have the same introductory routine and exit routine).
- Reinforce positive behaviours.
- Communicate with parents/caregivers and participants.
- Establish class rules, and be consistent.
- Set up the environment to promote good behaviour (e.g., have participants face the gymnasium walls to avoid distractions).
- Examine the antecedents for possible causes of the behaviour.
- Examine the possible functions of the behaviour.
- Explore the consequences of the behaviour. (What happened after the behaviour occurred? Who reacted? How did they react? What was the punishment?)
- Consider simple alternatives that might prevent or reduce the behaviour.

PHE Canada
Physical & Health Education Canada

In their Community Coach's resource, **Special Olympics Canada** has outlined some key strategies for dealing with various behaviours that are useful in both educational and sporting contexts when working with individuals with intellectual disabilities.

Instructional Strategies to Promote Appropriate Behaviours

Source: Special Olympics Canada (2008)

1. Be concise, be consistent, and do not give lengthy directions.
2. Start with single teachable tasks, and add sequence tasks gradually.
3. Structure success-oriented tasks in small sequential steps that are achievable by the athlete.
4. Deliberately plan and schedule for repetition and practice of skills learned in situations outside of the gymnasium (pool, track, arena and so on).
5. Vary verbal and non-verbal communication in instruction, assisting, prompting, and fading as needed.
6. Provide repetition and practice in a variety of instructional activities, correlating word concepts and motor skills.
7. Give choices of activity participation.
8. Use controlled change when shifting from one task activity to another or when changing the student's or athlete's location.
9. Limit the length of work periods.
10. Reinforce appropriate behaviours promptly.
11. Encourage peer reinforcement and planned ignoring of inappropriate behaviours (i.e., not all behaviour needs to be acted on if safety is not a factor).
12. Reduce sound and visual distractions.
13. Define limits of behaviour, set consequences, and reinforce consistently.
14. Use contraction or contingency management (reinforcers must be appropriate for age).
15. Set up a reinforcement schedule, and document change of behaviours over time.
16. Identify student/athlete preferences and interests in activities and related motor skills.
17. Use the buddy system and peer modelling.
18. Use planned ignoring when behaviour will not cause serious problems on a short-term basis.
19. Know the prior history of a student's or athlete's hypersensitivity to the conditions (e.g., music in a gymnasium may send some children into hysterics).

For More Challenging Behaviours

The poor behaviour of children with severe cognitive limitations may be due to any number of factors. For example, they simply may not understand the instructions; or the task may be too difficult, so they are expressing their frustration in the form of yelling or other tantrum-like behaviour. Children with severe disabilities who are non-verbal may not be feeling well but cannot communicate this to anyone (e.g., stomach flu or a cold coming on). Or it may be as simple as the corner of their sock is digging into their toe and it hurts (something to consider for children with decreased sensation, such as children with spina bifida).

It can be challenging to play detective and try to decipher exactly what is causing the behaviours, but communication with the child's homeroom teacher in a school setting (if a physical education specialist is employed at the school), with the child's educational assistant and with parents can help get to the root of certain behaviours. Once all the potential health reasons are ruled out, try to examine the behaviour. Is the child trying to get your attention (albeit inappropriately)? Is the child trying to get the attention of his or her classmates? Is the child exhibiting a repetitive behaviour that is targeted for elimination by his or her IEP (e.g., running to doors, self-stimulation)? Being familiar with the child and the types of behaviours he or she exhibits on a regular basis will also help — not all behaviours need to be acted on.

It may be useful to conduct a behavioural survey whereby you observe the child and document what happened before the behaviour arose, during what task the behaviour occurred, with which other children, at what time of day and so on. This type of information can lead the team of educators responsible for the child (homeroom teacher, educational assistant, principal) to more fully understand the child's behavioural needs and challenges. For examples of behaviour surveys, we recommend Lavay, French and Henderson's *Positive Behavior Management in Physical Activity Settings* or Block's *A Teacher's Guide to Including Students With Disabilities in General Physical Education, Second Edition*.

After a particularly difficult behavioural episode, it is recommended that the teacher/instructor/coach take a moment with a trusted colleague to debrief and process the situation. This will allow everyone involved to learn from every situation and not have one person bear the entire burden.

Off-task behaviours (e.g., acting out, tantrums) exhibited by some children may, in fact, be avoidance strategies to hide poor motor skill proficiency!

Keep in mind that some of the off-task behaviours that can occur (e.g., clowning around, persistent water breaks, pestering other children) may in fact have a very specific purpose — avoidance. Children with higher cognitive and communication skills can present completely different behavioural challenges to a teacher than can children with severe cognitive limitations. Many children with poor motor skills (e.g., children with DCD, ASD and ADHD) often experience failure in physical activity settings because of lack of skill, lack of coordination or both. These repeated failures and negative feelings can lead to a cycle of withdrawal from physical activity settings, and in turn these children never improve their motor skills (Bouffard et al., 1996; Harvey, Fagan, & Kassis, 2003). This is important to keep in mind when disciplining some children; a time out may be exactly what they were trying to accomplish.

Importance of Self-Determination

Fostering and promoting independence and its many related constructs is a vital part of learning. Children with disabilities are often not given the same opportunities to be autonomous and make choices for themselves. Historically, people with disabilities and their families were offered few, if any, choices in their lives — recently the rights and capabilities of people with disabilities to make choices have moved to the forefront. It is critical that parents/caregivers and the child contribute to the IEP to decide on goals and objectives.

Providing reasonable choices within sessions is one way to facilitate self-determination and feelings of competence. If the child is able to make choices, he or she is more likely to be intrinsically motivated to engage in the activity. Therefore, an important concept for physical education teachers, generalist teachers and coaches to keep in mind is building choice into their sessions. For a more in-depth review of self-determination theory, please refer to the works of Deci and Ryan (e.g., Deci & Ryan, 1987; Ryan & Deci, 2000a, 2000b).

Continuum of Prompts

Prompts are instructions, demonstrations or manipulations that increase the chances of getting the desired response from the child. Following is an example of the continuum of prompts that can be used for children with developmental and behavioural disabilities. For each of the motor skills included in this resource, a specific continuum of prompts is presented.

For any skill, the continuum of prompts can be used when teaching/instructing. Where to start on the continuum is based on the child's level of comprehension and skill. The table describes the continuum and gives some generic examples. This is, however, just a guide — each child will respond differently to your teaching techniques. For example, a child with a severe and profound intellectual disability and ASD would require the teacher and the coach to start at the top of the continuum when introducing a new skill; a child with mild ADHD might be able to start farther down the continuum — again, which scenario applies depends on the skill of the individual child.

At the end of the continuum is free play. This is the ultimate goal — for children to actively practise their "skills" during free play without prompting. Free play is important because it allows for choice and social interactions. Canadian Sport for Life's Long-Term Athlete Development model emphasizes free play in the Active Start and FUNdamentals phases. Although very important, free play can cause anxiety in some children who thrive on routine and structure. Free play can also be a challenge for children with behavioural management difficulties. That is not to say it should be eliminated; however, it should be used when appropriate and as part of the continuum.

Continuum of Prompts

Physical Prompts	Physical prompts should be paired with verbal prompts.
- Complete manipulation	Teacher physically moves the child's body throughout the complete motion.
- Manipulative prompting	Provide assistance only during critical parts of the desired movement (e.g., holding hands only during dismount).
- Minimal guidance	Teacher makes contact with a relevant body part to initiate a movement (e.g., tapping knees to initiate jumping).
Visual Prompts	**Visual prompts should be paired with verbal prompts.**
- Complete skill demonstration	Accurate, often exaggerated demonstration of the complete skill by teacher or other participants.
- Partial skill demonstration	Accurate demonstration of a component of the skill (e.g., without the equipment, or just the beginning or end).
- Gestural prompting	Teacher uses a gesture that is not part of the skill (e.g., points at the floor to signal the child to jump down).
Verbal Prompts	
- Skill cue	Statements that focus the child's attention on a key component of the task (e.g., "Swing your arms") — try using familiar analogies, such as animal movements.
- Action command	Verbal description of the desired skill (e.g., "Jump down").
- Action cue	Motivational statement to help the child perform the skill (e.g., "One, two, three").
No Prompts	
- Initiation with environmental cue	Placement of equipment that encourages the participant to engage in the activity without using any verbal communication.
- Imitative initiation	Child performs the skill after watching other participants performing it.
- Initiation in free play	Child performs the skill at an appropriate time in free play but with no peer demonstration.

Adapted from Reid, O'Connor, & Lloyd (2003).

CHAPTER 4:
Balance and Stability Skills

The category of balance and stability skills refers to the first and most basic area of movement literacy; it is a prerequisite to all other skills. The ability to balance and remain stable in stillness and while moving are crucial skills for children to develop. If we are not stable in holding a body position, we'll lose our balance and fall over, perhaps hurting ourselves, but also forfeiting the opportunity to complete the movement.

The progression of stability and balancing skills are most evident through infancy and toddlerhood. Infants typically learn to sit at six months of age, stand with some assistance around ten months of age, and walk at about 12 months. At three years of age, the child is typically ready to run—a skill which is defined by flight, as neither foot is in contact with the ground. All of these developmentally predictable skills require many opportunities for the child to engage in them. These skills may range in difficulty from holding a still position (eg. standing, waiting to catch a ball) to holding a position while moving (as in swinging on a rope) to a far more difficult challenge of maintaining one's body shape, while balanced while travelling (as in high jumping).

In aesthetic movement forms such as gymnastics and dance, balancing in stillness is required on one foot and other body parts. In gymnastics, balance is the focal challenge on the balance beam, with legs or hands taking the weight. A dancer must hold an unusual shape on his or her back, chest, or buttocks. These types of balances are more difficult as the base of support is typically small, such as in ballet when a dancer balances on pointe.

The most common challenges in remaining stable and balanced are in athletic activities, where the body shape has to compensate for the changing centre of gravity and bases of support as the body travels through space. Dodging opposition while maintaining balance is typical of this skill; making tag-type games excellent opportunities to practice this skill. In more complex movement patterns, a receiver's stance becomes wider as he/ she reaches to catch the ball; an equestrian rider shifts his/her body forward as the horse jumps over the fence; a diver powerfully springs from a high diving board, successfully maintaining control of their body's shape while travelling through the air. As well, when flight is involved, balance is crucial in the pre-flight action (eg. bending of knees, arms low) to prepare for both the positions of stillness in the air and the safe landing (bending knees to absorb the force and arms swing down). ex. Sauté

Holding a shape in stillness

The most basic of balance and stability skills occur when the child can hold a position of stillness on two feet. The demands of this skill are increased when the stillness is required upon landing (after jumping up or out) or after running and stopping (to catch a baseball).

STANDING ON ONE FOOT: *a one-foot balance with sole of the non-support foot placed against the support leg*

A. Characteristics of

STANDING ON ONE FOOT:	Cue Words for Children
ACTION:	
Head neutral, look forward; stare at a spot for increased stability	Look forward
Back straight	
Arms straight at shoulder height and parallel to ground	Arms at shoulder height
Weight on one foot	
Sole of foot placed against knee and thigh of opposite foot	Foot flat against leg
Position held for three seconds	Hold

B. Teaching Tips

(i) Developmental changes to watch for prior to a mature balance on one foot:

- Initially, children will only balance momentarily without support. Children will look at their feet when balancing.
- Later, they will be able to balance while looking ahead. They will use their arms for balance, i.e., large exaggerated movements.
- In the mature balance, the children will be able to balance with their eyes closed.
- At a mature stage, the arms will be used as required to maintain balance. The ability to balance on either leg will also develop.

(ii) Difficulties to watch for:

If...	Then...
Children are clapping one arm to the side of their body.	Encourage children to use both arms for balance.
	Allow them to perform the skill in front of a mirror so they can check the position of their arm.
	A partner can provide feedback on arm positioning
Children have difficulty using both legs.	Encourage children to try balancing on each leg.
	They can add a little support (e.g., hold partner's shoulder, hold Chair) when balancing with their non-dominant leg.
Children are visually checking support leg.	Encourage children to keep their head up by looking at something on the wall.
	A partner can hold up fingers for the balancing child to count.
Children have difficulty holding the balance.	Add support, e.g., by lightly touching a wall or partner with one outstretched hand. Ensure the children don't put too much weight on the wall or partner.

(iii) Static balances with two feet touching the ground can build children's confidence and comprehension of the concept of balance before proceeding to one-leg balances.

(iv) When practicing standing on one foot, children need to completely move the weight onto one foot before they try to lift the other leg.

To view and analyze video for this skill, and all the skills in this manual online, please visit:

↘ **www.phecanada.ca**

C. Activities for Balancing

Skill: Balancing on one foot
Children: Individual
Equipment: None
Area: Gymnasium, court or field
Activity: The children take a balancing position. Ask them to add some of the following movements:

- keep their arms by their sides
- hold their arms up high
- cross their arms across their chest
- close their eyes

- place their hands on their head
- keep their arms out
- hold their hands behind their back
- throw a scarf up and catch it on their head.

Change legs and try again. Invite the children to suggest tricky things to do while holding the balance on one foot.

Balance touch

Skill: Balance
Children: Individual
Equipment: Beanbags
Area: Gymnasium, court, or field
Activity: The children adopt a balance on one foot with a beanbag on the floor beside them. Then, they reach their elevated foot out to touch the beanbag before resuming the balance on one foot. The aim is to perform the movement without losing balance and without putting weight on the beanbag.

Traffic Light

Skills: Balance, skip, hop
Children: Individual
Equipment: Three sheets of coloured paper (Green, Amber and Red)
Area: Gymnasium, court, or field
Activity: Children pretend to be vehicles responding to the colour of the traffic signal. The teacher/coach holds up a colour and the children respond with an action. For green, the children skip in free space; for amber, they hop on the spot; and for red, they adopt a balance on one foot.

Inuit Owl Hop

Skills: Balance, hopping

Children: Individual

Equipment: None

Area: Gymnasium, court, or field

Activity: The children adopt the following starting position. Balance on one foot (the hopping leg) with the other foot behind the knee of the hopping leg. Bend the knee of the hopping leg to approximately a 45 degree angle. Arms out to side with hands clenched into fists and thumbs pointing upward. Invite children to hop several times on the spot or hop across the room. Change feet and try again.

Standing on One Foot Tag

Skills: Balance, running

Children: Pairs

Equipment: None

Area: Gymnasium, court, or field

Activity: Designate a playing area and choose two or three children as taggers. Other children are scattered in the playing area. The taggers run to tag other players. When tagged, this child becomes the new tagger. Children can be safe from being tagged by balancing on one foot. As long as the child maintains the balance he/she cannot be tagged.

STORK STAND
- Look forward
- Back straight
- Wings out - arms straight out to sides
- Hold position

STORK STAND: *A one-foot balance with the ankle of the non-support foot placed against the knee of the support leg*

Balance is attained when the centre of gravity is over the base of support. There are two types of balance: 1. static balance – involves maintaining a desired shape in a stationary position (e.g. stork stand); and 2. dynamic balance – involves the control of the body as it moves in space (e.g. kicking ball).

Characteristics of the STORK STAND	*Cue Words for Children*
Head neutral, look forward	"Look forward" (Reminder: pick a spot on the wall to look at)
Back straight	"Stand up straight"
Arms straight and parallel to ground	"Reach arms out"
Weight on one foot	"Stand on one foot"
Inside of ankle of one foot placed against the knee of the support leg (foot placed either below the knee or above the knee depending on child's flexibility)	"Bottom of foot to leg"
Position held for three seconds	"Balance 1,2,3"

Adaptations of the STORK STAND for:

Children in wheelchairs	• The stork stand is not generally congruent with the IEP goals of children in wheelchairs. • Alternate activities that fit with the child's IEP should be planned.
Children with mobility aids	• Children who use mobility aids will have poor balance, therefore adaptations to the stork stand should include the use of their crutches or walker as needed. • Encourage the child to keep one hand on their aid (instead of two hands) and perform the rest of the skill (i.e. one leg up and one arm out straight). • Slowly encourage the child to use less and less support (if possible). • Encourage the children to practice the stork stand on each foot (especially their weaker side). • *Always keep safety in mind. Children, who use a walker or crutches, have poor balance. Balance activities are good for them, but can also be problematic – <u>be aware of falls</u>.*

Children with mobility limitations	• Children with club feet, amputations, or mild cerebral palsy are all likely to have balance difficulties. The stork stand is an excellent activity to work on balance but also poses some challenges.
	• Allow children with extreme balance issues to practice their stork stand with some sort of support nearby for security. Don't allow the child to become dependant on this support – but it will facilitate success in the early teaching stages. Slowly remove the support as balance improves.
	• Encourage children to start by lifting their non-support leg just above the ground at the ankle (not at their knee in the beginning). As they get more proficient, instruct them to raise their non-support leg higher.
	• Be aware that these children may have a weaker leg. Allow them to practice on the strong leg but also encourage practice on the weaker leg to build strength and balance skills.
Children with visual impairments	• Ensure the students understand the instructions using verbal and tactile cues.
	• This skill may or may not be more difficult for children with visual impairments.
	• Allow for a physical support to be nearby (a wall or an educational assistant) especially in the ear ly stages of learning.
Children who are deaf	• Deaf children may have increased balance difficulties making the stork stand a great opportunity to practice.
	• Allow the child to use physical supports during the early stages of learning (as necessary).
	• If an interpreter is not available (or necessary) have a cue card at each station (or for each Physical Education lesson) with the task or plan clearly outlined at the child's level of understanding.
	• Be prepared to give extra demonstrations of skills and activities.
	• Consider using an FM loop system (microphone worn by the teacher to amplify the voice into the hearing aid worn by the Deaf student).
	• Avoid excess noise in the learning environment.

Difficulties to watch for:

If...	Then...
Children are clapping one arm to the side of their body.	Encourage children to use both arms for balance. Allow them to perform the skill in front of a mirror so they can check the position of their arm. A partner can provide feedback on arm positioning.
Inability to balance unaided.	Spot activities carefully, but only as needed. Offer your hand for assistance, encouraging the child to grasp it less and less securely as balance is gained.
Children have difficulty using both legs.	Encourage children to try balancing on each leg. They can add a little support (e.g., hold partner's shoulder, hold chair) when balancing with their non-dominant leg.
Children are visually checking support leg.	Encourage children to keep their head up by looking at something on the wall. A partner can hold up fingers for the balancing child to count.
Children have difficulty maintaining balance.	Add support, e.g., by lightly touching a wall or partner with one outstretched hand. Ensure the children don't put too much weight on the wall or partner.

To view and analyze video for this skill, and all the skills in this manual online, please visit:

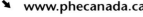 **www.phecanada.ca**

"what has worked in real life...."

Tanis was born with club feet; this means she has decreased mobility and flexibility in her feet and ankles. To help Tanis practice the stork stand, her teacher started off holding both her hands while Tanis tried to balance. As she got better, her teacher slowly decreased the amount of support by moving to one hand, then one finger, then having Tanis hold onto a rope where the teacher had the other end. This progression of physical aids has allowed Tanis to explore her own boundaries when it comes to balance. Now Tanis is quite good at balancing on her right foot, but still is off-balance on her left foot. However Tanis has progressed to the point where her teacher allows her to practice near the wall so that if Tanis needs to reach out for some extra support it is right there and the risk of Tanis falling in front of her whole class is reduced. This simple modification to the level of support has allowed Tanis to significantly progress in terms of her stork stand and her teacher is noticing improvements in other dynamic balance tasks.

Activities for the STORK STAND

Exploring the stork stand

Skill: Balance
Children: Individual
Equipment: None
Area: Gymnasium, court or field
Activity: The children take the stork stand position. Ask them to add some of the following movements: keep their arms by their sides, place their hands on their head, hold their arms up high, keep their arms out, cross their arms across their chest, hold their hands behind their back, close their eyes, throw a scarf up and catch it on their head. Change legs and try again. Invite the children to suggest tricky things to do while holding the stork balance.

Specific Modifications:
- Children in wheelchairs can be encouraged to do the arm actions of this activity.

Balance touch

Skill: Balance
Children: Individual
Equipment: Beanbags
Area: Gymnasium, court or field
Activity: The children adopt a stork stand with a beanbag on the floor beside them. Then, they reach their elevated foot out to touch the beanbag before resuming the stork position. The aim is to perform the movement without losing balance and without putting weight on the beanbag.

Specific Modifications:
- Children with mobility limitations with and without aids, may find this activity difficult if they are required to let go and balance. They could use a 'pool noodle' or a short racquet to touch the beanbag instead of their hand.
- Children in wheelchairs can use a stick or a pole to reach down and touch the beanbag on the floor.

Puzzle Balances

Skills: Static balance, balancing on different body parts, problem solving, body and space awareness.

Equipment: Mats.

Prepare a set of small cards with two or more symbols on each card, chosen so that it is possible to achieve a balance from that combination. Below are some ideas for symbols that could be used.

- *two feet and two elbows*
- *head, two hands, two feet*
- *bottom and two hands*
- *one knee and one foot*

Area: Gymnasium, court or field

Activity: Children take a sheet with a series of puzzle balances and see how many balances they can do to solve the puzzle, using mats provided.

Variations

Create a sequence: Move from puzzle balance to puzzle balance to create a sequence.

Work in pairs or small groups: Group members instruct each other (verbally) about how to do the puzzle balances.

Specific Modifications:

- Children with movement limitations should be encouraged to do this activity to the best of their ability on the mats.
- Some children in wheelchairs will do very well on the mat with the other children doing this task. Make sure to vary the "puzzle" instructions to the skill level and strength of the child who uses a wheelchair (e.g. instead of balancing on their feet they might use their bottom).

Cooperative Balances

Skills: Static balance, counterbalance, body and space awareness, problem solving and relationships (with others).

Equipment: Benches, box tops, mats and balls.

Children are in pairs of approximately the same height and size. Each pair has a mat or a defined area to work in.

Area: Gymnasium, court or field

Activity: With a partner, explore how many ways you can balance.

Repeat with only one base of support for each partner.

Repeat one more time, this time without using your foot as a base of support (e.g. using back or hands).

Can you balance with your partner – on a line, bench/box top, or crash pad with only …?

- two feet on the ground.
- two hands and one foot.
- one foot and two knees.
- one back and one foot.

Safety tip: *In some instances a "spotter" may be required depending on the level of difficulty and the skill level of the students. Safety is always a priority.*

Specific Modifications:

- Children in wheelchairs can be encouraged to do the arm actions of this activity and facilitate the balancing of a classmate – (e.g. classmate balances by holding onto the child's chair).

STORK STAND: *A one-foot balance with the ankle of the non-support foot placed against the knee of the support leg.*

Balance is attained when the centre of gravity is over the base of support.

INCLUSION ADAPTATIONS

Continuum of Prompts for the STORK STAND

Physical Prompts	**Physical prompts should be paired with verbal prompts.**
- Complete manipulation	Have the child hold onto the wall, a bar or another assistant, and physically bring one leg up to get the child into the stork position.
- Manipulative prompting	Try to hold onto the child's fingers less and less over time.
- Minimal guidance	Use a gentle tap to the non-support foot to indicate the child should raise his or her foot off the ground.
Visual Prompts	**Visual prompts should be paired with verbal prompts.**
- Complete skill demonstration	Demonstrate the stork stand with the child watching — maintain the position until you are certain the child has really watched.
- Partial skill demonstration	Demonstrate where to put your hands (hips) and where to put your foot (beside support leg knee) separately.
- Gestural prompting	Point to the child's foot to indicate he or she should lift it off the floor — or point to the hips to indicate the hands should be there.
Verbal Prompts	
- Skill cue	Tell the child to look ahead and focus, to hold the leg up and to put hands on hips.
- Action command	Give a verbal description of the desired skill (e.g., "Balance for 5 seconds," "Look forward").
- Action cue	Make a motivational statement to help the child perform the skill (e.g., "One, two, three").

PHE Canada
Physical & Health Education Canada

No Prompts

- Initiation with environmental cue	Pictures on the wall that show either stick figures or human figures balancing may initiate practice of balancing; an X on the floor near the walls could also be balance cues.
- Imitative initiation	Child performs the skill after watching other participants performing it.
- Initiation in free play	Child performs the skill at an appropriate time in free play but with no peer demonstration.

Behaviour Management and Pedagogical Considerations for the STORK STAND

ASD	• If a child uses pic-syms in the classroom, find pic-syms for balance-related activities and tasks, and create a storyboard of activities for each day. • Reduce distractions. • Avoid the child's sensitive aversions (e.g., loud noises, certain textures or colours). • Use structure and "sameness" for consistency (e.g., follow the same warm-up routine, the same general lesson structure). • Capitalize on the child's preferences as motivation (e.g., have the child focus on a poster or picture of a favourite character, such as Thomas the Tank Engine, that is taped to the wall).
DS	• Keep instructions clear and simple. • Encourage positive behaviours. • Visual demonstrations are highly recommended. • Balance may be limited in children with DS; therefore, practice is encouraged, but try to avoid repeated failure experiences. Allow children with DS to use a wall or a bar to hold if they need it. • Peer tutors can be effective for modelling and promoting on-task behaviour.
ADHD	• Reduce distractions: use small groups, keep space smaller. • Keep instructions clear and simple. • Maintain good "timing" — boredom may result in off-task behaviours. • Create an environment of success; provide enough of a challenge to maintain interest and motivation. • Set clear boundaries, both physical and task related. • Place something on the wall for the child to look at to maintain focus. • Reinforce respect, teamwork and sportsmanship concepts in all aspects of the lesson.

ID	• Use a peer tutor or educational assistant to keep the child on task. • Keep instructions simple and concise. • Repetition may be needed of both instructions and demonstrations. • Start with a simple task and add difficulty as the child progresses.
DCD	• Create an environment of success to prevent frustration. • Ensure the class rules are consistently enforced and the expectations are very clear. • Allow for and encourage repetition and practice. • Use self-rehearsal strategies, talk-aloud strategies (e.g., have the child assign words to the parts of the skill and say them aloud during practice). • Discourage off-task behaviours such as excessive water breaks, time outs and "clowning around" by keeping groups small and tasks age- and skill-level appropriate.

Characteristics of the STORK STAND	Cue Words for Children
Head neutral, looking forward	"Look forward." "Pick a spot on the wall to look at."
Back straight	"Stand up straight."
Arms straight and parallel to ground	"Reach arms out — it will help you balance."
Weight on one foot	"Stand on one foot."
Inside of ankle of one foot placed against the knee of the support leg	"Put your ankle next to your knee."
Position held for 3 seconds	"Hold still."

Difficulties to Watch For

If...	Then...
Children are not able to keep one or both arms on hips.	Encourage children to use both arms for balance.
	Allow them to perform the skill in front of a mirror so they can check the position of their arm.
	A peer tutor can provide feedback on arm positioning.
	Use a belt or a string around the waist for the children to hold.

Children have difficulty balancing on both legs (one at a time).	Encourage children to try balancing on each leg.
	Allow for an external support (e.g. peer tutor to hold onto or a wall or bar).
Children are visually checking support leg.	Encourage children to keep their head up by looking at something on the wall.
	A peer tutor can hold up fingers for the balancing child to count.
Children have difficulty holding the balance.	Add support, e.g., by lightly touching a wall or partner with one outstretched hand. Ensure the children don't put too much weight on the wall or partner.
	Start with short time periods and gradually increase time.

To view and analyze video for this skill, and all the skills in this manual online, please visit:

↘ **www.phecanada.ca**

What Has Worked in Real Life

At our school, the physical education students are given the opportunity to select their activity blocks. Many students benefit from having a choice in their activities, but where I notice a significant empowerment is with the students with intellectual disabilities. Kurt is a 17-year-old student who normally would go to the outside or far back when in large groups. Part of his course requirement is to document 50 hours of moderate to vigorous exercise during the semester. At the beginning of the school year, we were considering modifying some of the course requirements, but Kurt has proven us wrong. He is excelling in performing and documenting his moderate to vigorous exercise program. His self-esteem has flourished, with him wanting to be in the front row during the yoga unit or be the first to demonstrate/ instruct a pose for the students to follow (e.g., the stork stand). In our one-on-one meetings that take place approximately twice a month, Kurt has expressed how much fun he is having and that he likes the idea that he picked his activity blocks, not the teacher or the teacher assistant. This independence has made him a different physical education student — one who looks forward to class, wants to be involved and wants to be a part of the group activity.

Activities for the STORK STAND

Exploring the Stork Stand

Skill: Balancing
Children: Individual
Equipment: None
Area: Gymnasium, court or field
Activity: The children take the stork stand position. Ask them to add some of the following movements:
* keep their arms by their sides,
* place their hands on their heads,
* hold their arms up high,
* keep their arms out,
* cross their arms across their chests,
* hold their hands behind their backs,
* close their eyes,
* throw a scarf up and catch it on their heads.

Have the children change legs and try again. Invite the children to suggest tricky things to do while holding the stork balance.

Balance Touch

Skill: Balancing
Children: Individual
Equipment: Beanbags
Area: Gymnasium, court or field
Activity: The children adopt a stork stand with a beanbag on the floor beside them. Based on individual skill level determine the distance and positioning of the bean bag. For example, a highly skilled child might place the bag in front, behind, to the side and vary the distances. A child who has more difficulty with the stork stand might place the bean bag very close to his or her standing leg. Then, they reach their elevated foot out to touch the beanbag before resuming the stork position. The aim is to perform the movement without losing balance and without putting weight on the beanbag.

Traffic Light

Skills: Balancing, skipping, hopping
Children: Individual
Equipment: Three sheets of coloured paper (green, amber and red)
Area: Gymnasium, court or field
Activity: Children pretend to be vehicles responding to the colour of the traffic signal. The teacher/coach holds up a colour, and the children respond with an action. For green, the children skip in free space; for amber, they hop on the spot; and for red, they adopt the stork stand.

Puzzle Balances

Skills: Static balancing, balancing on different body parts, problem solving, body and space awareness
Children: Individual
Equipment: Mats, balance cards.
Prepare a set of small cards with two or more symbols on each, chosen so that it is possible to achieve a balance from that combination. Following are some ideas for symbols.
Examples of cards and balance
* *two feet and two elbows*
* *head, two hands and two feet*
* *bottom and two hands*
* *one knee and one foot*

Area: Gymnasium, court or field
Activity: Children take a sheet with a series of puzzle balances and see how many they can do, using mats provided.
Variations:
* Create a sequence: Players move from puzzle balance to puzzle balance to create a sequence.
* Players work in pairs or small groups. Group members instruct each other (verbally) about how to do the puzzle balances.

Individual Hoop Challenges

Skills: Balancing, jumping
Children: Individual
Equipment: One hoop per child
Area: Gymnasium, court or field
Activity: Children are scattered throughout the activity area, standing in their hoops. Announce a movement sequence using the words *in*, *out*, *over*, and *around (or others that are appropriate for skill level)*. Participants execute the movements as quickly or slowly as you would like. The goal is for the students to use the hoop to move in and out of different positions, many of which will require the student to balance in different positions, especially when the sequences are to be performed slowly.

Variations:

Challenge participants to come up with their own sequences.

Hoop Body-Part Balance

Skill: Balancing
Children: Individual
Equipment: One hoop per child
Area: Gymnasium, court or field
Activity: Children place their hoops on the ground and attempt the following challenges.

- Challenge children on all fours to:
  - demonstrate movements with the feet inside and the hands outside the hoop,
  - demonstrate movements with the hands inside and the feet outside the hoop, and
  - demonstrate movements with one foot and one hand inside the hoop while the other hand and foot are outside the hoop.
- Challenge participants to balance on:
  - two body parts inside the hoop,
  - three body parts inside the hoop,
  - two body parts inside and one outside the hoop, and
  - two body parts outside and one inside the hoop.
- Challenge participants to invent their own ways to balance.

HOLDING A SHAPE WHILE TRAVELLING

There are numerous skills that require a combination of maintaining a body shape while travelling. An example of this in the preschool years is sliding down a slide at a park. The locomotion involved may be primary or secondary to the skill. For example, there are skills such as snowboarding, skiing, and diving where gravity propels the body to travel and the challenge is to defy gravity with some finesse. However, there are other activities in which the primary challenge of the skill is to maintain momentum while travelling. Examples of this are skills which also involve locomotion such as the log roll, riding a bicycle, skating and skateboarding.

LOG ROLL: *a straight body rotating around the long axis.*

A. Characteristics of the mature LOG ROLL	Cue Words for Children
GET READY:	
Lie on stomach with arms stretched overhead	
Legs together and straight	Be as **long** as you can
Palms facing floor	
ROLLING ACTION:	
Roll to side, tummy, side and then back	
Keep body rigid	**Stiff** like a pencil

B. Teaching Tips

(i) Developmental changes to watch for prior to mature log roll:

- Increasing control and coordination of the body parts.
- Increasing ability to roll in a straight line.
- Crossing of arms and legs is less evident.

(ii) Difficulties to watch for:

If...	Then...
Children have difficulty generating momentum for the roll.	Coach them to start on their side or elevate one end of the mat to create a little "hill" to roll down.
Children have difficulty rolling in a straight line.	Encourage the children to control the force generated and rotate all body parts at the same time.
Arms or legs are crossing.	Coach the children to keep their legs and arms parallel.

To view and analyze video for this skill, and all the skills in this manual online, please visit:
www.phecanada.ca

C. Activities for LOG ROLLING

Three Rolls
Skill: Log roll
Children: Individual
Equipment: Mat per child
Area: Gymnasium
Activity: Ask the children to log roll three times in a row.

There and Back Again
Skill: Log roll
Children: Individual
Equipment: Mat per child
Area: Gymnasium
Activity: Ask the children to log roll one complete turn to the left and then return with a complete roll to the right.

No Hands, No Feet
Skill: Log roll
Children: Individual
Equipment: Mat per child
Area: Gymnasium
Activity: Coach the children to roll without letting their hands and feet touch the mat.

Floor Sequence
Skills: Log roll, balance
Children: Individual
Equipment: Mat per child
Area: Gymnasium
Activity: Invite the children to perform a more challenging sequence that links two static positions with a log roll. For example: long sit, to rear lying position, 1.5 log rolls, push up to front support. Extend this activity by having the children link together other static balances with a log roll.

LOG ROLL
- Arms straight over head
- Be as long as you can
- Body stiff like a pencil

Partner Roll

Skill: Log roll
Children: Pairs
Equipment: One mat per pair
Area: Gymnasium
Activity: The children lie on their stomach facing each other. They hold hands and roll in the same direction down the mat.

Seals in The Sea

Skill: Log roll
Children: Individual
Equipment: Mat per child
Area: Gymnasium
Activity: Ask the children to pretend they are seals rolling in the sea by keeping their arms and shoulders off the mat as they roll. When they are performing seal rolls, children should try to keep their back straight and avoid arching it.

LOG ROLL: *A straight body rolling around the long axis.*

Continuum of Prompts for the LOG ROLL

Physical Prompts	Physical prompts should be paired with verbal prompts.
- Complete manipulation	Have the child lie down on a mat, and physically roll the child along the mat (having the child wrapped in a blanket is also effective).
- Manipulative prompting	Provide a slight push to give the child the momentum to initiate the roll.
- Minimal guidance	Give a slight push if the child needs help with rolling more than one time in a row, if he or she doesn't have the momentum to keep going, if he or she can't get started.
Visual Prompts	**Visual prompts should be paired with verbal prompts.**
- Complete skill demonstration	Give a demonstration of the log roll slowly with a straight body.
- Partial skill demonstration	Demonstrate the log roll by standing up and "spinning" to illustrate the rolling action, or try rolling one roll at a time on the mat.
- Gestural prompting	Give a gesture that indicates the child should roll over (e.g., an arched gesture with the hand).

Verbal Prompts

- Skill cue	Try focusing the child's attention on a key component of the task (e.g., "Keep your body straight like a board," "Try to make your body long").
- Action command	Give a verbal description of the desired skill (e.g., "Roll over").
- Action cue	Make a motivational statement to help the child perform the skill (e.g., "One, two, three, roll").

No Prompts

- Initiation with environmental cue	Place mats out on the floor to encourage the child to explore his or her movements on the mats.
- Imitative initiation	Child performs the skill after watching other participants performing it.
- Initiation in free play	Child performs the skill at an appropriate time in free play but with no peer demonstration.

Behaviour Management and Pedagogical Considerations for LOG ROLLING

ASD	• If a child uses pic-syms in the classroom, find pic-syms for rolling-related activities and tasks, and create a storyboard of activities for each day. • Some children with ASD may really enjoy log roll activities for sensory reasons. Log rolls could actually be a fixation activity if allowed. Log rolls using blankets may give some children with ASD a calming sensation; therefore, log rolls could be used as an appropriate activity to bring a child out of a behavioural episode. • Conversely, it is also possible that some children may have a sensory aversion to log rolls (dizziness). • Use structure and "sameness" for consistency (e.g., follow the same warm-up routine, the same general lesson structure).
DS	• Keep instructions clear and simple. • Encourage positive behaviours. • Visual demonstrations are highly recommended. • Peer tutors can be effective for modelling and promoting on-task behaviour. • Children with DS are hyperflexible, and so it is important to demonstrate and teach proper form to prevent injuries when working on the floor.

ADHD	• Reduce distractions: use small groups, keep space smaller. • Keep instructions clear and simple. • Maintain good "timing" — boredom may result in off-task behaviours. • Create an environment of success. • Set clear boundaries, both physical and task related. • Reinforce respect, teamwork and sportsmanship concepts in all aspects of the lesson.
ID	• Use a peer tutor or educational assistant to keep the child on task. • Keep instructions simple and concise. • Repetition may be needed of both instructions and demonstrations. • Start with a simple task and add difficulty as the child progresses.
DCD	• Ensure the class rules are consistently enforced and the expectations are very clear. • Allow for and encourage repetition and practice. • Use self-rehearsal strategies, talk-aloud strategies (e.g., have the child assign words to the parts of the skill and say them aloud during practice). • Discourage off-task behaviours such as excessive water breaks, time outs and "clowning around" by keeping groups small and tasks age- and skill-level appropriate.

Characteristics of the LOG ROLL	Cue Words for Children
Lying on stomach with arms stretched overhead	"Make yourself as long as you can."
Legs together and straight	"Legs together."
Rolling to side, tummy, side and then back	"Roll over." "Roll onto your stomach (or back)."
Keep body rigid	"Stiff like a pencil."

Difficulties to Watch For:

If...	Then...
Child has difficulty generating momentum for the roll.	Coach the child to start on his or her side, or elevate one end of the mat to create a little "hill" to roll down.
Child has difficulty rolling in a straight line.	Encourage the child to control the force generated and rotate all body parts at the same time. Encourage the child to keep his or her body very straight.
Child's arms or legs are crossing.	Coach the child to keep his or her legs and arms parallel.

To view and analyze video for this skill, and all the skills in this manual online, please visit:
www.phecanada.ca

What Has Worked in Real Life

Michael has Asperger syndrome and is eight years old. When Michael feels overwhelmed, his teachers can often find him squeezed into a small space, behind a chair or under a cushion. His parents have indicated that deep pressure and small spaces provide the right kind of sensory stimulation he needs to calm down. When teaching log rolls, I sometimes like to allow the students who are having difficulty to be rolled up in a blanket and then unrolled so they can experience the log roll passively. When I first rolled Michael up in the blanket, I had no idea he was going to like it so much. That first day he asked to be rolled up and unrolled probably 15 times. At first I was so glad that Michael was engaged in an activity that I complied. The next physical education class he asked to do rolls again. Once again, I was so happy he was engaged that I did not realize he was becoming fixated on getting rolled up in a blanket. I quickly started to limit the log roll activities and began to use them as a reward. For example, if Michael successfully completed 10 log rolls on his own on the mat, he could have one blanket log roll. This type of motivation worked well for Michael.

Activities for the LOG ROLL

* Children with ASD or other sensory affinities may really enjoy the log roll activities, especially using a blanket. Be careful not to let these activities become fixations or obsessions to the exclusion of other educational topics.

Blanket Roll

* Suitable for very young children with developmental delays.

Skills: Rolling

Children: Pairs

Equipment: One mat and one blanket per pair

Area: Gymnasium

Activity: Children work in pairs, where one child lies on the ground and is rolled up in the blanket. The second child unrolls the first by pulling on the loose end of the blanket, and then they switch roles.

Triple Roll

Skill: Rolling

Children: Individual

Equipment: One mat per child

Area: Gymnasium

Activity: Ask the children to log roll three times in a row.

There and Back Again

Skill: Rolling

Children: Individual

Equipment: One mat per child

Area: Gymnasium

Activity: Ask the children to log roll one complete turn to the left and then return with a complete roll to the right.

Body Bowling

Skill: Rolling

Children: Whole class

Equipment: Floor mats, plastic or foam bowling pins

Area: Gymnasium

Activity: Set up the bowling pins at one end of the mat. Each player lies on his or her tummy at the other end of the mat, across from the pins. Tell the children they are bright, colourful bowling balls. Each "ball" log rolls the distance of the mat to knock over the pins.

Variations:

Vary the distance to the pins for different skill levels.

Partner Roll

Skill: Rolling

Children: Pairs

Equipment: One mat per pair

Area: Gymnasium

Activity: The children lie on their tummies facing each other. They hold hands and roll in the same direction down the mat.

No Hands, No Feet

Skill: Rolling

Children: Individual

Equipment: One mat per child

Area: Gymnasium

Activity: Coach the children to roll without letting their hands and feet touch the mat.

CHAPTER 5: Locomotor Skills

The second category of fundamental movement skills is *locomotion* or *locomotor skills*, which comprise all of the ways in which the body can travel. The primary locomotor skills include walking, running, skipping, galloping, and jumping (which includes hopping and leaping). These skills most typically develop during the preschool and early primary school years. Between ages six and eight, the child usually performs these skills with ease and effectiveness in a myriad of situations. For this reason, games and activities that involve running and stopping, dodging, racing and chasing, and travelling to music are popular. Children learn to travel in different directions (forwards or backwards) at different speeds (slowly and quickly) and at different levels (high and low levels). They can increase in difficulty through sequencing (eg. walk, hop, jump); foot patterning (eg., slide-step); rhythm (eg., walk 4 beats, hop 4 beats, jump 4 beats, freeze); and cooperating with others (eg. do it together, matching). Locomotor skills can be made more complex as in games when equipment to carry or propel an object is added- as in lacrosse, hockey, basketball and soccer— and even more complex when competition is present (eg. 2 vs. 2).

RUN: *travel fast by using one's feet, with one foot off the ground at any given time*

A. Characteristics of the mature RUN — Cue Words for Children

A. Characteristics of the mature RUN	Cue Words for Children
LEG ACTION:	
Foot contact is with the heel, or as speed increases, with the ball of the foot under the body	Balls of feet
Swing knee is raised high	High knees
Support leg moves from slight bend to complete extension	
ARM ACTION:	
Elbow is bent at right angles (stay at this angle) and move in opposition to legs	Hands brush hips in backswing
Upper arm drives forward and back	Drive arms; elbows in

B. Teaching Tips

(i) Developmental changes to watch for prior to the mature run:

- As the running stride develops, the length of the stride increases as does the amount of extension of the hip, knee and ankle during the push off.
- The length of time when the body is in flight increases.
- The height of the heel increases as the knee drives forward.
- The height of the knee drive increases.
- The base of support narrows and the amount of vertical movement decreases.

(ii) Difficulties to watch for:

If...	Then...
Children have very small steps with little or no flight.	Show them how to exaggerate the length of the stride to get a flight phase.
Children have their feet spread wide apart.	Coach them to run along a line trying to keep their feet on the line.
Children have short strides.	Place beanbags or markers at a distance that is a bit longer than their stride and see if they can place each foot at a marker.
Children have low heel recovery.	Ask them to run over a short distance with their heels coming up and touching their rear end.
Children have their arms swinging from side to side.	Coach children to stand still but move their arms so they have a 90 degree angle at their elbow and their hands don't cross the midline of the body; their hands should lightly touch the top of their hips.
Children are leaning too far forward.	Lead children to walk on their toes swinging their arms and keeping as tall as possible; this can be followed by a high knee running motion but not moving forward very quickly.

To view and analyze video for this skill, and all the skills in this manual online, please visit:
www.phecanada.ca

C. Activities for RUNNING

Straight Line Shadow Tag

Skills: Running, dodging
Children: Pairs
Equipment: None
Area: Large gymnasium or outside field
Activity: One partner is a leader with their 'shadow' standing behind them. The leader accelerates and decelerates and the shadow tries to keep a constant distance behind the leader. Children may need to be reminded that this is a cooperative activity.

Pie

Skills: Running, dodging
Children: Individual
Equipment: Three flags
Area: A snow covered field
Activity: Mark off a giant pie on half a soccer field covered in snow. Children play a game of tag, and they must stay within the lines established by making the pie. Two or three children are 'it' and carry the flags so the other children can see who is 'it.'

RUN

- Contact with heels of feet
- Go faster – increase contact with balls of feet
- Lift knees
- Extend your leg
- Hands brush hips
- Elbows at right angles
- Drive arms – elbows in

Beanbag Scramble

Skill: Running
Children: Teams of four
Equipment: Large number of beanbags and six hula hoops
Area: Large gymnasium or playing field; place one hoop in the centre with all the beanbags inside the hoop.
Activity: Each team has a hula hoop designated as their home hoop, placed an equal distance from the centre hoop and from the other teams' hoops.

On a signal, one person from each team runs to the centre and grabs one beanbag and returns it their home hoop. The next person can then go to the centre hoop or another team's hoop to collect one beanbag. This repeats with children taking their turn to run. Once the pattern is learned, two children can go at once.

Run and Stop

Skills: Running and stopping
Children: Individual
Equipment: Music
Area: Open space
Activity: Teacher plays music while children run. Children stop suddenly when the music stops. This can be made more challenging if the teacher instructs children to; "Run backwards"; "Now run in a zig-zag pathway". Teacher can call out various directions (forward, backwards, sideways), pathways (straight, zig-zag, curved), and speeds (slow, medium, sprint)or with older children, a combination of these.

Belly Run

Skill: Running

Children: Pairs

Equipment: Four cones marking two lines about 20 meters apart

Area: Gymnasium or playing field

Activity: Partners line up, one behind the other on one of the lines. They start by lying face down; at the teacher's signal, they scramble to a running position and sprint to the other line. The second group repeats this.

Crows and Cranes

Skill: Running

Children: Two teams

Equipment: Four cones marking two lines about 2 meters apart in the centre of the play space; four cones marking end lines about 20 meters from the centre lines

Area: Gymnasium or playing field

Activity: One team (the crows) lines up between one set of cones and the other group (the cranes) lines up between the other set of cones, facing the other team. The teacher calls out "cranes" and the cranes turn and run to their end line before being tagged by the crows who are chasing them. If caught before they reach the end line those tagged join the other team. The teacher can try to trick the groups by dragging out the "crrrrrrr" part.

RUN: *Locomotor skill where one foot is off the ground at any given time*

Characteristics of the mature RUN	Cue words for children
Trunk maintains a slight forward lean throughout the stride pattern	"Lean forward"
Foot contact is with the heel or as speed increases with the ball of the foot under the body	"Heels first or toes first"
Swing knee is raised high	"High knees"
Support leg moves from slight bend to complete extension	"Push forward"
Both arms swing through a large arc close to the body and are synchronized opposite to the leg action	"Brush hips"

Adaptations of the RUN for:

Children in wheelchairs	• Encourage the child to wheel quickly in the same direction as the other classmates are running. • Have the child work on controlling his or her chair at different speeds negotiating different terrains.
Children with mobility aids	• Instruct the child to find the most appropriate rhythm of using his or her crutches or planting their crutches or walker to run fast, but also efficiently and effectively. • Allow the child to move at their own pace to ensure success and safety. • Shorten running games or distances for children who use mobility aids as fatigue could present as an issue due to the demands of using his or her upper body to help run.
Children with mobility limitations	• Allow the child to move at his or her own pace, emphasizing control during a change of direction. • Be aware that the child's movements may appear jerky or out of control. Encourage the child to move smoothly. • Children with hemiplegic cerebral palsy will likely have one stronger side and changing direction can be more difficult on the weaker side.
Children with visual impairments	• If possible, set up a guide-wire course for the child to have a tactile guide while running. • Use a bell or a sound to indicate it is time to change directions (e.g. two rings of a bell could mean go left, on right could mean go right etc.). • Have a partner or education assistant run parallel to the child giving real-time instructions. • Allow the child to "walk the course" first to enable familiarization. • Provide very clear verbal instructions about the task and the environment for safety purposes.

Children who are deaf	• If an interpreter is not available (or necessary), have a cue card at each station (or for each physical education lesson) with the task or plan clearly outlined at the child's level of understanding.
	• Be prepared to give extra demonstrations of skills and activities.
	• Consider using an FM loop system (microphone worn by the teacher to amplify the voice into the hearing aid worn by the Deaf student).
	• Avoid excess noise in the learning environment.
	• Be aware that some Deaf children may have balance difficulties and therefore stopping while at full speed may be a challenge.

Difficulties to watch for:

If...	**Then...**
Children have very small steps with little or no flight.	Show them how to exaggerate the length of the stride to get a flight phase (moment when both feet are off the ground). Have them reach forward with their legs.
Children have their feet spread wide apart.	Instruct them to run along a line trying to keep their feet close to the line – one foot in front of the other.
Children have short strides.	Place floor markers at a distance that is slightly longer than their stride and see if they can place each foot at a marker.
Children have low heel recovery.	Ask them to run over a short distance with their heels coming up and touching their rear end.
Children have their arms swinging from side to side.	Coach children to stand still but move their arms so they have a 90 degree angle at their elbow and their hands don't cross the midline of the body; their hands should lightly touch the top of their hips.
Children are leaning too far forward.	Lead children to walk on their toes swinging their arms and keeping as tall as possible. This can be followed by a high knee running motion but not moving forward very quickly.

To view and analyze video for this skill, and all the skills in this manual online, please visit:
➤ **www.phecanada.ca**

"what has worked in real life...."

Rose began her kindergarten year last September. When I met Rose, she was a happy cheerful little girl who enjoyed coming to physical education classes, but she was always in her wheelchair and often felt apprehensive to venture out and try new activities. Leigh's Syndrome is a rare inherited Neuro-metabolic disorder characterized by degeneration of the central nervous system, brain, spinal- cord and optic nerve. The central nervous system gradually loses its ability to function properly. Rose was included in our regular PE classes. As time went on you could see that she became eager to move and wanted out of her chair. With the help of her educational assistant she was taken out of her chair and she started to participate in daily PE activities. Her means of mobility is crawling, walking with aid and running with aid. Her limitations are not slowing her down. Her classmates are wonderful with her and often are the first to choose her for a partner when we are doing partner activities. Including a child like Rose into the class has definitely helped her fellow classmates learn patience and compassion.

Activities for RUNNING

Waves of runners

Skill: Running

Children: Pairs

Equipment: Four cones establishing two lines about 20 meters apart

Area: In the gymnasium however a field is more suitable

Activity: Children are in pairs, standing one behind the other at the starting line. On a signal the first group accelerates to the target line. The second partner repeats this when the first person crosses the line. Repeat coming back.

Specific Modifications:

- Encourage children in wheelchairs to explore their environment using their chair, changing directions quickly and safely.

Straight line shadow tag

Skill: Running at varying speeds

Children: Pairs

Equipment: None

Area: Large gymnasium or outside field

Activity: One partner is a leader with their 'shadow' standing behind them. The leader accelerates and decelerates and the shadow tries to keep a constant distance behind the leader.

Safety: Instruct students to pay attention when shadowing a wheelchair in case the child in the wheelchair stops quickly.

Specific Modifications:

- Encourage children in wheelchairs to explore their environment using their chair, changing directions quickly and safely.

PHE Canada
Physical & Health Education Canada

Pie

Skill: Running
Children: Individual
Equipment: Three flags
Area: A snow covered field
Activity: Mark off a giant pie on half a soccer field covered in snow. Children play a game of tag, and they must stay within the lines established by making the pie. Two or three children are 'it' and carry the flags so the other children can see who is 'it.'

Specific Modifications:

- For Deaf children, use flashcards, with the instructions on them or a Sign Language interpreter to ensure the instructions/changes are communicated.
- Encourage children in wheelchairs to participate if possible. When it is not snowing, this game may be better suited for the playground.

RUN: *Locomotor skill where one foot is off the ground at any given time.*

Continuum of Prompts for the RUN

Physical Prompts	Physical prompts should be paired with verbal prompts.
- Complete manipulation	Hold hands with the child and try to increase the pace by running with the child. If the child has difficulty increasing the pace, external motivators can be used in conjunction with physical prompts.
- Manipulative prompting	Provide assistance only during critical parts of the run (e.g., holding hands only during initiation — getting the child started).
- Minimal guidance	Make contact with a relevant body part to initiate running (e.g., soft pull on hand to signal it's time to run, or a tap to the foot).

Visual Prompts	**Visual prompts should be paired with verbal prompts.**
- Complete skill demonstration	Accurately and slowly demonstrate running, exaggerating the flight phase and the arms. Slowly speed up the demonstration based on the skill level of the child.
- Partial skill demonstration	Accurately demonstrate a component of the skill (e.g., demonstrate just the arms or just the heel strike).
- Gestural prompting	Gesture to remind participant of key component (e.g., point to the destination or at the child's feet).
Verbal Prompts	
- Skill cue	Try focusing the child's attention on a key component of the task (e.g., "Swing your arms," "Lift your feet").
- Action command	Give a verbal description of the desired skill (e.g., "Run to the red line," "Run fast").
- Action cue	Make a motivational statement to help the child perform the skill (e.g., "One, two, three, go").
No Prompts	
- Initiation with	Having a wide-open space may be the best way to encourage running, or having different patterns of lines on the floor.
- Imitative initiation	Child performs the skill after watching other participants performing it.
- Initiation in free play	Child performs the skill at an appropriate time in free play but with no peer demonstration.

Behaviour Management and Pedagogical Considerations for RUNNING

ASD	• If a child uses pic-syms in the classroom, find pic-syms for running and running-related activities (e.g., games that involve running), and create a storyboard of activities for the lesson. • Avoid the child's sensitive aversions (e.g., loud noises, certain textures or colours). • Use structure and "sameness" for consistency (e.g., follow the same warm-up routine, the same general lesson structure). • Physical activity and exercise can have a positive impact on repetitive and stereotyped movements common in children with ASD; therefore, starting a lesson with vigorous physical activity may be effective at increasing on-task behaviours for the rest of the lesson or practice.
DS	• Keep instructions clear and simple. • Encourage positive behaviours. • Visual demonstrations are highly recommended. • Force production, strength and balance may be limited in children with DS, making physical education a critical component of a child's education plan. • Peer tutors can be effective for modelling and promoting on-task behaviour. • Children with DS are very socially motivated; therefore, having the child work in pairs or in groups where he or she can follow the group may be a very effective motivator for running activities.
ADHD	• Reduce distractions: use small groups, keep space smaller. • Keep instructions clear and simple. • Maintain good "timing" — boredom may result in off-task behaviours. • Create an environment of success. • Set clear boundaries, both physical and task related. • Reinforce respect, teamwork and sportsmanship concepts in all aspects of the lesson.
ID	• Use a peer tutor or educational assistant to keep the child on task. • Keep instructions simple and concise. • Repetition may be needed of both instructions and demonstrations. • A motivating object or activity may be needed to engage a child with a severe and profound disability in running.
DCD	• Create an environment of success to prevent frustration. • Ensure the class rules are consistently enforced and the expectations are very clear. • Allow for and encourage repetition and practice. • Use self-rehearsal strategies, talk-aloud strategies (e.g., have the child assign words to the parts of the skill and say them aloud during practice). • Discourage off-task behaviours such as excessive water breaks, time outs and "clowning around" by keeping groups small and tasks age- and skill-level appropriate.

Characteristics of the RUN

Characteristics of the RUN	Cue Words for children
Trunk maintains a slight forward lean throughout the stride pattern	"Lean your chest into where you're going."
Foot contact is with the heel or, as speed increases, with the ball of the foot under the body	"Land on your heels."
Swing knee is raised high	"Keep your knees high."
Support leg moves from slight bend to complete extension	"Push through the floor with your legs."
Both arms swing through a large arc close to the body and are synchronized opposite to the leg action	"Your hands brush your hips."

Difficulties to Watch For

If...	Then...
Child takes very small steps, with little or no flight.	Show the child how to exaggerate the length of the stride to get a flight phase; have him or her reach forward with the legs.
Child has his or her feet spread wide apart.	Instruct the child to run along a line, trying to keep his or her feet close to the line — one foot in front of the other
Child has short strides.	Place floor markers at a distance that is slightly longer than the child's stride, and see if he or she can place each foot at a marker.
Child has low heel recovery.	Ask the child to run over a short distance while lifting the heels up to touch his or her rear end.
Child has his or her arms swinging from side to side.	Coach the child to stand still but move his or her arms to make a 90-degree angle at the elbow. The child's hands don't cross the midline of the body and should lightly touch the top of the hips.
Child is leaning too far forward.	Instruct the child to walk on his or her toes while swinging the arms and keeping as tall as possible; this can be followed by a high-knee running motion while moving forward slowly.

To view and analyze video for this skill, and all the skills in this manual online, please visit:
www.phecanada.ca

What Has Worked in Real Life

I teach a class of 11 students who have a variety of unique needs, including autism, developmental delays, Down syndrome and oppositional defiant disorder. As part of our routine in physical education class, the students do laps around the gym. This acts as a great warm-up for the students as well as an avenue for them to expend some energy and simply get active. Individuals decide whether they will walk, jog or do a combination of both. For every lap they do, they get a token. After all the tokens have been distributed, they each count their own, and we keep track on a poster. Once the chart is completed, we have a special treat or activity for the students. The tokens serve as a great reinforcement or instant reward for the work they do, and the high level of activity at the beginning of the class promotes on-task behaviour for the rest of the lesson.

Activities for the RUN

Waves of Runners

Skill: Running
Children: Pairs
Equipment: Four cones establishing two lines about 20 metres apart
Area: Large gymnasium or outside field (a field is preferable)
Activity: Children are in pairs, standing one behind the other at the starting line. On a signal, the first group accelerates to the target line. The second partner starts outs when the first person crosses the line. Repeat coming back.

Straight-Line Shadow Tag

Skill: Running
Children: Pairs
Equipment: None
Area: Large gymnasium or outside field
Activity: One partner is a leader, with his or her "shadow" standing behind. The leader accelerates and decelerates, and the shadow tries to keep a constant distance behind the leader.

Safety tip: Instruct participants to pay attention when shadowing a wheelchair in case the child in the wheelchair stops quickly.

Spinning Wheel

* Suitable for very young children with developmental delays.

Skills: Running, jogging, skipping
Children: Whole class
Equipment: Parachute
Area: Gymnasium, court or field
Activity: The children stand sideways to the parachute, holding the edge with the right hand. On a signal, the children begin walking clockwise. Gradually have participants "accelerate" the spinning wheel to faster modes of travel (e.g., skipping, jogging, running). After a few moments, the children "decelerate" the spinning wheel gradually, bringing it to a full stop. Repeat the activity with the children travelling in the opposite direction.

Automobile

Skills: Running, skipping, marching, shuffling, hopping, jumping, leaping, dodging

Children: Individual

Equipment: One hoop per child

Area: Gymnasium, court or field

Activity: The children are scattered in a designated activity area, each with a hoop. Participants imagine the hoop is an automobile and they are the drivers (imagine Fred Flintstone's car). Each participant stands inside his or her automobile (hoop), holds it at waist height and buckles up! On a signal, participants travel about the street, avoiding other traffic.

The following commands can be used:

Green light — begin moving

Yellow light — move slowly

Red light — stop

School zone — skip

Neighbourhood — march

Highway — run

Reverse — move backward making "beeping" sounds

Emergency vehicle — move to the side of the activity area and stop

One way — move clockwise

Oil slick — swerve and make a quick turn

Pothole — leap

Tunnel — duck down

Flat tire — hop

Traffic jam — shuffle

* Automobiles that collide must report to the "body shop" before they can resume participating. The "drivers" involved must

a) stop and put their hoops down next to each other,

b) do "repair" work (e.g., five jumping jacks or some other activity), and

c) shake hands and say, "I'm sorry. Please drive safely!"

Pie

Skills: Running, dodging

Children: Individual

Equipment: Three flags

Area: A snow-covered field

Activity: Mark off a giant pie on half a soccer field covered in snow. Children play a game of tag, and they must stay within the lines established by the pie. Two or three children are "it" and carry the flags so the other children can see who is "it."

Beanbag Scramble

Skill: Running

Children: Teams of four

Equipment: Large number of beanbags; one hoop per team plus one extra

Area: Large gymnasium or playing field

Activity: Place one hoop in the centre of the gym or field, with all the beanbags inside it. Each team has a hoop designated as their home hoop, placed an equal distance from the centre hoop and from the other teams' hoops. On a signal, one person from each team runs to the centre hoop, grabs one beanbag and returns it to his or her home hoop. The next person can then go to the centre hoop or another team's hoop to collect one beanbag. Each child takes a turn retrieving a beanbag. Once every child has a turn, two children can go at once.

DODGE: *a rapid shift of the body from one line of travel to another*

A. Characteristics of the mature DODGE

the mature DODGE	Cue Words for Children
DODGING ACTION:	
Eyes focused in direction of travel	Look where you are running
Body lowered during change of direction	Get low
Change direction by pushing off outside foot	Push off
Change of direction occurs in one step	One step
Can change direction in both directions	Go left, go right

B. Teaching Tips

(i) Developmental changes to watch for leading up to mature dodge:

- Initially, children run to a point and then take several steps to turn their whole body to the new intended direction of travel.
- Children do not bend their knees.
- Transfer of weight becomes more rapid; spatial and directional awareness improve.
- Timing of movement improves.
- Improving ability to deal with complex and unpredictable environments while dodging (e.g. fleeing in chase games).
- Developmental changes also include increasing ability to dodge off of either foot, the ability to perform several dodging movements in a row, and the ability to include a head and shoulder fake.

(ii) Difficulties to watch for:

If...	Then...
Children have difficulty judging the distance to stationary or moving objects.	Give the children more opportunities to vary the distance to the object and vary the angle of approach and exit. Start with stationary objects to dodge and gradually increase the level of unpredictability.
Children are crossing their feet.	Ensure they understand the footwork sequence. Use coloured tape on the ground to indicate when to step with the left foot and when to step with the right foot.
Children take several small steps to change direction of travel.	Encourage the children to push off and change direction in one step. The children will need to plant their outside foot next to a cone or line and take the next step on another path. Provide opportunities to master the skill in predictable environments (e.g. ask the children to run to a line and back, before including the skill in less predictable environments such as in a game of tag).

(iii) When practicing the dodge, avoid slippery surfaces.

To view and analyze video for this skill, and all the skills in this manual online, please visit:
↘ **www.phecanada.ca**

C. Activities for DODGING

Exploring the Dodge
Skills: Dodging, running, sidestepping
Children: Individual
Equipment: Cones
Area: Gymnasium, court, or field
Activities:
- Run to a line and back, dodge as they reach the line.
- Place cones in a zigzag pattern and dodge at each one.
- Place two cones 5 meters apart, sidestep between them and dodge sideways back to the other cone.

Push Off
Skills: Dodging, running
Children: Individual
Equipment: Cones
Area: Gymnasium, court, or field
Activity: Place cones in a designated area and invite the children to jog between the cones and push off with their outside foot as they reach one.

Locomotor Circuit

Skills: Dodging, skipping, jumping

Children: Individual

Equipment: Cones, hula-hoops, skipping ropes

Area: Gymnasium, court or field

Activity: Set up a circuit and invite the children to hop over the skipping ropes, jump across the hoops, dodge from cone to cone, and crabwalk back to the beginning.

Rats and Rabbits

Skills: Dodging, running

Children: Pairs

Equipment: Cones

Area: Gymnasium, court, or field

Activity: Children form two parallel lines, one meter apart, opposite their partner. The "rats" are facing the "rabbits." A further set of lines are set up 5 meters from each line. The teacher/coach calls "rats" or "rabbits." If "rats" is called, the rats try to run through the "rabbits" and over the line before being tagged by their rabbit partner; and vice versa. To ensure this is a dodging activity, the children should face forward and push off with a dodging motion.

Safety tip: Ensure there is plenty of room so that there is no risk of children running into a solid object such as a wall or fence.

What Time is it, Tricky Wolf?

Skills: Dodging, running

Children: Whole class

Equipment: None

Area: Gymnasium, court, or field

Activity: The child chosen to be Tricky Wolf stands at one end of the playing area, facing away from the children who are at the other end of the space.

The aim is for the children to move closer to the wolf without getting caught. The children chant in unison "What time is it, Tricky Wolf?" and Tricky Wolf will answer in one of two ways:

- If Tricky Wolf calls a time on the clock; e.g.
  "Three o'clock!" The children will then take that number of steps towards Tricky Wolf, counting the steps out loud as they go ("One, Two, Three!"). They then ask the question again.
- Tricky Wolf may answer "Dinner Time!" At this point, Tricky Wolf turns and chases the children back to their starting point. If Tricky Wolf successfully tags someone, that child is the new Tricky Wolf for the next round. If a child does get all the way to Tricky Wolf without getting caught, everyone goes back to the start and the game begins again. Encourage the children to use their dodging action when chasing or fleeing.

Zigzag Relay

Skills: Dodging, running

Children: Pairs

Equipment: Cones

Area: Gymnasium, court, or field

Activity: The first partner runs the zigzag pattern, using a dodging action at each cone. After reaching the end, the child runs back to the beginning and tags his/her partner.

DODGE

- Look where you are running
- Get low
- Change direction:
  .. Push off
  .. Take one step
- Go left
- Go right

DODGE: *Dodging involves quick, deceptive changes in direction to evade, chase or flee from an opponent.*

PHOTO BY DAVE ARNOLD, COMPLIMENTS OF PARASPORT ONTARIO

Characteristics of the DODGE	Cue Words for Children
Eyes focused in direction of travel	"Look or Aim for the cone"
Body lowered during change of direction (athletic stance)	"Get low or Bend"
Change direction by pushing off outside foot	"Push"
Change of direction occurs in one step	"One step or Look first"
Can change direction in both directions	"Left, right"

Adaptations of the DODGE for:

Children in wheelchairs	• Encourage the child to wheel toward the cone, stop the wheelchair and change directions toward the next cone.
	• Encourage the child to stop the chair and change directions rather than do a big "arc turn".
	• Instruct the children to focus on the pivot rather than speed.
	• Ensure the "course" is widened and extended to accommodate the chairs.
Children with mobility aids	• Encourage the child to move quickly towards the target (cone) in an "athletic stance" (feet shoulder width apart, bend in ankles, knees and hips, chest up, weight on the heels of feet, slight forward bend in spine, hands out in front with elbows slightly bent, relaxed shoulders, head level with ground).
	• Instruct the child to plant their crutches or walker to help with the pivot and change of direction.
	• Allow the child to move at their own pace to ensure success and safety.
	• To facilitate success, narrow the field at first. As skill progresses, increase the field and the level of difficulty.

Children with mobility limitations	• Allow the child to move at his or her own pace, emphasizing control at the pivot.
	• Be aware that the child's movements may appear jerky or out of control. Encourage the child to move smoothly.
	• Children with hemiplegic cerebral palsy will likely have one stronger side, making the pivot more difficult on the weaker side. Encourage the child to practice the dodge by pivoting on both sides of the body. This allows them to practice balance and coordination on both the strong and weaker side.
	• Try narrowing the "dodge course" for children with mobility limitations.
Children with visual impairments * *Dodging may be more appropriate for children who have partial vision; and may not be advisable for children with complete vision loss.*	• If possible, set up a rope course for the child to have a tactile guide while running through the dodge course.
	• Use a bell or a sound to indicate it is time to change directions.
	• Have a partner or education assistant run parallel to the child giving real-time instructions.
	• Allow the child to "walk the course" first to allow for familiarization.
	• Provide verbal instructions about how many "steps" to take before the pivot in order to help the student during the running phase.
Children who are deaf	• If an interpreter is not available or necessary, have a cue card at each station (or for each PE lesson) with the task or plan clearly outlined at the child's level of understanding.
	• Print off pages from the online teaching tool for the dodge.
	• Be prepared to give extra demonstrations of skills and activities.
	• Consider using an FM loop system (microphone worn by the teacher to amplify the voice into the hearing aid worn by the deaf student).
	• Avoid excess noise in the learning environment.
	• Be aware that some deaf children may have balance difficulties therefore the pivot part of the dodge may be more challenging.

Difficulties to watch for:

If...	Then...
Children have difficulty judging the distance to stationary or moving objects.	Give the children more opportunities to vary the distance to the object to dodge and vary the angle of approach and exit. Start with stationary objects to dodge and gradually increase the level of unpredictability.
Children are crossing their feet.	Ensure they understand the footwork sequence. Use coloured tape on the ground to indicate when to step with the left foot and when to step with the right foot.
Children take several small steps to change direction of travel.	Encourage the children to push off and change direction in one step. The children will need to plant their outside foot next to a cone or line and take the next step on another path. Encourage the children to slow down and anticipate the change of direction. Provide opportunity to master the skill in predictable environments. e.g., ask the children to run to a line and back, before including the skill in less predictable environments such as a game of tag.

To view and analyze video for this skill, and all the skills in this manual online, please visit:
www.phecanada.ca

"what has worked in real life...."

Billy is eight years old and has mild cerebral palsy and uses crutches to assist with walking. When practicing the dodge he was having great difficulty with the pivot portion. To assist Billy in coordinating his crutches and his legs for the pivot, his teacher used gym tape to place markers on the floor to guide Billy on where to put both his crutches and his feet when executing the pivot. After several weeks of practice with the floor markings, Billy's dodge became much more proficient and he no longer needed the visual cues on the floor for assistance.

Activities for the DODGE

Exploring the dodge

Skills: Dodging, running, side-stepping

Children: Individual

Equipment: Cones

Area: Gymnasium, court or field

Activities:
- Run to a line and back, dodge as they reach the line.
- Place cones in a zigzag pattern and dodge at each one.
- Place two cones 5 meters apart, sidestep between them and dodge sideways back to the other cone.

Line tag

Skills: Dodging, running

Children: Pairs

Equipment: Line

Area: Gymnasium, court or field with marked lines

Activity: Children face each other in each side of a line. One partner is the dodger, the other is the tagger. On a signal to begin, the dodger moves left and right, trying to get out of reach of the tagger. When the teacher/coach blows a whistle as the signal to stop (about 15 seconds), both children stop and the tagger reaches out to see if he/she can tag the dodger. Swap roles; repeat a few times.

Specific Modifications:
- For deaf children make the start signal a visual signal (lights flickering).
- For children with visual impairments make the start signal auditory.

Travelling to Dodge

Skills: Dodging, running

Children: Individual

Equipment: Carpet squares, cones or ropes (obstacles) spread out around gymnasium

Area: gymnasium

Activities: On the signal, travel around the space without touching any obstacles or any other students. Slowly increase the speed of the game.

Locomotor circuit

Skills: Dodging, skipping, jumping

Children: Individual

Equipment: Cones, hula hoops, skipping ropes

Area: Gymnasium, court or field

Activity: Set up a circuit and invite the children to hop over the skipping ropes, jump across the hoops, dodge from cone to cone, and crabwalk back to the beginning.

Specific Modifications:
- If a child who uses a wheelchair is included – instead of using hoola hoops use gym tape or lines on the floor so it is easier for the child in the chair to "enter the circle".

Zigzag relay

Skills: Dodging, running

Children: Pairs

Equipment: Cones

Area: Gymnasium, court or field

Activity: The first partner runs the zigzag pattern, using a dodging action at each cone. After reaching the end, the child runs back to the beginning and tags his/her partner.

Specific Modifications:

- For deaf children, use flashcards, with the instructions on them, or a sign language interpreter to ensure the instructions/changes are communicated.
- For deaf children make the start signal a visual signal (lights flickering), for children with visual impairments make the start an auditory signal.

What time is it, Tricky Wolf?

Skills: Dodging, running

Children: Whole class

Equipment: None

Area: Gymnasium, court or field

Activity: The child chosen to be Tricky Wolf stands at one end of the playing area, facing away from the children who are at the other end of the space.

The aim is for the children to move closer to the wolf without getting caught.

The children chant in unison "What time is it, Tricky Wolf?" and Tricky Wolf will answer in one of two ways:

- If Tricky Wolf calls a time on the clock, e.g., "Three o'clock!", the children will then take that number of steps towards Tricky Wolf, counting the steps out loud as they go ("One, Two, Three!"). They then ask the question again.
- Tricky Wolf may answer "Dinner Time!" At this point, Tricky Wolf turns and chases the children back to their starting point. If Tricky Wolf successfully tags someone, that child is the new Tricky Wolf for the next round.

If a child does get all the way to Tricky Wolf without getting caught, everyone goes back to the start and the game begins again. Encourage the children to use their dodging action when chasing or fleeing.

Specific Modifications:

- Ensure the "time" is communicated in a visual manner as well as verbally (e.g. hold up the fingers to indicate 'what time it is').
- For children with visual impairments use a buddy/peer tutor system, or use educational assistants to facilitate inclusion – especially when the Tricky Wolf turns around to run.

DODGE: *Quick, deceptive changes in direction to evade, chase or flee from an opponent.*

Continuum of Prompts for the DODGE

Physical Prompts	**Physical prompts should be paired with verbal prompts.**
- Complete manipulation	Slowly run with the child while holding hands; when changing direction, tap on the leg to indicate which direction, and gently pull the child's hand in the desired direction.
- Manipulative prompting	Run with the child; give a gentle pull on the hand to indicate the change of direction.
- Minimal guidance	Run beside the child; tap his or her hand or knee when a change of direction is needed.
Visual Prompts	**Visual prompts should be paired with verbal prompts.**
- Complete skill demonstration	Demonstrate the dodge with a slow-motion change of direction (pivot) that is exaggerated.
- Partial skill demonstration	Demonstrate only the pivot part.
- Gestural prompting	Gesture to the spot where you would like the child to change directions.
Verbal Prompts	
- Skill cue	Try focusing the child's attention on a key component of the task (e.g., "Plant your foot"; "Look where you're going").
- Action command	Give a verbal description of the desired skill (e.g., "Go this way").
- Action cue	Make a motivational statement to help the child perform the skill (e.g., "This way now"). Teacher should be positioned so the child changes direction to run towards him or her.

No Prompts

- Initiation with environmental cue	Use cones or flat floor markers to act as obstacles that the child must avoid when running.
- Imitative initiation	Child performs the skill after watching other participants performing it — allow the child with a disability to observe his or her classmates and then join in.
- Initiation in free play	Child performs the skill at an appropriate time in free play but with no peer demonstration — this could be observed during game play such as basketball or football and in various cooperative games where the dodge is used.

Behaviour Management and Pedagogical Considerations for DODGING

ASD	• If a child uses pic-syms in the classroom, find pic-syms for dodging-related activities (e.g., tag games) and tasks, and create a storyboard of activities for each day.
	• Reduce distractions.
	• Avoid the child's sensitive aversions (e.g., loud noises, certain textures or colours).
	• Use structure and "sameness" for consistency (e.g., follow the same warm-up routine, the same general lesson structure).
	• Capitalize on the child's preferences for motivation when dodging (e.g., certain colours).
	• Physical activity and exercise can have a positive impact on repetitive and stereotyped movements common in children with ASD; therefore, starting a lesson with vigorous physical activity may be effective for increasing on-task behaviours for the rest of the lesson or practice.
DS	• Keep instructions clear and simple.
	• Encourage positive behaviours.
	• Visual demonstrations are highly recommended.
	• Force production, strength and balance may be limited in children with DS; therefore, the controlled pivot and change of direction in dodging may be difficult. Allow for extra repetitions for learning.
	• Peer tutors can be effective for modelling and promoting on-task behaviour.

ADHD	• Reduce distractions: use small groups, keep space smaller, use structural barriers (e.g., portable walls to reduce the gym space). • Keep instructions clear and simple, and set clear behavioural boundaries. • Maintain good "timing" in the lesson — boredom may result in off-task behaviours. • Begin with dodging inanimate objects (not other participants). • Reinforce respect, teamwork and sportsmanship concepts in all aspects of the lesson.
ID	• Use a peer tutor or educational assistant to keep the child on task. • Keep instructions simple and concise. • Repetition may be needed of both instructions and demonstrations. • Start with a simple task and add difficulty as the child progresses.
DCD	• Create an environment of success to prevent frustration. • Ensure the class rules are consistently enforced and the expectations are very clear. • Allow for and encourage repetition and practice. • Use self-rehearsal strategies, talk-aloud strategies (e.g., have the child assign words to the parts of the skill and say them aloud during practice). • Discourage off-task behaviours such as excessive water breaks, time outs and "clowning around" by keeping groups small and tasks age- and skill-level appropriate.

Characteristics of the DODGE	*Cue Words for Children*
Eyes focused in direction of travel	"Look where you are going" "Aim for the cone"
Body lowered during change of direction (athletic stance)	"Get low, bend your knees"
Change direction by pushing off outside foot	"Push off your leg and then go the other way"
Change of direction occurs in one step	"One step only" "Turn your head to look where you want to go now"
Can change direction in both directions	"Go left, go right"

Difficulties to watch for:

If...	Then...
Child has difficulty judging the distance to stationary or moving objects.	Give the child more opportunities to vary the distance to the object to dodge, and vary the angle of approach and exit. Start with stationary objects to dodge, and gradually increase the level of unpredictability.
Child is crossing his or her feet.	Ensure the child understands the footwork sequence. Use coloured tape on the ground to indicate when to step with the left foot and when to step with the right foot.
Child takes several small steps to change direction of travel.	Encourage the child to push off and change direction in one step. The child will need to plant the outside foot next to a cone or line and take the next step on another path. Encourage the child to slow down and anticipate the change of direction. Provide opportunities to master the skill in predictable environments (e.g., ask the child to run to a line and back before including the skill in less predictable environments such as a game of tag).

To view and analyze video for this skill, and all the skills in this manual online, please visit:
↘ **www.phecanada.ca**

What Has Worked in Real Life

Marcus is six years old and has Down syndrome. I tried to teach dodging by having Marcus run towards cones or objects and avoid them, but he was never interested or focused on the "dodge" part of what I was teaching him. I noticed that Marcus was drawn to another little boy in our class named Will, who was quite a skilled and talented child. Will was a very good peer mentor to Marcus. I asked Will to allow Marcus to follow him as he went through the dodging exercises. I told Marcus to "chase" Will and do what he did. Remarkably, by giving Marcus permission to imitate and chase Will, Marcus imitated him so closely that he was executing the dodge quite well. By allowing Marcus to practise this way at first, he became more proficient at the dodge and will have a sense of accomplishment and belonging because of his learning. I don't normally allow the children to just "chase" each other; however, the skill of dodging is used in most chase games, such as basketball, football, rugby and ultimate Frisbee, so I felt more comfortable with allowing this. I did, however, ensure that Marcus knew that the chasing was allowed only when I said so. I did not want Marcus to think it was appropriate to chase Will all the time.

Activities for the DODGE

Exploring the dodge

Skills: Dodging, running, sidestepping
Children: Individual
Equipment: Cones
Area: Gymnasium, court or field
Activities:
- The children run to a line and back, dodging as they reach the line.
- Place cones in a zigzag pattern. The children dodge at each cone.
- Place two cones 5 metres apart. The children sidestep between them and dodge sideways back to the other cone.
- Place 4 cones in a square and have the children dodge in a X's and O's pattern of their choice changing directions at each cone (suitable for children with a higher skill level).

Travelling to Dodge

Skills: Dodging, running
Children: Individual
Equipment: Carpet squares, cones or ropes (obstacles) spread out around gymnasium
Area: Gymnasium
Activities: On the signal to begin, the children travel around the space without touching any obstacles or any other participants. Slowly increase the speed of the game.

Locomotor Circuit

Skills: Dodging, hopping, jumping
Children: Individual
Equipment: Cones, hoops, skipping ropes
Area: Gymnasium, court or field
Activity: Set up a circuit, and invite the children to hop over the skipping ropes, jump across the hoops, dodge from cone to cone, and crabwalk back to the beginning.

Line Tag

Skills: Dodging, running
Children: Pairs
Equipment: Line
Area: Gymnasium, court or field with marked lines
Activity: Children face each other on either side of a line. One partner is the dodger, the other is the tagger. On the signal to begin, the dodger moves left and right, trying to get out of reach of the tagger. When the teacher/coach blows a whistle as the signal to stop (after about 15 seconds), both children stop and the tagger reaches out to see if he or she can tag the dodger. Swap roles; repeat a few times.

SPRINT: *running at full or close to one's full speed*

A. *Characteristics of the mature SPRINT*	*Cue Words for Children*
Head to toe posture should be like a pillar. The head should be over the shoulders, shoulders over hips, and hips over feet.	Form a straight pillar
Contact the ground mainly with the balls of the feet (not the heels).	Run mainly on the balls of your feet
Run light by avoiding pounding down on the ground and keep chest, neck, and chin slightly elevated.	Run light. Spend minimal time in contact with the ground
"Pawing" Leg Action: Flex the knee more by having the heel pull up close to the buttocks so the knee (thigh) is parallel to the ground.	Paw using a 90-degree knee
Arm Action: Elbows at 90 degrees with the arms acting as alternating pendulums. The hands swing up to cheek height ("pulling down an apple") and then brush along one's side ("putting the apple in the side pocket").	90-degree elbows Pull down an apple with the hand and put it in your side pocket

Arm and leg motion should be in line with the direction of travel not sideways.	Straight ahead arm and leg motion
Stride: Widen stride length (extend slightly) and increase stride frequency.	Run fast
Maintain a relaxed facial expression and hands.	Run relaxed

B. Sample Activities for SPRINTING

Note: For all sprinting activities, ensure adequate warm-up prior to sprinting. Ensure the running surface is safe (e.g., no holes, flat and even, and not slippery). Do not proceed too soon, too fast, or for too long. Provide adequate recovery and rest time.

Sample Guided Discovery Activities

1. Can you "paw" like a bull? Stand sideways having one hand on the side wall while standing on the near leg. With the swing leg, perform the "pawing" leg action for the run. Switch legs.
2. Walking A's: Begin by standing like a pillar. Use the same pawing action as above while moving forward in a walking motion (alternating legs). Add the corresponding arm action. Emphasize the key cues of pillar, run light, paw, and apple pull.
3. Can you run six 30 m sprints with a 30 m walk in-between?
4. Mirroring: "Can you do this..."

Accelerations

Skills: Sprint technique and pacing

Children: In pairs or triples

Equipment: Cones

Area: 75 m flat area. Cones marking the start, 20 m line, 50m line, and the 70 m line.

Activity: Inform students of the three zones: Gradual acceleration zone (20 m), pacing zone (30 m), and the gradual deceleration zone (20 m). In one running lane each, have 2-3 students (of relatively matched ability) at a time accelerate gradually through the first 20 m to establish the pace that they are assigned (e.g., 40% maximum speed), sustain the pace through the pacing zone, and then gradually decelerate in the final zone so they are jogging lightly at the finish. Speed walk back to the start and repeat at a different (slightly increased pace like 50% maximum). Once the group ahead reaches the 20 m line the next group can begin.

Modifications: Have each student in the group take turns setting the pace (increasing with each repetition) for their group. Add the official start (e.g., crouched start) to the activity.

Safety Tip (if applicable): In addition to the safety consideration noted earlier, do not ask students to run 100% unless they are warmed up and it is safe to do so. Avoid students competing with one another and discretely try to have groups of relatively similar ability so slower students are not obvious. Avoid long wait lines so people are not standing and watching others.

Relays

Skills: Sprinting technique and baton exchange

Children: In groups of 2-4

Equipment: Batons

Area: A long grass field or track.

Activity: Have students brainstorm how they can most effectively exchange the baton between 2-4 sprinters so that the baton maintains close to full speed for the duration of the run. Give some additional suggestions and a demonstration.

Remind them that exchanges must occur with a 20 m zone; however, the next runner can begin running up to 10 m before that exchange zone.

Have them practice in pairs first (in a 40-50 m area) and then (if desired) in groups of 2-4 around a track. Remind them of the key sprinting cues.

Modification(s): Have students jog around the track slowly in a line of 4 people. The person at the back starts with the baton and says "stick" when they are ready to exchange it with the person ahead of them. The person ahead then puts their hand back to receive it. This is repeated until the front person receives the baton. They then gently place the baton down to the side and the person in the back retrieves it and repeats the cycles.

Safety Tip (if applicable): Practice all exchanges together (teacher calls out "all ready," "all go") so students are not crossing into other lanes while others are sprinting and practicing their exchanges.

Chasing and Fleeing Tag Games

Skill: Sprinting

Children: Large groups

Equipment: Pinnies

Area: Gymnasium or field space

Activity: Tag, educational gymnastics, and various developmental games (e.g., lead-up territorial and striking-fielding games) include some opportunities for sprinting and can be used to foster sprinting competence in children. For example, one effective tag games for this is Team Tag. Divide the class into teams of four and give them a pinnie (identification) with a distinct color for their team. Set up a few safe zones within the playing area. Students may be in a safe zone for a maximum of 5 seconds of every 20 seconds. If they are tagged by a member of another team they must stop moving and stay standing (but can still tag others if they come within their reach) where they are tagged until someone from their team touches them so they can once again move. The winning team is the last team to still have members that are still free and moving.

Modification(s): For other sprinting activities see the other relevant activities listed in this manual.

Skip and Gallop

Skipping and galloping typically develop at about the same time in children ages four to six. Both movement patterns involve flight and are used in various forms in diverse situations and are thus, presented together.

SKIP: *a rhythmical flow of the step-hop pattern*

Skipping combines two fundamental motor skills; the step and the hop. The skip is the rhythmical flow of the step and hop on one foot, then step and hop on the other foot; flight occurs on the hop.

GALLOP: *a rhythmical flow of the step-together, step- together pattern with the same foot always leading; flight occurs when both feet are together in the air.*

Note: It may be helpful to instruct the fundamentals of the HOP before or along with skipping. Children who have difficulty galloping may find it helpful to have their hand held by an adult to feel the upwards motion while both feet are airborne.

A. Characteristics of the mature SKIP

Characteristics of the mature SKIP	Cue Words for Children
A rhythmical repetition of the step-hop on alternate feet	Step-hop, step-hop
Foot of non-support leg is carried near surface during hop	Keep back foot near the ground
Arms move alternatively in opposition to legs	Arm/leg opposite
Toes and ball of foot are first landing	Land toes first

B. Teaching Tips

(i) Developmental changes to watch for prior to mature skip:

- Coordination of the step-hop pattern from initial distinct and exaggerated actions to a rhythmical transfer of weight.
- Greater involvement of the arms in the skipping action. Initially, there is very little arms action.
- Gradually, children will include rhythmical action of the arms in opposition to the legs, but this action may not generate much forward momentum.
- In a mature skip, the arms will be used for momentum. Vertical height of the skip reduces as the skill develops.

(ii) Difficulties to watch for:

If...	Then...
There is an inconsistent step-hop pattern.	The skip involves a combination of two fundamental movement skills: the hop and the step. Make sure the children have mastered both skills before teaching the skip.
	When ready, practice the new step-hop pattern slowly in a predictable environment.
	Use coloured tape to mark footsteps on the floor and help establish the pattern.
There is a lack of rhythm in the skip.	Again, ensure children have mastered both the hop and step and they understand the step pattern for the skip.
	Clap the rhythm for children.
	Give plenty of opportunities to practice the skill in free space.
Movements are exaggerated.	Encourage the children not to lift their feet too high.
Children are landing flat-footed.	Review the parts of the foot with the children. Ensure they understand how to locate the ball of the foot so they can practice walking on it.
	Practice landing on the ball of the foot while hopping.
	Encourage children to be light on their feet.

To view and analyze video for this skill, and all the skills in this manual online, please visit:
www.phecanada.ca

C. Activities for SKIPPING and GALLOPING

Basic Step Pattern

Skills: Skipping or galloping
Children: Individual
Equipment: None
Area: Gymnasium, court, or field
Activity: Children practice the step-hop (or step-together) pattern in their own space. It can be helpful to have the children say, "step-hop, step-hop" (step-together) as they travel. Gradually increase the pace and encourage the children to connect the step and hop (step-together) by putting the weight onto the ball of their foot at the end of the step. Encourage children to swing their arms in opposition to their legs and try to gain flight.

Gallop (or Skip) a Pathway

Skills: Galloping or skipping
Children: Individual
Equipment: Hula hoop (optional)
Area: Gymnasium, court, or field
Activity: Invite the children to gallop (or skip) in free space.

Call out a pathway such as a circle or triangle. Coach the children to gallop or skip in this pathway twice, and then return to skipping in free space.

Vary the activity by regularly calling out different pathways. Ask the children to suggest different shapes to skip. Tip: you could use hula hoops to create circular skipping spaces for students.

Word Sequence

Skills: Skipping, galloping and other locomotor and balance skills
Children: Individual
Equipment: None
Area: Gymnasium, court, or field
Activity: Coach the children to create and execute a three part movement sequence of locomotor and balance skills. For example, SKIP – BALANCE – GALLOP. Encourage them to write the words on paper. Extensions of this activity may include: making up the sequence in pairs, or incorporating a change of direction or level or both.

Skip or Gallop and Freeze

Skills: Skipping and galloping
Children: Individual
Equipment: Children's music, music player
Area: Gymnasium or indoor open space
Activity: To music, the children gallop or skip, copying the teacher. When the music stops, the children freeze in an interesting shape.

SKIP
- Step-Hop-Step-Hop
- Bend knees
- Opposite arm to leg
- Heel to toe weight transfer
- Stretch up in flight

Far or High?

Skills: Skipping and galloping
Children: Individual
Equipment: Children's music (optional)
Area: Gymnasium or indoor open space
Activity: Teacher calls out "far" or "high", to which the children respond by skipping or galloping to gain distance or height with their actions. Teacher can encourage strong feet, use of knees, heads up, and arms swinging.

Pathfinder

Skills: Skipping, galloping, jumping, other locomotor skills (crabwalk, hop, etc.)
Children: Individual
Equipment: Beanbags or small cones
Area: Gymnasium, court, or field
Activity: The children each place a beanbag in a space in a designated area. When directed, the children skip to touch five other beanbags and then return to their own. Ask the children to suggest other ways to move between beanbags (e.g., jump, crabwalk).

fashion, one at a time to the next hoop.

Numbers

Skills: Skipping or Galloping
Children: Class
Equipment: Drum or tambourine
Area: Gymnasium
Activity: Children skip or gallop in free space to the rhythm of the beat. Two loud drumbeats is the signal to skip or gallop toward another child, join hands and continue to skip in free space together. When they hear one loud drum beat they separate. When the children hear three loud drumbeats they form a circle of three and skip in a clockwise direction. Again, one loud drumbeat is the signal to separate and skip in free space.

Grand Portage

Skills: Skipping or galloping
Children: Pairs
Equipment: Hula-hoops and beanbags
Area: Gymnasium, court, or field
Activity: Each pair places one hula-hoop 5 meters from the start line and a second hoop 10 meters from the start line. Provide each pair with three beanbags. The aim of the game is to move all of the beanbags from the start line into the furthest hoop. To start, the first child carries a beanbag to the closest hoop and returns to the start line to tag their partner. The second child may choose to move the beanbag from the closest hoop to the furthest hoop or to add a second beanbag to the closest hoop, and so on. Partners take turns skipping or galloping and moving the beanbags in a relay.

GALLOP
- Step-Together-Step-Together
- Bend knees
- Opposite arm to leg
- Heel to toe weight transfer
- Stretch up in flight

SKIP: *A rhythmical flow of the step-hop pattern*

Skipping combines two fundamental motor skills, the step and the hop. The skip is the rhythmical flow of the step and hop on one foot, then step and hop on the other foot.

Characteristics of the SKIP	*Cue Words for Children*
A rhythmical repetition of the step-hop on alternate feet	"Step-hop, step-hop" (Reminder: Hop on the same foot that you stepped with)
Foot of non-support leg is carried near surface during hop	"Knees half way up"
Arms alternatively moving in opposition to legs	"Opposite arms and legs"
Toes and ball of foot are landing first	"Land tippy toes first"

Adaptations of the SKIP for:

Children in wheelchairs	• While able-bodied classmates are practicing the skip encourage the child in an electric wheel chair to move the direction of the other classmates while practicing the skip.
	• Introduce the rhythmical aspect of the skip into the wheelchair's movements. Encourage head movements in the same rhythmical pattern.
	• For children in manual wheelchairs, encourage them to move in the same directions as the able-bodied children while practicing the skip.
	• Encourage the children in manual chairs to use short and long pushes to mimic the rhythm of the step-hop pattern of the skip.
	• Have a peer push the chair while skipping to facilitate social inclusion. Encourage the peer to use a rhythmical pushing pattern (use discretion when having peers push a classmate who uses a wheelchair – an educational assistant or para-professional can also serve in this capacity).

Children with mobility aids	• Allow the child who uses a mobility aid to execute the step-hop pattern while keeping the aid planted to the ground (i.e. legs execute the action but aid serves as a stabilizing device).
	• Encourage the child to experiment with the timing of using the mobility aid, but also executing the timing of the step-hop to perform a skip. Having the child verbalize the pattern out loud may facilitate the emergence of the skill. For example – "lift walker, plant, step, hop, lift walker …."
	• Practice the hop in isolation for children with a prosthesis or cerebral palsy and slowly integrate the step component.
	• Be aware that some children with cerebral palsy will be wearing braces on the lower leg limiting ankle flexibility. This will affect propulsion at the ankle and balance on landing.
Children with mobility limitations	• Some children with mobility limitations will be stronger on one side making the skip pattern more difficult (e.g. cerebral palsy) – encourage the child to slow down and practice the step hop pattern on both feet.
	• Initially allow the child to practice the skip holding onto the wall or a person's hand for balance. This will allow the child to experiment without fear of falling down.
	• Often the legs of a child with cerebral palsy will be quite stiff or rigid. Encourage the child to have relaxed legs.
	• A child with a lower leg prosthesis may have difficulty with balance and hopping on the leg with the prosthesis. Allow the child to use a mobility aid if warranted or use the wall for support while gaining confidence in learning how to skip.
	• Encourage the child to use his or her arms for balance (extending arms out) at the initial stages of the skip.
	• Practice the hop in isolation for children with prosthesis or cerebral palsy then slowly integrate the step component.
	• Have the child use verbal cues "step, hop, step, hop" to practice the rhythm.

Children with visual impairments	• Children with visual impairments will benefit from detailed auditory cues to learn how to skip as it is not an intuitive motor skill used in every day life. • Explain the skip in every detail to help the child understand the nuances of the skip that are not available without a visual – verbalize "left foot step, left foot hop, right foot step, right foot hop". • Have an educational assistant work with the child especially at the early stages for safety. • Gradually have the student perform the skill with more independence, allowing the child to use a wall or a guide-wire for support and direction.
Children who are deaf	• If an interpreter is not available (or necessary) have a cue card at each station (or for each PE lesson, practice or coaching session) with the task or plan clearly outlined at the child's level of understanding. • Be prepared to give extra demonstrations of skills and activities. • Consider using an FM loop system (microphone worn by the teacher to amplify the voice into the hearing aid worn by the Deaf student). • Avoid excess noise in the learning environment.

Difficulties to watch for:

If...	Then...
There is an inconsistent step-hop pattern, or the child is only proficient on one side.	The skip involves a combination of two fundamental movement skills: the hop and the step. Make sure the children have mastered both skills before teaching the skip.
	When ready, practice the new step-hop pattern slowly in a predictable environment.
	Use coloured tape to mark footsteps on the floor and help establish the pattern.
There is a lack of rhythm in the skip.	Again, ensure children have mastered both the hop and step and they understand the step pattern for the skip.
	Clap the rhythm for children.
	Give plenty of opportunities to practice the skill in free space.
Movements are exaggerated.	Encourage the children to lift their feet just off the ground.
Slight loss of balance from time to time.	Have the child slow the skip down and exaggerate the hop portion of the skip – lots of practice at different speeds.
Children are landing flat-footed.	Review the parts of the foot with the children. Ensure they understand how to locate the ball of the foot (tippy toes) so they can practice walking on the ball of their foot.
	Practice landing on the ball of the foot while hopping.
	Encourage children to be light on their feet.
	Ask children to see if they can make their skip as "quiet" as possible.

To view and analyze video for this skill, and all the skills in this manual online, please visit:
⤵ **www.phecanada.ca**

"what has worked in real life...."

Samir is nine years old and although he has some vision, he is legally blind. To ensure Samir is fully included in physical education classes, his teacher made sure that there were no burnt out bulbs in the gymnasium and the curtains are always open to ensure the most light possible. His teacher also ensured that there was never any clutter around the perimeter of the gymnasium for Samir to trip on and his teacher takes care to set up the gymnasium in a consistent manner for each class. The balls are always a fluorescent colour for increased visibility and sometimes it is necessary to slow down games so Samir can keep up with the pace. Samir is always seated at the front when his teacher gives instructions and when necessary his teacher will help Samir understand the skill (such as skipping) by using tactile prompts. On occasion, Samir's teacher will video tape a motor skill so that Samir can use video technology to zoom in on the image and look closely at the screen for as long as he needs.

Activities for the SKIP

Basic step pattern

Skill: Skipping

Children: Individual

Equipment: None

Area: Gymnasium, court or field

Activity: Children practice the step-hop pattern in their own space. It can be helpful to have the children say "Step-hop, step-hop" as they move. Gradually increase the pace and encourage the children to connect the step and hop by putting the weight onto the ball of their foot at the end of the step. Encourage children to swing their arms in opposition to their legs.

Word sequence

Skills: Skipping, other locomotor and balance skills

Children: Individual

Equipment: None

Area: Gymnasium, court or field

Activity: Coach the children to make up and execute a three word movement sequence of locomotor and balance skills. For example, JUMP – SKIP – GALLOP. Encourage them to write the words on paper. Extensions of this activity may include: making up the sequence in pairs, or incorporating a change of direction or level or both.

Shuttle relay

Skill: Skipping
Children: Groups of four
Equipment: Cones
Area: Gymnasium, court or field
Activity: Use cones to mark out two lines 8 – 10 meters apart. Set up the activity with two children behind the line facing the other two behind the other line. One child starts by skipping to the other line. When the first child crosses the line the next child skips and the first skipper joins the back of the line, and so on.

Specific Modification:

- For children who move very slowly when skipping, allow that child to skip a shorter distance before tagging off their teammate.
- If children with wheelchairs are included in this activity spread the cones out a little bit to give more room – conversely for children who use mobility aids or have mobility limitations it may be appropriate to make the cones closer together.

SKIP: *A rhythmical flow of the step-hop pattern.*
Skipping combines two fundamental motor skills: the step and the hop. The skip is a rhythmical flow of a step and hop on one foot, followed by a step and hop on the other foot.

Continuum of Prompts for the SKIP

Physical Prompts	Physical prompts should be paired with verbal prompts.
- Complete manipulation	Hold hands with the child and start to skip, bringing the child with you to try to convey the rhythmical component.
- Manipulative prompting	Provide assistance only during critical parts of the desired movement — skip beside the child and touch hands every time the extra hop occurs.
- Minimal guidance	Make contact with a relevant body part to initiate a movement (e.g., tap feet to initiate the hopping action).

Visual Prompts	**Visual prompts should be paired with verbal prompts.**
- Complete skill demonstration	Perform the skip in slow motion, only one skip at a time, to illustrate the "step then hop" aspect.
- Partial skill demonstration	Slowly demonstrate the step and then the hop separately.
- Gestural prompting	Use gestures to illustrate the rhythm (e.g., a long arc with the finger for the step and a short arc to illustrate the hop).

Verbal Prompts	
- Skill cue	Try focusing the child's attention on a key component of the task (e.g., "Step and hop on the same foot," "Step-hop").
- Action command	Give a verbal description of the desired skill (e.g., "Skip five times over here," "Step-hop, step-hop").
- Action cue	Make a motivational statement to help the child perform the skill (e.g., "One, two, three"), or use a musical or rhythmical beat to facilitate the step-hop pattern.

No Prompts	
- Initiation with environmental cue	Place cones around the gym to encourage the child to explore the movement by skipping around the cones.
- Imitative initiation	Child performs the skill after watching other participants performing it.
- Initiation in free play	Child performs the skill at an appropriate time in free play but with no peer demonstration.

Behaviour Management and Pedagogical Considerations for SKIPPING

ASD	• If a child uses pic-syms in the classroom, find pic-syms for skipping-related activities and tasks, and create a storyboard of activities for each day. • Reduce distractions. • Avoid the child's sensitive aversions (e.g., loud music). • Use structure and "sameness" for consistency (e.g., follow the same warm-up routine, the same general lesson structure). • Capitalize on the child's preferences for motivation (e.g., certain colours). • Use music or a rhythmical beat to facilitate the rhythmical aspect of the skip (assuming the noise is not too much for the child with ASD). • Physical activity and exercise can have a positive impact on repetitive and stereotyped movements common in children with ASD; therefore, starting a lesson with vigorous physical activity (including skipping) may be effective at increasing on-task behaviours for the rest of the lesson or practice.
DS	• Keep instructions clear and simple. • Encourage positive behaviours. • Visual demonstrations are highly recommended. • Force production, strength, balance and coordination may be limited in children with DS, making skipping a challenge. Use music or a beat to help facilitate the skipping pattern. • Peer tutors can be effective for modelling and promoting on-task behaviour.
ADHD	• Reduce distractions: use small groups, keep space smaller. • Keep instructions clear and simple. • Maintain good "timing" — boredom may result in off-task behaviours. • Create an environment of success. • Set clear boundaries, both physical and task related. • Reinforce respect, teamwork and sportsmanship concepts in all aspects of the lesson.
ID	• Use a peer tutor or educational assistant to keep the child on task. • Keep instructions simple and concise. • Repetition may be needed of both instructions and demonstrations. • Start with a simple task and add difficulty as the child progresses.
DCD	• Create an environment of success to prevent frustration. • Ensure the class rules are consistently enforced and the expectations are very clear. • Allow for and encourage repetition and practice. • Use self-rehearsal strategies, talk-aloud strategies (e.g., have the child assign words to the parts of the skill and say them aloud during practice). • Discourage off-task behaviours such as excessive water breaks, time outs and "clowning around" by keeping groups small and tasks age- and skill-level appropriate.

Characteristics of the SKIP	Cue Words for Children
A rhythmical repetition of the step-hop on alternate feet	"Step-hop, step-hop." "Hop on the same foot that you stepped with."
Foot of non-support leg carried near surface during hop	"Keep back foot near the ground." "We're not doing "knees up" — bring your knees only halfway up."
Arms alternatively moving in opposition to legs	"Right leg, left arm." "Left leg, right arm."
Toes and ball of foot landing first	"Land on your tippy toes."

Difficulties to Watch For:

If...	Then...
There is an inconsistent step-hop pattern, or the child is proficient on only one side.	The skip involves a combination of two fundamental movement skills: the hop and the step. Make sure the child has mastered both skills before teaching the skip. When the child is ready, have him or her practise the new step-hop pattern slowly in a predictable environment. Use coloured tape to mark footsteps on the floor to help establish the pattern.
There is a lack of rhythm in the skip.	Again, ensure the child has mastered both the hop and step and understands the step pattern for the skip. Clap the rhythm for the child. Give plenty of opportunities to practise the skill in free space.
Movements are exaggerated.	Encourage the child to lift the feet just off the ground.
There is a slight loss of balance from time to time.	Have the child slow the skip down and exaggerate the hop portion of the skip — allow for lots of practice at different speeds.

Child is landing flat-footed.	Review the parts of the foot with the child. Ensure he or she understands how to locate the ball of the foot (tippy toes) so he or she can practise walking on the ball of the foot.
	Ask the child to practise landing on the ball of the foot while hopping.
	Encourage the child to be light on his or her feet.
	Ask the child to see if he or she can make the skip as "quiet" as possible.

To view and analyze video for this skill, and all the skills in this manual online, please visit:
www.phecanada.ca

What Has Worked in Real Life

Tanis is seven years old and has been diagnosed with fetal alcohol syndrome, which for Tanis has meant attention difficulties, behavioural problems and a lower cognitive level than her peers; she is eager to fit in and wants to be friends with her classmates, but her immaturity and methods are often off-putting, so she does not have many friends in her class. Tanis has the most difficulty in physical education when the lesson or the task is open and dynamic; if the students are playing a large game; or if the class is working on skills such as skipping in a big, open setting. To help keep Tanis on task, I put a very basic schedule of what we are going to do that day on the wall. The first thing Tanis does is go and look at the schedule. This way she knows what is coming, and she doesn't have to keep asking. To keep her on task during the lesson, I give her very clear boundaries as to where she can practise skipping. If allowed to skip around the entire gym, she becomes overwhelmed and her behaviour deteriorates, so I give her a smaller space with concrete directions, such as skip back and forth six times and then sit down on this square. Knowing the boundaries helps Tanis participate to the best of her ability.

Activities for the SKIP

Basic Step Pattern

Skill: Skipping

Children: Individual

Equipment: None

Area: Gymnasium, court or field

Activity: Children practise the step-hop pattern in their own space. It can be helpful to have the children say, "Step-hop, step-hop," as they move. Gradually increase the pace, and encourage the children to connect the step and hop by putting their weight onto the ball of the foot at the end of the step. Encourage children to swing their arms in opposition to their legs.

Word Sequence

Skills: Skipping, other locomotor skills (e.g., jumping, running, galloping, hopping)

Children: Individual

Equipment: None

Area: Gymnasium, court or field

Activity: Coach the children to make up and execute a four-word movement sequence of locomotor and balance skills. For example, JUMP — SKIP — GALLOP — HOP. Encourage them to write the words on paper. Extensions of this activity may include making up the sequence in pairs and incorporating a change of direction or level or both.

Grand Portage

Skill: Skipping

Children: Pairs

Equipment: Hoops and beanbags

Area: Gymnasium, court or field

Activity: Each pair places one hoop 5 metres from the start line and a second hoop 10 metres from the start (distances can be modified depending on the skill level of the participants). Provide each pair with three beanbags. The aim of the game is to move all of the beanbags from the start line into the farthest hoop. To start, the first child carries a beanbag to the closest hoop and returns to the start line to tag his or her partner. The second child may choose to move the beanbag from the closest hoop to the farthest hoop or to add a second beanbag to the closest hoop, and so on. Partners take turns skipping and moving the beanbags in relay fashion, one at a time to the next hoop.

Musical Hoops

Skills: Skipping, other locomotor skills (e.g., hopping, jumping, dodging, running)

Children: Individual

Equipment: One hoop for every two children

Area: Gymnasium, court or field

Activity: On the signal (music starts), call out a locomotor pattern (e.g., skipping). Children move randomly throughout the activity area; they may not enter any hoops while the music is playing. Stop the music after 30 to 60 seconds; children immediately move inside a hoop. More than one participant can be in a hoop at the same time. Challenge children to move to a hoop quickly and to share hoops.

Variations:

- Call out another locomotor pattern (running, jumping, hopping).
- Decrease the number of hoops or increase the distance between the hoops to promote physical activity.
- For older children, try to increase the amount of time spent moving.

Shuttle Relay

Skill: Skipping

Children: Groups of four

Equipment: Cones

Area: Gymnasium, court or field

Activity: Use cones to mark out two lines 8 to 10 metres apart. Set up the activity with two children standing behind one line and facing the other two children behind the other line. One child starts by skipping to the other line. When the first child crosses the line, the next child skips and the first skipper joins the back of the line, and so on.

Pathfinder

Skills: Skipping, other locomotor skills (e.g., crabwalking, hopping, jumping, running)

Children: Individual

Equipment: Beanbags or small cones

Area: Gymnasium, court or field

Activity: The children each place a beanbag in a space in a designated area. When directed, the children skip to touch five other beanbags and then return to their own. Ask the children to suggest other ways to move between beanbags (e.g., jumping, crabwalking).

Jump

Jumping is a fundamental movement skill that is required in many movement situations. All true jumping involves flight which means that no body part is touching the ground or any equipment. The child's first jumping actions are typically with the help of an adult on a soft surface such as a bed or couch. The first independent jumping actions usually involve jumping down from a height such as stairs or a footstool. As the child matures, various forms of jumps will develop (eg. hopping, leaping) and can be practiced for height or distance as well as from heights, over objects, or onto objects.

The mature jumping form takes on many diverse movement patterns. Consider the variations in jumping among a diver's preparation off a springboard, a basketball player's rebound, a soccer goalie's save, or a triple-jumper's take-off. Despite these differences, all jumps involve a preparation phase (knees bend), an airborne phase (flight), and a recovery phase (knees bend), and are generally intended to gain height or distance.

The Five Basic Jumps

There are five basic jumps which are created with the variations of foot patterns in take-offs and landings. They include jumping (three forms), hopping, and leaping, all of which may be accomplished for height or distance.

Jump: take-off from two feet and land on two feet
take-off from two feet and land on one foot
take-off from one foot and land on two feet

Hop: take-off from one foot and land on the same foot

Leap: take-off from one foot and land on the opposite foot

JUMP: *horizontal: two-foot take-off with two-foot landing*

A. Characteristics of the mature Horizontal JUMP

Characteristics of the mature Horizontal JUMP	Cue Words for Children
GET READY:	
Lower hips to sitting position (hips, knees, ankles flex in crouch)	Bend ankles, knees, and hips
Shoulders lean forward	Crouch forward
Feet together in balance stance	Arms back
Bend knees, with toes staying in front of knees	
Swing arms back	Arms back
TAKE-OFF:	
Simultaneous forceful extension at hips, knees, and ankles as arms thrust forward and upward	Explode with legs
Aim for 45-degree angle in flight path	Swing up and forward with arms
As body moves forward, hips, knees, ankles extend in succession	
FLIGHT:	
Full body extension	Look ahead and stretch out
Thighs parallel to ground	Knees up
Eyes focused ahead on target	
LANDING:	
Lower legs extend prior to landing	
Balanced landing with feet apart, heels on ground, knees bent, arms out	
Force taken on balls of feet, ankles, knees and hips on impact	Quiet knees on landing
Arms reach forward to keep centre of gravity moving in direction of flight	Reach forward

B. Teaching Tips

(i) Developmental changes to watch for prior to mature jump:
- Progressive increase in initial crouch prior to take-off.
- Arms lifted and extended more vigorously.
- Greater extension through jumping action.
- Knees become less rigid on landing, with feet in balanced position.

(ii) Difficulties to watch for:

If...	Then...
Child is showing insufficient extension of legs and body on take-off.	Ask the child to jump over a horizontal target (e.g., jump over a skipping rope), gradually increasing the distance between take-off and rope.
Child is using ineffective arm swing in the jump.	Encourage the child to rock forward in a heel-to-toe motion while coordinating arm swing. Partner holds an object (e.g., scarf) ahead of the jumper in a high enough position to encourage him/her to jump toward object, thus swinging arm forward during jumping motion.
Child is falling backward on landing. Arms are beside or behind on landing.	Encourage the child to reach forward on landing. Use cue words as a reminder (e.g., reach forward).

(iii) Warm up to make sure muscles and joints are ready for action. Cool down after.

(iv) Allow safe distance for landing.

(v) Emphasize coordinated action of arms and legs.

(vi) Practice jumping on different surfaces.

(vii) Use exploration activities in early stages of practice.

To view and analyze video for this skill, and all the skills in this manual online, please visit:
↘ **www.phecanada.ca**

C. Activities for the Horizontal JUMP

The following section provides a selection of individual, partner, small group, and large group activities that focus on development of the vertical jump. (Note: in several instances the activities may be adapted and used to practice hopping.)

Exploration Activities

Skill: Jumping
Children: Individual
Equipment: Beanbag and rope
Area: Outdoors or large indoor area
Activity: Try to...

- Jump high and land lightly. (Question: What part of foot lands first?)
- Jump as far as you can and land softly
- Jump and reach up
- Jump and reach out
- Jump up and forward, high and far
- Jump up and land in same place
- Jump and turn (quarter, half)
- Jump forward with a partner
- Jump over the rope
- Jump like a bouncing ball
- Jump with your feet straddled then together, slowly then increase speed
- Jump forward then backward, slowly then increase speed

- Jump and make shapes while in the air: wide, narrow, star
- Jump and mark your landing with your beanbag. Try to jump farther than your beanbag.
- Jump over the rope; increase distance of rope each time
- Jump to drum beat
- Jump three times forward, three times backwards
- Land with your feet wide apart, and close together
- Jump like a frog, a rabbit...
- Jump in a zigzag pattern, in a circle...
- Jump quickly, slowly, quickly, and slowly...
- Alternate jump, hop, jump, hop
- Jumping jacks
- Jump and turn in the air
- Jump in different patterns on the floor
- Jump and clap your hands above your head

Island Jumping

Skills: Jumping, hopping, leaping
Children: Individual or partners
Equipment: Gymnastics mats scattered throughout gym (close enough to jump from mat to mat)
Area: Gymnasium
Activity: The object of the game is to jump to all islands without falling in the water (gym floor).

Gradually increase distance between mats. Tip: make sure mats have a good grip to the floor so they do not slide during game (yoga mats work well).

Jump the Creek

Skills: Jumping, hopping, leaping
Children: Groups of 3-4
Equipment: Skipping ropes (two per group)
Area: Gymnasium or outdoor field space
Activity: Each group stretches out the two skipping ropes in parallel about a meter apart. Distance between the ropes represents the creek. Traveling in single file, each team member jumps over creek. Gradually increase the width of the creek. Ask "How wide can you make the creek before you fall in?"

Stones in the Creek

Skills: Jumping, hopping, leaping

Children: Individual

Equipment: Non-slip rubber "spot" markers (stones) scattered between two long mat areas (shore)

Area: Gymnasium

Activity: Starting on one side, children must jump from stone to stone without falling in the creek. Change the patterns of the stones to increase or decrease the challenge. If a jumper falls in the creek, he or she starts at the beginning. Each time a player starts over he/she may move one stone in any direction.

Jump the Shot

Skill: Jumping

Children: Groups of 5-8

Equipment: Beanbag on the end of a 3-metre rope

Area: Outdoors or large indoor area

Activity: Groups form a single circle. One child kneels in the centre and swings the rope around about 10-15 cm off the ground. Other children attempt to jump over rope as it passes by. Remind centre person to keep rope low to ground.

JUMP

- Get ready
- Crouch forward and arms swing back
- Take off! Explode with legs, swing forward with arms
- Look ahead and stretch out in flight
- Bend knees on landing
- Heels stay on ground in landing

Go the Distance (team jumping)

Skills: Jumping, hopping, individual rope jumping

Children: Groups of 3-4

Equipment: Four cones

Area: Gymnasium or outdoor field space

Activity: From a common start line, the first person jumps as far as possible and marks landing with a cone; the next person jumps from this point and marks with a cone. Continue until each team member has jumped. Which team covers the greatest distance? How many jumps does it take each team to cross the gym? To cross the field?

Bunny Hop/Jump

Skills: Jumping, hopping

Children: Individual, small groups, large groups

Equipment: 4/4 music with strong beat (or Bunny Hop song)

Area: Gymnasium

Activity:
- Stand single file, with hands on hips or shoulders of person in front
- Touch right toe to right side
- Step right foot in place
- Repeat
- Touch left toe to left side
- Step left foot in place
- Repeat
- Jump forward
- Jump backward
- Jump forward three times then pause
- Start again from the beginning

JUMP: *A locomotor pattern in which the body propels itself off the floor or apparatus (two foot take-off) in to a momentary period of flight finishing with a two-foot landing.*

Characteristics of the Horizontal JUMP	Cue Words for Children
Lower hips to sitting position (hips, knees, ankles flex in crouch)	"Bend ankles, knees, and hips"
Shoulders lean forward	"Lean forward"
Bend knees, with toes staying in front of knees	"Knees bent"
Swing arms back	"Arms back"
Simultaneous forceful extension at hips, knees, and ankles as arms thrust forward and upward	"Explode with legs"
Aim for 45-degree angle in flight path	"Swing up and forward with arms"
Full body extension	"Look ahead and stretch out"
Eyes focused ahead on target	"Look or eyes ahead"
Lower legs extend prior to landing	"Legs out"
Balanced landing with feet apart, knees bent, arms out	"Quiet or soft landing"
Force taken on balls of feet, ankles, knees and hips on impact	"Absorb (bend on) landing"
Arms reach forward to keep centre of gravity moving in direction of flight	"Reach forward"

Adaptations of the horizontal JUMP for:

Children in wheelchairs	• Encourage children in wheelchairs to make the upper body portion of the jump if possible – bending over at the waist, swinging the arms back and forward.
	• Children with severe spastic cerebral palsy can participate by making the head motions and even the arm actions to the best of their ability.
	• Some children with muscular dystrophy or a spinal cord injury may actually lift their bodies off the seat of their chair when executing the upper body portion of the jump.
	• Children with severe mobility limitations may enjoy and benefit from movement exploration activities on a trampoline (ensure school safety procedures are always followed when using a trampoline).
Children with mobility aids	• Allow the child who uses crutches or a walker to use the aid while executing the jump for stability.
	• Encourage the child to reach forward and plant the aid and then execute the jumping action with his or her lower body – their distance is likely to be limited by the reach of their aid.
	• Be aware that some children with cerebral palsy will be wearing braces on the lower leg limiting ankle flexibility and will impact on take off and landing.
	• If possible encourage the child to try jumping without his or her aid, although it is best to try this on a mat to support likely falls.
	• Some children may be wearing braces on their ankles which will restrict their range of motion, balance, and stability when landing. Encourage these children to start off with a short jump.
Children with mobility limitations	• Children with mobility limitations are likely to have limited flexibility in their lower body (e.g. cerebral palsy, amputee, and club feet). This has implications for "proper" form of the jump.
	• Encourage the children to crouch down and swing their arms to the best of their ability.
	• Use verbal and tactile cues to facilitate the jumping form.
	• During the initial learning stages encourage the children to experiment with the length of their jumps to determine the best length which ensures success.
	• It is a good idea to have the children jump on or onto a mat that will support them if they fall.

Children with visual impairments	• Utilize very specific verbal and tactile cues to convey the goals and expectations of the jumping lesson.
	• Provide very specific feedback about his or her jump e.g. "you just jumped 1meter - great job!" – rather than – "look how far you've jumped…"
	• Ensure the environment is clear of clutter for a child with a visual impairment to prevent injury when jumping.
	• A peer tutor jumping along side a child with a visual impairment can be a good motivator.
Children who are deaf	• If an interpreter is not available (or necessary) have a cue card at each station (or for each PE lesson) with the task or plan clearly outlined at the child's level of understanding.
	• Be prepared to give extra demonstrations of skills and activities.
	• Consider using an FM loop system (microphone worn by the teacher to amplify the voice into the hearing aid worn by the Deaf student).
	• Avoid excess noise in the learning environment.

Difficulties to watch for:

If...	Then...
Child is showing insufficient extension of legs and body on take-off.	Ask the child to jump over a horizontal target (e.g., jump over a skipping rope or a line on the floor), gradually increasing the distance between take-off and rope.
Child is using ineffective arm swing in the jump.	Encourage the child to rock forward in a heel-to-toe motion while coordinating arm swing. Partner holds an object (e.g., scarf) ahead of the jumper in a high enough position to encourage him/her to jump toward object, thus swinging arm forward during jumping motion.
Child is falling backward on landing.	Encourage the child to reach forward on landing.
Arms are beside or behind on landing.	Use cue words as a reminder (e.g., reach forward).

To view and analyze video for this skill, and all the skills in this manual online, please visit:
www.phecanada.ca

"what has worked in real life...."

Oscar is 10 years old and lost his left leg below the knee in a farm accident when he was eight. He has a lower leg prosthesis and after two years any limp or differences in his locomotion are minimal. When it comes to practicing the horizontal jump Oscar often falls over to the right side on the landing and it became apparent that Oscar was avoiding the jumping exercises (he would go to the washroom, go for a drink or act out in order to receive a time-out – effectively reducing his practice time). His teacher realized what he was up to and decided that the constant falls were because he was compensating for the missing lower limb. Even though he always wears his prosthesis the impact of the jump is hard for Oscar to judge and accommodate. To improve this skill his teacher would hold Oscar's left hand while he practiced the jump to provide an extra element of balance/security. This forced Oscar to actually practice landing on his prosthetic leg and explore how it feels and understand what his limitations are. By providing that little extra support Oscar's confidence improved with his skill and now Oscar enjoys jumping lessons even though he occasionally loses his balance.

Activities for the horizontal JUMP (for distance)

Jumping Exploration

Skill: Jumping

Children: Individual

Equipment: Beanbag and rope

Area: Outdoors or large indoor area

Activity: Try to...
- Jump high and land lightly. (Question: What part of foot lands first?)
- Jump as far as you can and land softly.
- Jump and reach up.
- Jump and reach out.
- Jump up and forward, high and far.
- Jump up and land in same place.
- Jump and turn (half, quarter).
- Jump forward with a partner.
- Jump over the rope.
- Jump like a bouncing ball.
- Jump with your feet straddled then together, slowly then increase speed.
- Jump forward then backward, slowly then increase speed.
- Jump and make shapes while in the air: wide, narrow, star.
- Jump and mark your landing with your beanbag. Try to jump farther than your beanbag.

- Jump over the rope; increase distance of rope each time.
- Jump to drum beat.
- Jump three times forward, three times backwards.
- Land with your feet wide apart and then close together.
- Jump like a frog, a rabbit...
- Jump in a zigzag pattern, in a circle...
- Jump quickly, slowly, quickly, and slowly...
- Alternate jump, hop, jump, hop.
- Jumping jacks.
- Jump and turn in the air.
- Jump in different patterns on the floor.
- Jump and clap your hands above your head.

Specific Modifications:
- Have children in wheelchairs execute the upper body portion of the hop. For some children, such as those with muscular dystrophy, they may even be able to leave their seat a little bit.

PHE Canada
Physical & Health Education Canada

Jump the creek

Skills: Jumping, hopping, leaping

Children: Groups of three to four

Equipment: Skipping ropes (two per group)

Area: Gymnasium or outdoor field space

Activity: Each group stretches out the two skipping ropes in parallel about a meter apart. Distance between the ropes represents the creek. Traveling in single file, each team member jumps over creek. Gradually increase the width of the creek. Ask "How wide can you make the creek before you fall in?"

Specific Modifications:
- This activity is difficult for children in wheelchairs. Use gym tape to put the lines on the floor to allow the child to roll right over the lines easily.

Jump the shot

Skill: Jumping

Children: Groups of five to eight

Equipment: Beanbag on the end of a three-metre rope

Area: Outdoors or large indoor area

Activity: Groups form a single circle. One child kneels in the centre and swings the rope around about 10-15 cm off the ground. Other children attempt to jump over rope as it passes by. Remind centre person to keep rope low to ground.

Specific Modifications:
- This activity may not be too difficult for children who use walkers or crutches depending on the speed of the rope.
- For children in wheelchairs – instead of jumping over the rope, they should be allowed to roll over the rope while executing the upper body motion of the horizontal jump.

JUMP (Horizontal): *A locomotor pattern in which the body propels itself off the floor or apparatus (two-foot takeoff) into a brief period of flight finishing with a two-foot landing.*

Continuum of Prompts for the JUMP (Horizontal)

Physical Prompts	Physical prompts should be paired with verbal prompts.
- Complete manipulation	Physically lift the child and jump with him or her, or stand in front of, or behind, the child and provide maximal assistance for jumping.
- Manipulative prompting	Provide assistance when necessary, such as holding hands during jumping or during a dismount.
- Minimal guidance	Make contact with a relevant body part to initiate a movement (e.g., tap knees to initiate jumping).

Visual Prompts	Visual prompts should be paired with verbal prompts.
- Complete skill demonstration	Demonstrate the jump in slow motion with exaggerated movements; have peers demonstrate as well — be sure to demonstrate the landing so children do not fall forward.
- Partial skill demonstration	Demonstrate the arm swing slowly and separately; demonstrate bending knees; demonstrate straightening legs.
- Gestural prompting	Gesture to remind participant of key component (e.g., point at the floor to signal the child to jump down).

Verbal Prompts	
- Skill cue	Try focusing the child's attention on a key component of the task (e.g., "Swing your arms," "Chin up," "Eyes up," "Bend your knees").
- Action command	Give a verbal description of the desired skill (e.g., "Jump down," "Jump up").
- Action cue	Make a motivational statement to help the child perform the skill (e.g., "One, two, three, jump").

No Prompts	
- Initiation with environmental cue	Place lines on the floor of the gym (e.g., in the shape of boxes, hopscotch), or place flat floor shapes close enough in a pattern to entice jumping from one to the other, or place short boxes around the gym to jump off.
- Imitative initiation	Child performs the skill after watching other participants performing it.
- Initiation in free play	Child performs the skill at an appropriate time in free play but with no peer demonstration.

Behaviour Management and Pedagogical Considerations for JUMPING

ASD	<ul><li>If a child uses pic-syms in the classroom, find pic-syms for jumping-related activities and tasks, and create a storyboard of activities for each day.</li><li>Some children with ASD really enjoy jumping on trampolines. This is likely a sensory preference, but it can be an effective way to practise jumping.</li><li>Reduce distractions.</li><li>Avoid the child's sensitive aversions (e.g., loud noises, certain textures or colours).</li><li>Use structure and "sameness" for consistency (e.g., follow the same warm-up routine, the same general lesson structure).</li><li>Capitalize on the child's preferences for motivation (e.g., certain colours on the floor to jump to and from).</li></ul>
DS	<ul><li>Keep instructions clear and simple.</li><li>Encourage positive behaviours.</li><li>Visual demonstrations are highly recommended.</li><li>Force production, strength and balance may be limited in children with DS — jumping may be difficult or not a natural movement. Lots of encouragement is often effective.</li><li>Peer tutors can be effective for modelling and promoting on-task behaviour.</li></ul>
ADHD	<ul><li>Reduce distractions: use small groups, keep space smaller.</li><li>Keep instructions clear and simple.</li><li>Maintain good "timing" — boredom may result in off-task behaviours.</li><li>Create an environment of success.</li><li>Set clear boundaries, both physical and task related.</li><li>Reinforce respect, teamwork and sportsmanship concepts in all aspects of the lesson.</li></ul>
ID	<ul><li>Use a peer tutor or educational assistant to keep the child on task.</li><li>Keep instructions simple and concise.</li><li>Repetition may be needed of both instructions and demonstrations.</li><li>Start with a simple task and add difficulty as the child progresses.</li></ul>
DCD	<ul><li>Create an environment of success to prevent frustration.</li><li>Ensure the class rules are consistently enforced and the expectations are very clear.</li><li>Allow for and encourage repetition and practice.</li><li>Use self-rehearsal strategies, talk-aloud strategies (e.g., have the child assign words to the parts of the skill and say them aloud during practice).</li><li>Discourage off-task behaviours such as excessive water breaks, time outs and "clowning around" by keeping groups small and tasks age- and skill-level appropriate.</li></ul>

Characteristics of the Horizontal JUMP | Cue Words for Children

Characteristics of the Horizontal JUMP	Cue Words for Children
Hips lowered to sitting position (hips, knees, ankles flex in crouch)	"Bend ankles, knees and hips."
Shoulders lean forward	"Lean forward."
Knees bent, with toes staying in front of knees	"Bend knees."
Arms swing back	"Arms back."
Simultaneous forceful extension at hips, knees and ankles as arms thrust forward and upward	"Explode with legs."
45-degree angle in flight path	"Swing up and forward with arms."
Full body extension	"Look ahead and stretch out."
Eyes focused ahead on target	"Look where you're going." "Eyes ahead."
Lower legs extended before landing	"Put your legs out to land."
Balanced landing with feet apart, knees bent, arms out	"Quiet landing." "Soft landing."
Force taken on balls of feet, ankles, knees and hips on impact	"Bend your knees on landing."
Arms reach forward to keep centre of gravity moving in direction of flight	"Reach forward to brace for the landing."

Difficulties to Watch For

If...	Then...
Child is showing insufficient extension of legs and body on takeoff.	Ask the child to jump over a horizontal target (e.g., jump over a skipping rope or a line on the floor), gradually increasing the distance between takeoff and target.
Child is using ineffective arm swing in the jump.	Encourage the child to rock forward in a heel-to-toe motion while coordinating arm swing. A partner holds an object (e.g., scarf) ahead of the jumper in a high enough position to encourage him or her to jump towards the object, thus swinging arms forward during jumping motion.
Child is falling backward on landing.	Encourage the child to reach forward on landing.
Arms are beside or behind body on landing.	Use cue words as a reminder (e.g., "Reach forward").

To view and analyze video for this skill, and all the skills in this manual online, please visit:
➤ **www.phecanada.ca**

What Has Worked in Real Life

Joey is 9 years old and is a very clumsy, awkward child. I've had Joey in my physical education class for several years, and he has always been clumsy and not very skilled; in fact, he has always been a bit of a class clown, picking on other children, asking for water breaks, showing off the things he can do and generally being disruptive. I have come to realize that Joey is likely avoiding having to perform any skill that might reveal his lack of coordination. His parents, maybe sensing his lack of coordination on land, have always encouraged Joey's love of swimming, and he is getting quite good for his age group. To motivate Joey in physical education class, I recently tried to relate what we were doing to swimming and how it would help him. For example, during our track and field unit when we were working on jumping, I explained to him that the same power used for jumping is used for pushing off the wall in swimming, and if he kept working on his jumping he might get a better push-off during races. To help encourage this, I worked with Joey to verbally label all the parts of jumping (standing long jump): bending the knees, swinging the arms back, pushing down through the legs, bringing arms forward and extending forward. Joey seemed more engaged in the track and field unit, and so I will try to make other lessons relevant and give him verbal rehearsal strategies to help him become more proficient in his motor skills.

Activities for the Horizontal JUMP (for Distance)

Exploring the Jump

Skills: Jumping, hopping

Children: Individual

Equipment: One beanbag and one rope per child

Area: Outdoors or large indoor area

Activity: Ask the children to try to . . .

- Jump high and land lightly. (Question: What part of the foot lands first?)
- Jump as far as you can and land softly.
- Jump and reach up.
- Jump and reach out.
- Jump up and forward, high and far.
- Jump up and land in the same place.
- Jump and turn (half, quarter).
- Jump forward with a partner.
- Jump over the rope.
- Jump like a bouncing ball.
- Jump with your feet straddled and then together; slowly and then with increasing speed.
- Jump forward and then backward; slowly and then with increasing speed.

- Jump and make shapes while in the air: wide, narrow, star.
- Jump and mark your landing with your beanbag. Try to jump farther than your beanbag.
- Jump over the rope, increasing the distance of the rope each time.
- Jump to a drumbeat.
- Jump three times forward, three times backward.
- Land with your feet wide apart and then close together.
- Jump like a frog, like a rabbit, and so on.
- Jump in a zigzag pattern, in a circle, and so on.
- Jump quickly, slowly, quickly, slowly.
- Alternate jump, hop, jump, hop.
- Do jumping jacks.
- Jump and turn in the air.
- Jump in different patterns on the floor.
- Jump and clap your hands above your head.

JUMP for distance: *one-foot take-off with two-foot landing*

A. *Characteristics of the mature JUMP for Distance*

Characteristics of the mature JUMP for Distance	Cue Words for Children
GET READY:	
Determine your preferred (dominant) take-off foot.	
Mark and stand a distance (10-12 running steps) so that you can comfortably accelerate to full speed by the time you arrive at the take-off zone.	Stand far enough away to get to full speed.
Eyes and thoughts are focused on the runway and take-off zone.	Focus.
Eliminate distractions and imagine a successful jump before attempting it.	Imagine a successful jump.
ACTION:	
Demonstrate the correct sprinting technique to get maximum speed.	Run like your best sprint (do you recall the technique for sprinting?)
Focus eyes on the take-off zone.	
Two steps before the take-off, slow-down *slightly* while lowering your center of gravity somewhat (*shorten* these two strides slightly) to generate jumping height (e.g., like the steps in a basketball lay-up).	Last two steps are lower, shorter, and slower to be able to jump.
Plant the take-off foot in the take-off zone yet not past it and push off forcefully. Have your arms bent at your sides	Plant firmly and drive forcefully with the arms and the take-off and kicking legs.
At the same time, forcefully drive with the kicking leg forward so that it is parallel with the ground.	
At the same time, drive both arms upward forcefully.	
Bend backwards like a banana and "hang" as you float forward in the air.	Reach high, arch body like a banana, and "hang."
On the way down, move both legs forward so they extend to the front, bend forward at the waist, and extend your arms forward.	Jackknife: Bend and stretch forward.

As you land, pull your straight arms back to slightly behind your back.

Land on your heels followed by the balls of your feet and bend your knees and waist to absorb the force of landing.	Heels land first. Absorb weight by finishing in a squat position.

FINISH:

Bend the knees fully absorb the force of the landing.	Squat to balanced stand.
Allow your torso to move forward over the feet while moving your arms forward.	
Stand up in a balanced position and move forward out of the landing area.	Step forward and then out of the landing pit.

B. Teaching Tips

(i) Developmental changes to watch for prior to mature jump:
- Progressive increase initial crouch prior to take-off.
- Arms in opposition to legs and extended more vigorously.
- Greater extension through jumping action.
- Knees become less rigid on landing, with feet in balanced position.

C. Activities for the JUMP for Distance

Sample Guided Discovery Activities
1. Can you take two steps and jump off of one foot and onto two feet?
2. Repeat while jumping as high as possible. What did you do to jump high?
3. Now try taking four steps. Go fast but jump high too.
4. Can you make a "C" while in the air?
5. How do you land so you go as far as possible ("jack-knife")?
6. How can you land safely so you absorb your weight and do not fall backward?
7. From which foot do you most like to jump? Why? How can you consistently jump off of that one? (E.g., Set a beginning mark while maintaining consistent stride length.) To do so, practice running from 10-12 strides away from the take-off zone and try to plant your take-off foot in that zone while running full speed (do not jump but instead run through the landing area).
8. Try sprinting and then jump high and long. Why is sprint speed so important to jumping far? What do you do in the final two steps to help you get higher? Should you reach for the take-off zone in your final step(s)?
9. Set two jump ropes a certain distance apart. Now try to sprint and jump over them from one foot onto two feet. If necessary, widen or narrow them so you can succeed.

All-Succeed Long Jump

Skill: Sprint and long jump

Children: In groups of 3-5

Equipment: Cones

Area: One long-jump runway and landing pit(e.g., non-slip gymnastics mat) per group.

Have a 1-2 foot take-off zone (not a line) so students fault less often.

Activity: Set-up three pairs of cones across from each other (different colors for each pair) at a distance everyone can attain (bronze criterion), a further distance most can attain (silver criterion), and a further distance that fewer can attain (gold criterion). Students perform several long jumps and try to attain their personal best. Students should determine where they will begin their sprint approach and place a mark at the side of the runway there. If they do not land in the landing zone they should adjust their mark or strides to do so.

Modifications: Have each student choose a figure and draw it on a sticky tab or an object. After they jump, they place their sticky tab or object beside the pit. On successive jumps they try to beat and move their personal best mark. If desired, they can measure the distance.

Safety Tip (if applicable): Warm-up adequately prior to beginning. To minimize the risk of leg or foot injuries from overuse, do not perform too often during one class. Consider using a non-slip gymnastics mat(s) for the landing area. Ensure runways are far enough apart and away from walls so students do not collide with each other or into walls.

Rock Pond Triple Jump

Skill: Long jumping rhythmically

Children: Groups of 4

Equipment: Jump ropes, Poly-spots

Area: Join 2-3 jump ropes and put them in a circle formation on the ground (small circle at first). Place four poly-spots down as rocks in the mock pond about two feet apart from each other in the pattern of the triple jump (two for successively for the left foot and then one for the right). Repeat for each group.

Activity: Hop, step, and jump over the pond using the rocks. First, have students repeat the Hop-step-jump rhythm by saying "same-same, other, both" or "left-left, right, both" (if left-foot dominant). Then clap and say it and finally step and say it. In their groups, have students try to clear the pond using the pattern of the rocks. If successful, widen the pond and alter the spacing of the poly-spots.

Modifications:
- Try to have students have relatively equal distances for their hop, step, and jump.
- Have students begin by completing the triple jump activity from a standing position before attempting it while running.
- Set up an obstacle course with several such ponds or obstacles over which students must jump. Design the challenges with several crossing widths so students can choose where they wish to cross and so that each student can succeed.
- Instead of this mock scenario, create another or use cones as markers for the approximate location of the hop, step, and jump. Have the whole class participate in one line to minimize public comparisons. Students can alter the position of their cones according to their ability level.

Safety Tip (if applicable): To minimize the risk of leg or foot injuries from overuse, do not perform too often during one class. Consider using a non-slip gymnastics mat(s) for the landing area.

HOP: *one foot take-off with same foot landing*

Note: It is recommended that the child can stand on one foot before practicing hopping.

A. Characteristics of the mature HOP | Cue Words for Children

Characteristics of the mature HOP	Cue Words for Children
GET READY:	
Body upright, look forward	Look ahead
Arms bent at side (90 degree angle)	Bend ankles, knees and hips
PUSH OFF AND MOTION:	
"Swing leg" flexed and swings forward and upward to produce thrust	Spring with legs Spring and swing
Arms lifted rhythmically as support leg leaves ground	Swing with arms
Push off on ball of foot	
Pendulum action of swing leg to increase force	
LANDING:	
Softly on balls of feet	
Ankle flexion	Soft touch down
Slight knee flexion	

B. Teaching Tips

(i) Developmental changes to watch for prior to mature hop:

- Greater range of motion in support leg.
- Decreased forward body lean; upward leg thrust to initiate hop rather than from flexion of knee.
- Reduced use of arms for stabilization and greater use for force production.

(ii) Difficulties to watch for:

If...	Then...
Child is using insufficient spring with hopping foot (flat-footed action).	Give the child an object to hop over (e.g., small cone) in order to encourage him/her to generate more force in the hop.
Children are unable to alternate hopping foot.	Encourage the child to hold non-hopping foot until he/she is comfortable with hopping motion.
Child is using insufficient arm swing.	Encourage the child to stand in a stationary position and swing arms to imitate a hop motion. Gradually introduce hop action with a cue to remind the child when to swing her/his arms.

(iii) Before introducing the hop, a child must be able to balance on one foot.

(iv) Provide activities that enable children to practice hopping on their dominant foot and non-dominant foot.

(v) Begin with exploration activities in the early stages of practice.

To view and analyze video for this skill, and all the skills in this manual online, please visit:
↘ **www.phecanada.ca**

C. Activities for HOPPING

The following section provides a selection of individual, partner, small group and large group activities that focus on development of the hop. (Note: in several instances the activities may be adapted and used to practice jumping.)

Exploration Activities

Skill: Hopping
Children: Individual
Equipment: None
Area: Outdoor pavement, gymnasium
Activity: Try to...
- Hop in place on right foot, left foot
- Hop side to side
- Hop forward, hop backward
- Hop forward and swing your arms
- Hop forward and keep your arms still
- Hop to the drumbeat
- Hop five times in a row and change feet
- Hop with hands on hips, hands around free leg, behind head
- Hop with arms straight out at sides, straight out in front
- Hop quickly, slowly
- Hop and turn in place
- Hop while holding non-hopping leg
- Hop, then jump, then hop, and then jump
- Hop with your eyes closed
- Hop forward on a straight line
- Hop in place ten times in a row, and then hop forward ten times
- Hop three times on right foot, three times on left foot, and continue
- Hop without using your arms
- Hop in rhythm with a partner
- Hop while bouncing a ball
- Hop in different patterns on the floor
- Hop softly so you don't make a sound
- Hop back and forth over a line
- Turn around while hopping in place

Hopscotch

Skills: Hopping, jumping
Children: Groups of 2-4
Equipment: One beanbag per child
Area: Outdoor pavement, hopscotch patterns
Activity:
- First player tosses beanbag on to first square, hops into this square, picks up beanbag and hops out. Second player completes the same and so on.
- Second round, throw beanbag into second square and complete same action as first round.
  A player must negotiate all squares in this way.
  If the toss does not land in the appropriate square, the turn is forfeited and players try again at same square for the next round.

Jiggle Rope

Skills: Hopping, jumping
Children: Groups of 2-4
Equipment: One long skipping rope per group
Area: Gymnasium or outdoor pavement
Activity: Two players at each end of long skipping rope. From a kneeling or sitting position, the rope holders jiggle in different ways – side to side, up and down, etc. Other players try to hop or jump over the rope without touching it.

Rope Mazes

Skills: Hopping, jumping, leaping
Children: Groups of 2-3
Equipment: One skipping rope per child
Area: Gymnasium or outdoor field space
Activity: Using their skipping ropes, each group makes a maze on the floor with their ropes, and makes a hopping or jumping challenge through the maze. Children try all the different mazes.

Hop, step, jump

Skills: Hopping, jumping
Children: Individual
Equipment: None
Area: Gymnasium or outdoor field space
Activity: Hop forward on right foot; step on to left foot, and spring forward to land on both feet.

Repeat until the hop-step-jump sequence is smooth. Perform sequence starting with left foot. Measure the distance you travel from start to finish. Try to increase the distance. Extend challenge by adding a short "run up" into the sequence.

Hop to the Beat

Skills: Hopping, jumping, leaping, skipping, jogging
Children: Individual
Equipment: Drum or tambourine
Area: Gymnasium
Activity: Listening to the drumbeat, children hop to the beat of the drum. Teacher varies tempo and rhythm. Add other locomotor movements.

HOP
- Arms bent, look ahead
- Spring with your legs and swing your arms
- Land on balls of feet
- Bend knees on landing

HOP: *One foot take-off with same foot landing*

Characteristics of the HOP	Cue Words for Children
Body upright, look forward	"Look ahead" (Reminder: Pick a spot on the wall and focus on it)
Arms bent at side (90 degree angle)	"Arms ready!"
Bend Ankle, Knee and Hip	"Bend ankles, knees, and hips"
"Swing leg" is bent and swings forward and upward to produce thrust	"Push down or spring and swing"
Arms lifted rhythmically as support leg leaves ground	"Swing arms up and forward"
Push off on ball of foot	"Push through your toes"
Pendulum action of swing leg to increase force	"Pump your arms"
Softly lands on balls of feet	"Quiet or soft landing"
Ankle flexion	"Bend ankles"
Slight knee flexion	"Bend knees"

Adaptations of the HOP for:

Children in wheelchairs	• Encourage the child to perform the upper body motions of the hop (arms and trunk action – increases strength and coordination). Depending on ability level, the child might be able to raise self out of wheelchair seat slightly – a wheelchair/whole body hop.
	• If child has limited mobility, an Education Assistant (EA) or para-professional can move the wheelchair up and down to be included in the activity, encouraging up and down head movements.
Children with mobility aids	• Encourage child to plant device and execute the leg portion of the hop (i.e. their arms are secured to the crutch or walker) using the upper body to maintain balance with assistive device.

- Have the child practice the skill on both the dominant and non-dominant leg to build strength (some children will be stronger on one side – it is important to work on both sides).
- If possible, encourage child to attempt the skill without assistive device.
- Be aware that some children with cerebral palsy will be wearing braces on the lower leg limiting ankle flexibility and range of motion.

Children with
visual impairments

- Ensure the environment is clear of obstacles and other students to prevent injury.
- In the early stages of skill development, have the child hold onto a secure bar for balance.
- Use both verbal and tactile cues to tell the child what is expected.
- Try having the child hold onto the teacher's foot as the teacher hops to convey the message of getting the foot off the ground without falling over.
- As the child becomes more proficient, a peer tutor could be used for safety.
- Have sighted children in the class participate with a blindfold on during hopping practice to demonstrate the challenges experienced by children with visual impairments. This exercise is intended to increase awareness and understanding of the challenges and barriers faced by children with visual impairments.

Children who are deaf

- If an interpreter is not available (or necessary), have a cue card at each station (or for each PE lesson) with the task or plan clearly outlined at the child's level of understanding.
- Be prepared to give extra demonstrations of skills and activities.
- Consider using an FM loop system (microphone worn by the teacher to amplify the voice into the hearing aid worn by the Deaf student).
- Avoid excess noise in the learning environment.
- Be aware of the potential for balance issues in Deaf children; however, skill adaptations (to hopping) may not be necessary if child is otherwise able-bodied.

Difficulties to watch for:

If...	Then...
Child is not actually getting off the ground (flat-footed action).	Give the child a target to try to touch above their head.
	Tell the child to push down into the ground and then up into the air.
	Provide flat obstacles for the child to try to hop over (e.g. rope, or a line).
	Encourage child to point toes down as he or she jumps off the floor.
Hopping appears very uncoordinated and awkward.	Have the child verbalize the parts of the hop out loud (e.g. knees bent, push up, arm swing, land).
Children are unable to alternate hopping foot.	Encourage the child to practice hopping on each foot separately (as applicable).
Child is using insufficient arm swing (as applicable).	Encourage the child to stand in a stationary position and swing arms to imitate a hop motion. Gradually introduce hop action with a cue to remind the child when to swing her/his arms.

To view and analyze video for this skill, and all the skills in this manual online, please visit:

↘ **www.phecanada.ca**

"what has worked in real life...."

Kristy has spastic diplegia cerebral palsy which means her lower limbs are affected more than her upper body. To assist Kristy in learning how to hop, it was necessary to have Kristy practice pushing down on her walker in order to lift her legs up off the ground. In Grade one Kristy did not have the strength to lift her legs off the ground at all, but by Grade four Kristy was able to plant her walker, lift one leg off the ground, bend her knee and using the walker for support, lift herself off the ground in a hopping fashion. She practiced this on both legs and gradually was able to do several "hops" in a row on each leg which was one of her Individual Education Plan goals. Taking the time to really break down the skill and really think about Kristy's strengths allowed her teacher to devise a plan to work on the skills components one at a time gradually putting them all together, Kristy is now quite proud of her hopping ability and has to be told not to hop down the hall!

Activities for the HOP

Hopping Exploration

Skill: Hopping
Children: Individual
Equipment: None
Area: Outdoor pavement, gymnasium
Activity: Try to...

- Hop in place on right foot. Left foot.
- Hop side to side.
- Hop forward. Hop backward.
- Hop forward and swing your arms.
- Hop forward and keep your arms still.
- Hop to the drumbeat.
- Hop five times in a row and change feet.
- Hop with hands on hips, hands around free leg, behind head.
- Hop with arms straight out at sides, straight out in front.
- Hop quickly, slowly.
- Hop and turn in place.
- Hop while holding non-hopping leg.
- Hop, then jump, then hop, and then jump.
- Hop with your eyes closed.
- Hop forward on a straight line.
- Hop in place 10 times in a row, and then hop forward 10 times.
- Hop three times on right foot, three times on left foot, and continue.
- Hop without using your arms.
- Hop in rhythm with a partner.
- Hop while bouncing a ball.
- Hop in different patterns on the floor.

- Hop softly so you don't make sound.
- Hop back and forth over a line.
- Turn around while hopping in place.

Specific Modifications:

- For children in wheelchairs, encourage the child to execute the upper body portion of the hop, while moving about the room in his or her chair. Allow the child to explore the movement and if possible to use his or her upper body strength to lift off the seat of the chair in a safe and comfortable way.

Bubble Hop

Skill: Hopping
Children: Whole class or groups of 10 (younger grades)
Equipment: Bubbles
Area: Gymnasium or outdoor yard
Activity: Teacher blows bubbles for children to pop. The students have to pop the bubbles by hopping up to pop them.

Specific Modifications:

- Children in wheelchairs could use paddles to reach up and pop the bubbles.
- For children with visual impairments, explain the task to the student and ensure success by blowing bubbles right above their head – as they hop up they can feel the bubbles popping on their hands.

Hopscotch

Skills: Hopping, jumping

Children: Groups of two to four

Equipment: One beanbag per child

Area: Outdoor pavement, hopscotch patterns

Activity: First player tosses beanbag on to first square, hops into this square, picks up beanbag and hops out. Second player completes the same and so on. Second round, throw beanbag into second square and complete same action as first round. A player must negotiate all squares in this way. If the toss does not land in appropriate square, the turn is forfeited and players try again at same square for the next round.

Specific Modifications:
- Allow modifications to hopping as needed for each student; modification of the game itself is not necessary – i.e. a child who uses crutches should be allowed to hop with his or her crutches during the game).
- Have a hopscotch template with slightly raised borders to allow for tactile cues for a child with a visual impairment. Allow the child to feel the general shape of the hopscotch field so they know the environment.
- Change the rules, as necessary, for the child with a disability so that they are allowed to hop on the lines without penalty (this may or may not be necessary).

Jiggle rope

Skills: Hopping, jumping

Children: Groups of two to four

Equipment: One long skipping rope per group

Area: Gymnasium or outdoor pavement

Activity: Two players at each end of long skipping rope. From a kneeling or sitting position, the rope holders jiggle in different ways – side to side, up and down, etc. Other players try to hop or jump over the rope without touching it.

Specific Modification:
- Children who use wheelchairs and children with visual impairments could be rope holders.
- For children with visual impairments a rope with bells attached could be used more slowly to allow the child to react appropriately.

Rope mazes

Skills: Hopping, jumping, leaping

Children: Groups of two to three

Equipment: One skipping rope per child

Area: Gymnasium or outdoor field space

Activity: Using their skipping ropes, each group makes a maze on the floor with their ropes, and makes a hopping or jumping challenge through the maze. Children try all the different mazes.

Specific Modifications:
- Ensure pathways or spaces are wide enough for a wheelchair.
- For children with visual impairments, a buddy system could be used to identify the obstacles/maze structure.
- Allow for auditory sounds or instructions to facilitate the inclusion of children with visual impairments. A buddy system or peer tutor could also be used.

HOP: *A one-foot takeoff with a same-foot landing.*

Continuum of Prompts for the HOP

Physical Prompts	Physical prompts should be paired with verbal prompts.
- Complete manipulation	Physically lift the child off the ground.
- Manipulative prompting	Hold onto hands (or one hand only) while child hops on one foot.
- Minimal guidance	Tap knees to signal the start of hopping; tap the foot to remind participant to keep it off the ground.

Visual Prompts	Visual prompts should be paired with verbal prompts.
- Complete skill demonstration	Demonstrate hopping in slow motion, exaggerating the arm swing and keeping one foot off the floor.
- Partial skill demonstration	Accurately demonstrate only the arm swing or the bending of knee on hopping leg in order to push off the ground.
- Gestural prompting	Gesture to remind participant of key component (e.g., point to non-hopping leg, point to arms, point to a spot on the floor).

Verbal Prompts	
- Skill cue environmental cue	Try focusing the child's attention on a key component of the task (e.g., "Swing your arms," "Bend your knee," "Push off the ground," "Keep your leg up").
- Action command	Give a verbal description of the desired skill (e.g., "Hop three times over here").
- Action cue	Make a motivational statement to help the child perform the skill (e.g., "One, two, three, up").

No Prompts

- Initiation with	Add equipment that encourages the participant to engage in the activity without using any verbal communication — place flat, coloured shapes on the floor close enough so the child can hop from one shape to the other; lines can also be used (e.g., gym-safe tape).
- Imitative initiation	Child performs the skill after watching other participants performing it — allow a child with a disability to freely observe for a moment what the other children are doing. This may or may not be effective.
- Initiation in free play	Child performs the skill at an appropriate time in free play but with no peer demonstration.

Behaviour Management and Pedagogical Considerations for HOPPING

ASD	• If a child uses pic-syms in the classroom, find pic-syms for hopping-related activities and tasks, and create a storyboard of activities for the lesson. • Use structure and "sameness" for consistency (e.g., follow the same warm-up routine, the same general lesson structure). • Reduce distractions. • Avoid the child's sensitive aversions (e.g., loud noises, certain textures or colours). • Capitalize on the child's preferences for motivation (e.g., certain colours on the floor to hop on).
DS	• Keep instructions clear and simple. • Encourage positive behaviours. • Visual demonstrations are highly recommended. • Force production, strength and balance may be limited in children with DS, making hopping a good skill to work on. • Peer tutors can be effective for modelling and promoting on-task behaviour.
ADHD	• Reduce distractions: use small groups, keep space smaller. • Keep instructions clear and simple. • Maintain good "timing" — boredom may result in off-task behaviours. • Create an environment of success. • Set clear boundaries, both physical and task related. • Reinforce respect, teamwork and sportsmanship concepts in all aspects of the lesson.
ID	• Start with a simple task and add difficulty as the child progresses. • Use a peer tutor or educational assistant to keep the child on task. • Keep instructions simple and concise. • Repetition may be needed of both instructions and demonstrations. • If hopping is not a favourite activity, negotiate that hopping comes first and then the favourite activity is second.
DCD	• Create an environment of success to prevent frustration. • Ensure the class rules are consistently enforced and the expectations are very clear. • Allow for and encourage repetition and practice. • Use self-rehearsal strategies, talk-aloud strategies (e.g., have the child assign words to the parts of the skill and say them aloud during practice). • Discourage off-task behaviours such as excessive water breaks, time outs and "clowning around" by keeping groups small and tasks age- and skill-level appropriate.

Characteristics of the HOP	Cue Words for Children
Body upright, looking	"Look ahead." "Pick a spot on the wall and focus on it."
Arms bent at side (90-degree angle)	"Arms ready!"
Ankle, knee and hip bent	"Bend your knee." "Bend over a little bit at the waist."
"Swing leg" is bent and swings and upward to produce thrust forward	"Push down into the ground." "Spring and swing."
Arms lifted rhythmically as support leg leaves ground	"Swing arms up and forward."
Push-off is from ball of foot	"Push through your toes."
Pendulum action of swing leg to increase force	"Pump your arms."
Softly lands on balls of feet	"Softly touch down."
Ankle flexion	"Bend at your ankle."
Slight knee flexion	"Bend at your knee."

Difficulties to Watch For:

If...	Then...
Child is not actually getting off the ground above his or her (flat-footed action).	Give the child a target to try to touch head. Tell the child to push down into the ground and then up into the air. Provide flat obstacles for the child to try to hop over (e.g., a rope or line). Encourage the child to point toes down as he or she jumps off the floor.
Hopping appears very uncoordinated and awkward.	Have the child verbalize the parts of the hop out loud (e.g., bent knees, push-off, arm swing, landing).
Child is unable to alternate hopping foot.	Encourage the child to practise hopping on each foot separately (as applicable).
Child is using insufficient arm swing.	Encourage the child to stand in a stationary position and swing arms to imitate a hopping motion. Gradually introduce hop action, with a cue to remind the child when to swing the arms.

To view and analyze video for this skill, and all the skills in this manual online, please visit:

↖ **www.phecanada.ca**

What Has Worked in Real Life

Jason has ADHD and has difficulty with impulse control and following directions. To keep Jason on task in physical education, his teacher has developed a very structured generic lesson plan. Much like children with ASD, Jason responds well when he knows the routine and what to expect, even if he doesn't know the exact lesson. By having a clear routine, with clear rules and expectations, Jason knows what is going to happen. When he is feeling overwhelmed and needs time to gather himself, he signals to his teacher that he needs a moment. When she gives him permission, Jason goes to the corner and skips rope for a minute, which helps him bring himself back to equilibrium. Jason's physical education teacher has been working on this self-control strategy over the past several years. Now that Jason is 12 years old and able to recognize when he needs a moment, the disruptions in class have decreased, and his ability to participate to his fullest potential has increased.

Activities for the HOP

Exploring the Hop

Skills: Hopping, jumping
Children: Individual
Equipment: None
Area: Outdoor pavement, gymnasium
Activity: Ask the children to try to . . .

- Hop in place on right foot, on left foot.
- Hop side to side.
- Hop forward, hop backward.
- Hop forward and swing your arms.
- Hop forward and keep your arms still.
- Hop to the drumbeat.
- Hop five times in a row and change feet.
- Hop with hands on hips, hands around free leg, hands behind head.
- Hop with arms straight out at sides, arms straight out in front.
- Hop quickly, slowly.
- Hop and turn in place.
- Hop while holding non-hopping leg.
- Hop, then jump, then hop, then jump.
- Hop with your eyes closed.
- Hop forward in a straight line.
- Hop in place 10 times in a row, and then hop forward 10 times.
- Hop three times on right foot, three times on left foot, and continue.
- Hop without using your arms.
- Hop in rhythm with a partner.
- Hop while bouncing a ball.
- Hop in different patterns on the floor.
- Hop softly so you don't make any sound.
- Hop back and forth over a line.
- Turn around while hopping in place.

Bubble Hop

Skill: Hopping

Children: Whole class or groups of 10 (younger grades)

Equipment: Bubbles

Area: Gymnasium or outdoor yard

Activity: Teacher blows bubbles for children to pop. The participants have to pop the bubbles by hopping up to pop them. Encourage children to run in between hops and jumping can also be used to pop the balloons.

Hopscotch

Skills: Hopping, jumping

Children: Groups of two to four

Equipment: One beanbag per child

Area: Outdoor pavement, hopscotch patterns

Activity: The first player tosses the beanbag onto the first square, hops into this square, picks up the beanbag and hops out. The second player does the same, and so on. In the second round, the player throws the beanbag into the second square and completes the same action as in the first round. The players must negotiate all squares in this way. If the toss does not land in the appropriate square, the turn is forfeited and the player tries again for the same square in the next round.

For children who have difficulty with hopping on one foot, jumping on two feet can be used for this activity.

LEAP: *one-foot take-off and landing on the opposite foot*

A. Characteristics of the mature LEAP   Cue Words for Children

GET READY:

Lower hips to sitting position (hips, knees, and ankles flex in crouch)	Bend ankles, knees, hips
May be preceded by a run or from a stand-still	Run fast and push off
Swing arms back	Arms back

TAKE-OFF:

Simultaneous forceful extension at hips, knees, and ankles as opposite arm to leg thrusts forward and upward	Explode with take-off leg
Aim for 45-degree angle in flight path	Swing up and forward with arms
As body moves forward, hips, knees, and ankles extend in succession	

FLIGHT:

Full body extension	Look ahead and chest up
Stretch legs forward and back	Knees up
Eyes focused ahead on target	

LANDING:

Landing leg extend prior to landing	
Balanced landing with toes, then heels, on the ground; knees bent, arms out	
Force taken on balls of feet, ankles, knees, and hips on impact	Bend knees on landing
Arms reach alternately to keep centre of gravity moving in direction of flight	Reach forward

Stability Skills Combined With Locomotor Skills

EDUCATIONAL GYMNASTICS

Educational gymnastics is a functional activity in which children attempt to maneuver their body in a variety of ways along the floor or on, over, around, and through apparatus in an aesthetically pleasing way (Wall & Murray, 1994). Compared to artistic and modern rhythmic gymnastics which tend to be standardized, competitive, and performance-oriented, educational gymnastics emphasizes the functional, cooperative (competing with self), process-oriented, and self-discovery aspect of acquired gymnastic movements for holistic and educational benefits. Rather than emphasizing the performance of specified skills or products, children respond to teacher-posed tasks to apply their movement knowledge as they design their own movement sequences. The use of small apparatus such as hoops and ropes, as well as larger apparatus such as benches, boxes, beams, ladders, and climbers, provide various contexts in which participants can explore what, where, and how their body can move. Educational gymnastics is generally taught both directly (i.e., reproduction) and indirectly (e.g., guided discovery, cooperative learning). A position statement by the National (U.S.) Association for Sport and Physical Education (in Graham, Holt & Parker, 2007) reports that it is *inappropriate* for teachers to "(1) require all students to perform the same predetermined stunts and routines on and off apparatus, regardless of their skill level, body composition, and levels of competence; (2) have students perform solo while the remainder of the class sits and watches and compares performances to other students; and, (3) use activities that require extensive teacher direction and spotting" (p. 627). Further, "spotting–the practice of physically assisting children as they perform a movement–isn't commonly used in educational gymnastics classes. Children who depend on such help are likely to be unsure and even afraid unless a teacher is nearby. And, conversely, spotting encourages children to attempt movements they may not be ready for" (p. 634). It is also critical for teachers to know, follow, and train, their students to adhere to their respective Ministry of Education safety guidelines.

THE EDUCATIONAL GYMNASTICS EXPERIENCE

The Physical Experience must be:	The Social Experience must be:		The Learning Experience must promote:
• Child-oriented	• Positive	• Encouraging	• Concentration
• Challenging	• Cooperative	• Pleasant	• Memory
• Safe	• Helpful	• Accepting	• Creativity
• Clean	• Observant	• Reinforcing	• Inventiveness
• Tidy	• Supportive	• Guiding	• Problem-Solving
• Predictable	• Advising	• Sincere	• Analysis
			• Observation

Table 2   *Wall & Murray, 1994, p. 369*

Although the emphasis in educational gymnastics is creative exploration, there are certain prescribed skills and sequences centered on balancing, rolling, jumping, landing, and transferring weight) at each developmental level (Graham, Holt & Parker, 2007). These skills are performed individually, with others, and/or with apparatus. Gallahue and Donnelly (2003) recommend an emphasis on control of the body during stability and locomotor movements at the first level; balancing (e.g., V-sit) and rolling (e.g., forward roll) at the second level; transferring weight (e.g., cartwheels, handstands, and handspring) at the third level; and, practicing advanced flight movements (e.g., vaulting) at the fourth level. Combinations and sequences of movements are promoted at each developmental level.

CRITICAL EDUCATIONAL GYMNASTIC SKILLS
for Elementary School Children

1. Five basic jumps
2. Sideways roll
3. Hand balance/body curled
4. Shoulder balance
5. Head/hand balance
6. Jump/land/roll basic sequence
7. Forward roll/shoulder roll
8. Backward roll/shoulder roll
9. Hand balance/body extended
10. Cartwheel
11. Jump for height

Table 3   *Allison & Barrett, 2000, p. 615*

It is beyond the scope of this resource to provide the descriptions of each skill. More generic movement frameworks, sample activities, and checklists for educational gymnastics may be found in the references.

A MOVEMENT FRAMEWORK FOR EDUCATIONAL GYMNASTICS

Weight Transference

On the Floor

- Run
- Jump
- Roll
- Slide
- Step

With Apparatus

- Climb
- Jump
- Roll
- Slide
- Step
- Swing

Weight Bearing

Balance

- Balance (static)
- Rock

Suspend

- Balance
- Rock
- Hang
- Swing

Each of the above may be developed through focus on:

Body Concepts

- Stressing specific body parts
- Stretching, curling, and twisting
- Changing or maintaining a body shape
- Flight

Space Concepts

- Direction
- Level
- Pathway

Effort Concepts

- Time
- Weight

Relationship Concepts

- Partner work
- In small groups

Table 4

Wall & Murray, 1994, p. 369

A. Sample Guided Discovery Activities for EDUCATIONAL GYMNASTICS

(Use according to developmental level)

Can you safely:

- From a standing position, tuck and roll in any way you like?
- Jump and land over a rope suspended between two cones? With a twist or turn (1/4, 1/2 or full) in the air? Off of a box? Jump very lightly, landing on your feet and roll forward, backward or sideways? Jump from the spring board with a two-foot take-off, land onto the mat with two feet, and do a forward roll to straddle balance position?
- Travel backwards using only your hands and feet? Travel along the bench at a low level? Travel over the bench, transferring your weight from one body part to another? Run very lightly, jump, land, and roll forward, backward, or sideways? Forward roll up an incline? Travel, jump, land on one foot, and freeze?
- Explore balancing on different body parts?
- Take your weight on your hands and stretch your feet to the ceiling? Transfer your weight onto your hands in different ways? From feet to hands to feet suddenly? By only allowing your hands inside a hoop on the floor so your feet travel over the hoop (hand-hand-foot-foot)?

- Travel around the room using flight to get over all of the mats and poly spots as you come to them?
- Jump over, onto, or off of your apparatus? Play on your apparatus as you like?
- Match (mirror) your partner's running, jumping, landing and freezing when following close behind?
- Perform combinations of movements like forward roll to 1/2 jump turn? Handstand to forward roll? Cartwheeling, land on 2 feet, t dive roll to V-sit? Back straddle roll to knee scale?
- Create a sequence of jumping, landing, rolling, and balancing with your apparatus? Design your sequence so you can do it twice without stopping. Show your sequence to a partner?
- Create a movement sequence where you use at least three pieces of apparatus and employ flight at least twice?

B. An Additional Sample Activity

Gymnastics Sequence

Skills: To create a logical sequence of gymnastic skills through cooperation and problem-solving that demonstrates contrast of levels (high, medium, and low).

Children: In pairs.

Equipment: Three large apparatus items, mats, small equipment (eg. hoops)

Area: Gymnasium

Activity: Groups choose three large apparatus items, mats, and desired small equipment. Encourage children to choose pieces that will help them demonstrate various levels in space. Create a sequence of movements that incorporates all of the selected apparatus and one movement or shape at each level. Be able to state the movement concepts we have discussed in educational gymnastics (e.g., body parts, levels, time, and relationship to others) into your sequence.

CREATIVE DANCE

The objective of creative dance (educational dance) is for the child to experience expression and communication through movement. Creative dance experiences should involve children exploring, responding, and refining their movement in a myriad of ways. According to the Council on Physical Education for Children (COPEC, 2000), teachers should foster quality dance experiences to stimulate children's diverse interests, imagination, and abilities to improve their rhythmic responses to a variety of age appropriate stimuli.

Children may explore various ways to travel or locomote (eg. skipping, jumping, and hopping) to music they enjoy or respond to expressive poetry, concepts (such as water and friendship), and musical instruments. Learners often experience delight and reward from these experiences in which they create and design their own movements and create sequences of various movements. Each child's interpretation, judgment, and authentic expression is welcomed and affirmed through helpful constructive feedback by the teacher and their peers.

It is the teacher's role to carefully construct a lesson in which the child feels capable and enthusiastic about the movement possibilities. For example the teacher may ask; "Can you show me three different shapes, each at a different level (high, medium, and low)?" After the children take some time to experiment, practice and refine with teacher feedback, this may form the basis for a movement motif. To further develop this dance idea, children could very suddenly change from one shape to the next to the beat of music, or with variation of sudden and sustained changes. Children could form groups of three, such that each child is at a different level from the others as they change levels in synchrony. Another idea to develop could be a focus on the children's relationship to one another-where each is facing to connote 'togetherness' or 'exclusion' in 2 vs. 1 situation. However, the teacher constructs the parameters for the movement problem; it is vital that each problem or teaching task is specific and finite. "Find or create three …" is a good parameter for every student. The focus can be on any aspect of Laban's Analysis (see Chapter 2) to create diversity and interest in the dance lesson and the final dance sequence or motif.

Conducive to integration with material from other subject areas, creative dance stimulus is highly varied and may be founded upon movement concepts (eg. body parts, directions) music (recorded, played and/or composed by the teacher or student, instruments), poetry or stories, or images and ideas (e.g., pictures, costumes, customs, festivals, or natural or scientific phenomena such as storms). Props in the form of a variety of small equipment such as inflated balls, individual ropes, rhythm sticks, hoops, and jump bands can also be very useful.

As teachers and children become increasingly comfortable in creative dance, the initiative and ideas will shift from the teacher to the student as the teacher supports, clarifies, suggests, and provides guidance and feedback. Dance ideas may be developed over a series of lessons, but each lesson should offer new problems to solve with clear parameters and stimulating movement material to develop.

Table 5 indicates the range of movement potential for dance lessons.

A MOVEMENT FRAMEWORK FOR CREATIVE DANCE

Body Actions	Body Concepts	Space Concepts	Effort Concepts	Relationship Concepts
• Locomotion • Stepping actions (foot patterns) • Gesturing • Jumping • Stillness • Turning	• Body parts • Body shapes	• Direction • Level • Pathway	• Time • Weight • Flow	• Partner work • In small groups

Table 5   *Adapted from Wall & Murray, 1994, p. 170*

A. Sample Problem Solving Activities for CREATIVE DANCE

1. Walk and then run to the beat of the drum. (Teacher can make it a 'game', increasing then decreasing the speed of the beat.)
2. Walk and then run to the beat of the drum, but make your movements strong when you hear a loud beat and light when you hear a soft beat. (Teacher can combine loud and slow with fast and soft beats).
3. Travel to the music, copying the movements of the teacher.
4. Travel to the music any way you like on your feet, starting and stopping (hold that shape!) when you want.
5. Pick a number between 4 and 8. Count that number out loud. Now take that many steps as you walk (eg. 6 walking steps). Freeze for that many counts (freeze for 6 beats). Now jump that many times. Let's do it to the music. (Walk, freeze, jump and repeat).
6. Let's each make up a poem. "My name is _____. I am very _____. I can _____ and _____." (eg. My name is Bart; I am very smart. I can jump and I can dart."

B. An Additional Sample Activity

Dance Sequence

Skills: To create a dance sequence that demonstrates a contrast of locomotion and body shape to music.

Children: Solo

Equipment: Any age appropriate music with a clear beat (4/4).

Area: Gymnasium

Activity: Teacher asks children what locomotor movements they can demonstrate—such as walk, run, skip, gallop, hop, jump, or leap to music. Children explore various locomotor movements with teacher providing refining cues ("Swing your arms as you leap"; "Stretch your legs and feet in the air when you gallop"). Children may observe one another to offer positive feedback as to what constitutes quality movement. Children are asked to each choose three different forms of locomotion; each one is to be performed for 8 counts and ordered into a logical sequence. The class should practice together with the teacher counting. Children are asked to stress a different body part for each form of locomotion (eg. feet in galloping, knees in jumping, and shoulders in walking). Add a starting shape and an ending shape to the sequence which is performed three times in a row without the child stopping. This sequence could be made more complex by performing it using a specific pathway, with changes in direction (forward, backwards), with a partner to demonstrate contrast, such as stillness and movement where one moves while the other freezes, and changes in time.

Chapter 6: Manipulative Skills in Games

While cooperative and lead up games may take many forms, all formal (adult) games involve the manipulation of an object. Some games such as soccer, volleyball, and rugby involve only a ball, while other games such as tennis, hockey, and lacrosse involve, an implement with which the ball is carried, struck, or propelled.

This chapter will focus on fundamental, manipulative, skills in games that are pre-requisite to advanced skill development. Game skills are typically categorized into the three options we have when playing the game: projecting (such as passing or shooting); receiving (being passed the object) and retaining (dribbling, carrying the ball).

PROJECTING SKILLS

UNDERHAND ROLL: *projecting an object underhand so it rolls or slides at or near an intended target.*

NOTE: Underhand roll is an application to target games like bowling, curling, etc.

A. Characteristics of the mature UNDERHAND ROLL

Characteristics of the mature UNDERHAND ROLL	Cue Words for Children
GET READY:	
Ball carried on palm of delivery hand with other hand supporting it.	Stand tall
Stand straight holding the ball at chest height.	Ball up chest height
Eyes are focused on the target spot.	Focus and imagine success
Eliminate distractions and imagine a successful shot before attempting it.	
RELEASE AND FINISH:	
Take three steps towards the line beginning with the foot opposite the delivery hand.	Three steps
On the second step, swing the arm with the ball straight back.	Backswing
On the third step, plant the lead foot opposite the delivery hand while bending at the knees (crouching).	Plant opposite foot to delivery hand
	Crouch

Release the ball low along the floor when it is 6-12 inches in front of the lead foot.	Release low
Use appropriate force and accuracy for meeting the objective.	
Follow-through with your swing so that your hand points to your target spot.	Follow-through and point

B. Sample Lead-Up Games

Box Bowl

Purpose: Accuracy and Technique; Tactic(s): Using a Sub-Target

Equipment: Pins and ball

Participants: Teams.

Area: Laneway about 15-25 feet long (no fixed boundaries).

Activity: Using a group of pins as the target, place one or two sub-targets (e.g., 2-way open cardboard box) halfway to the pins. Each member of the team can have a different responsibility (e.g., a pin setter, ball retriever, box setter, or a scorekeeper). Individuals get three attempts each to knock as many pins down as possible.

Beanbag Spot Bowling

Purpose: Release point and force; tactic(s): angles

Equipment: Tape, beanbags, balls

Participants: 2 vs. 2

Area: Laneway about 15-25 feet long (fixed boundaries).

Activity: Use three differently sized circles taped to the floor, each worth a different number of points (e.g., 1, 2, 5) in proportion to their size, and at least one foot apart and staggered (some closer than others). The non-releasing team should each have a responsibility (e.g., ball retriever or scorekeeper). Each individual gets five attempts to bowl the beanbag so it stops inside a circle thereby earning that number of points. Consider also using balls but allowing the balls to roll over the circles to earn points or adding a wall or sideline bench off which students must bounce the rolled ball.

Ricochet

Purpose: Release point, force, approach, accuracy.

Equipment: Small foam/nerf balls, utility balls

Participants: All

Area: Full gymnasium

Activity: Divide the class into two equal teams and line each on opposite sidelines (facing each other) of a large rectangular court. Give 10 small (foam/Nerf if possible) balls to each team and place 1-2 large utility balls on the centerline. Both teams must use the 3-step approach when underhand bowling their ball from behind their sideline in their attempt to strike the larger ball so that it rolls in the direction of the opposition sideline. Players may not touch the large ball and may only retrieve non-rolling balls from their own half of the playing area. They may not block rolled balls of the opponent's until the ball crosses their own sideline. Points are awarded when the ball is forced over the opponent's line.

Safety Tip (if applicable): Use appropriate balls, underhand throws, and width of playing area so students are not afraid of, nor injured by, released balls.

Underhand Beanbag Croquet

Purpose: Release point, force, and accuracy.

Equipment: Beanbags, hula-hoops

Participants: 1 vs. 1

Area: Full gymnasium or field

Activity: Each with beanbag playing alongside another. Position 10-15 pairs of cones ("gates") throughout the playing area. A pair begins at a hula-hoop positioned near a gate and selects another near gate that others are not using as a target. Count how many underhand rolls it takes for you to roll the beanbag along the floor and through the target gate. When there, move to the side so others can proceed through that gate and decide where to advance next. Each pair must go through 7 gates (pairs of cones) before they advance to the pinnacle (final) target cone. Keep track of your cumulative score.

Safety Tip (if applicable): Have two courses set up (one for each half of the class if the class is too large). Remind students to roll-not toss-the beanbags. Consider having them proceed through gates in a particular order if they are targeting gates that are too far away and potentially striking others.

Bocce

Purpose: Accuracy, levels, force, technique, relationships (e.g., guards, raises, take-outs).

Equipment: Cones, beanbags, and balls

Participants: Individually scored in groups of 4 (four some). Each player is a member of one of four teams in the class (one from each make a foursome at each hole).

Area: Gymnasium or large field

Activity:
- Set up 6-10 large cones as targets with a sheet of paper taped to it indicating the number of the hole and a hula-hoop somewhere approximately 5-12 m away and also having a sheet of paper taped to it indicating that same number of the hole.
- Use beanbags if indoors and balls if outdoors.
- Each player gets 2 beanbags (or balls) of the same color, but different in color from the other players. They shoot each beanbag/ball from the hula-hoop and try to get it to stop nearest the target cone. Beanbags/balls are released alternately until each in the four-some has released one. This is repeated for the second beanbag/ball.

- The player with the ball closest to the target cone will score two points and the player with the ball second closest to the target cone will score one point.
- If two or more balls of different colors are halfway from the jack and no other balls are closer, then each side will receive that point per ball.
- Individuals are responsible for ensuring that their scores are recorded accurately.
- At the completion of the 6-10 holes, the points scored on each hole by each player are given to the teacher, who then adds each team's points in private and reports each team's total score.

Modifications: Place some obstacles (e.g., garbage cans, mats, out-of-bounds) to serve as hazards.

Have groups design a hole, play it, and then rotate to play those designed by others.

Safety Tip (if applicable): Spread out the holes. Be wary that the longer the hole, the harder students will throw the beanbag thereby increasing the chances of an erratic throw that might contact others. Warn students to be well behind the person releasing the ball or beanbag.

C. Activities for ROLLING

Sample Guided Discovery Activities
1. Try rolling the ball when standing straight and again when your knees are bent. Which works better and why?
2. What can you do to make the ball roll as fast and straight as possible?
3. Roll the ball so that it bounces when it rolls. How did you do that?
4. Roll different-sized balls with control along a line, from your knees, or to targets of different size and distance.
5. Try mirroring the ball roll that your partner makes.

OVERHAND THROW: *propelling the ball toward a specific point with the hand and arm*

A. Characteristics of the mature OVERHAND THROW

the mature OVERHAND THROW	Cue Words for Children
GET READY:	
Side facing	Side
Weight on the right foot (back foot)	
Throwing arm circles downward and backward to make a W-shape with arms and body	Make a "W"
Eyes on the target	Look
THROWING ACTION:	
Left foot (opposite to throwing hand) steps forward	
Hips rotate first then the upper body	
Weight is transferred from right foot (back foot) to left foot (front foot)	Back to front
Release ball just in front of the head	
FOLLOW THROUGH:	
Point throwing hand to target	
Throwing hand drops down and points toward the opposite knee	Across body

B. Teaching Tips

(i) Developmental changes to watch for in throwing prior to the mature throw:

- Initially the object is thrown by extending the elbow with feet together and little or no preparation, rotation of the trunk or follow through.
- This is followed by an upward preparation to the throw.
- There is some trunk rotation and a step forward with the foot on the same side as the throwing arm.
- Finally there is a downward and backward preparation of the throwing arm, an opening up as the weight of the body is on the back foot and there is a step with the leg opposite the throwing arm.
- There is noticeable trunk rotation and a dramatic increase in the velocity and distance of the object being thrown.

(ii) Difficulties to watch for:

If...	Then...
Children are not standing sideways to the target.	They should straddle a line so that the shoulder opposite the throwing hand is facing the target.
Children are taking the object upwards in the preparation to throw.	They should make a downward circle and take the object behind the head.
Children are not keeping their eyes on the target.	A partner can hold some flash cards with letters or numbers on them as the thrower goes through the throwing action but does not throw anything.
Children are stepping forward with the foot on the same side as the throwing arm.	A partner can hold the object to be thrown behind the thrower so that the thrower has to reach behind them to initiate the throw.
Children are stepping with a small step with the opposite foot.	Place a skipping rope a bit further forward and coach the thrower to step across the rope. Gradually add more distance to increase the length of the step.
Children rotate their trunk and hips as a block.	Instruct the children to get into their final preparation position lead them in how to isolate some hip rotation, and then rotate the upper body and shoulders.
Children are ending their throw with their throwing hand pointing at the target.	Ask them to throw the object and then touch the outside of the knee opposite the throwing arm.

To view and analyze video for this skill, and all the skills in this manual online, please visit:
www.phecanada.ca

C. Activities for OVERHAND THROWING

Target Ball

Skill: Overhand throw

Children: Individual

Equipment: Class set of beanbags

Area: Gymnasium

Activity: Place targets of various sizes and shapes high on the wall of the gymnasium. Individually, have children move 10 -15 meters away from the wall and use the overhand throw for force to see how many times they can hit their target.

Clear Out

Skill: Overhand throw

Children: Teams of 3-4

Equipment: One foam ball/badminton bird per child

Area: Gymnasium or outdoor space; three or four games can be going on concurrently, with a 10-15 meter middle zone separating the two teams playing together.

Activity: Each team tries to keep the balls out of their area by throwing them into the other team's area. Tip: remind students to use their overhand throw.

Outdoor Darts

Skill: Overhand throw

Children: Pairs

Equipment: One beanbag per child; two hula-hoops spread 15-20 meters apart

Area: Soccer field

Activity: The children stand beside one of the hula-hoops; each child throws their beanbag aiming for the inside of the other hula-hoop; the beanbag that lands closest to the hoop scores a point. They retrieve their beanbags, then turn around and throw them, aiming for the other hula-hoop. Tip: remind students to use their overhand throw.

Mini Golf

Skill: Overhand throw

Children: Individual

Equipment: Hula-hoops designating the holes; one badminton bird or beanbag per child

Area: Large open outdoor area to accommodate 24 holes (or the number of children in your class); hoops must be spread apart far enough to necessitate overhand throws for force.

Activity: Each child starts at a different hole and proceeds to throw the badminton bird or beanbag into the hula-hoops. Children cannot go onto the next hole until the child in front of them has moved onto their next hole.

THROW

- Face your body to the side
- Put weight on the back foot
- Eyes on target
- Forward step with opposite foot
- Rotate your hips first then the upper body
- Release the ball in front of head
- Follow through – point hand toward target
- Follow through – hand to opposite knee

Ball's Eye

Skill: Overhand throw

Children: Pairs

Equipment: One large cone and one large ball that can rest on the cone; organize the cones close to the side wall of the gymnasium; one small ball for each child

Area: Gymnasium

Activity: Children stand behind a line that is 10-15 meters from the cone with a ball resting on top. Children throw the small ball at the large ball on the cone to try to knock it off. Children alternate throws and retrieve their own ball.

Bombardment

Skill: Overhand throw

Children: Teams of 3 vs. 3

Equipment: One large ball and 6-8 small balls per group of six

Area: Gymnasium divided into lanes for each game

Activity: Each group of three starts by standing on the end line of their play space facing the other team of three. Each child has a small ball; the large ball is placed in the middle of the play space. Children throw their ball at the large ball to roll the large ball across the end line of the opposing team. A point is scored each time this is accomplished.

Over the Top

Skill: Overhand throw

Children: Pairs

Equipment: One badminton bird or beanbag per pair

Area: Outdoor playing field

Activity: Children start close together at one end of the field. One partner throws the bird over the head of the partner. The partner picks up the bird where it lands and then throws it over the head of the first partner. Gradually, the partners work their way further and further apart until they can't throw over the head of their partner and the game restarts.

THROW: Overarm/Underarm:
Propelling the ball toward a given objective

OVERARM THROW

PHOTO BY DAVE ARNOLD, COMPLIMENTS OF PARASPORT ONTARIO

Characteristics of the Overarm THROW	*Cue Word for Children*
Side facing	"Face the side"
Weight on the right foot (back foot)	"Weight on back foot"
Throwing arm circles downward and backward	"Arms back"
Eyes on the target	"Look where you want to throw" or "Eyes on target"
Left foot (opposite to throwing hand) steps forward	"Opposite foot"
Hips rotate first then the upper body	"Hips first"
Weight is transferred from right foot (back foot) to left foot (front foot)	"Back to front"
Release ball just in front of the head	
Throwing hand drops down and toward the body	"Across"

Adaptations of the Overarm THROW for:

Children in wheelchairs	

- Allow the child in the wheelchair to experiment to find the most effective way to throw while in the wheelchair based on their own body and the size of their chair.
- Children with no upper-body limitations should be encouraged to practice all the typical throwing patterns.
- Explore the use of different size balls and balls of different weights.
- Encourage the children to rotate their trunk, and depending on the type of chair the child uses, the chair itself could be limiting range of motion. If this is the case you can have the child sit forward in his or her chair in order to have more room (assuming the task at hand does not require the child to be able to wheel somewhere quickly or loss of balance is not a concern).
- Children with upper body limitations, especially in the hands (e.g. children with severe spastic cerebral palsy) should experiment throwing weighted scarves, small bean bags, or very soft balls to provide better grip.

- Children with severe limitations can use a ramp to learn how to participate in games such as Boccia ball. These games require precision, distance and strategy.
- We suggest the use of suspended balls (balls on a tether) that will allow children in wheelchairs more independence as the ball will return to them without depending on others to retrieve the ball.
- Some children might have success by pushing the ball off their lap.

Children with mobility aids

- Children with cerebral palsy will likely have motor control difficulties; a heavier, but smaller ball could increase their success in throwing.
- Hand gripping reflexes may also impact the ability to grasp and release a ball.
- To allow the child greater opportunities to practice throwing, it may be appropriate at certain times to allow the child who uses crutches or a walker to sit down.
This will free up his or her hands to practice throwing. Alternatively, if the child is comfortable maintaining his or her balance with only one crutch or one hand on their walker, the other hand could be used as well.
- During the initial stages of learning the child may not be able to keep his or her balance with one hand holding on…gradually decrease the amount of support if possible.

Children with mobility limitations

- Allow the child with mobility limitations to experiment throwing with balls of different sizes and weights. Try using weighted scarves or balls that provide for increased grip.
- The child's throwing pattern may never reach the mature stage of throwing due to his or her mobility limitations; therefore accuracy and function should be emphasized keeping in mind the skill may never "look" perfect.

Children with visual impairments

- Use of a suspended ball (preferably one with a bell in it) will allow the child more opportunities to practice and less time chasing their balls (ensure there is a long enough rope).
- Use verbal as well as tactile cues to give instructions.

Children who are deaf	• If an interpreter is not available (or necessary) have a cue card at each station (or for each physical education lesson) with the task or plan clearly outlined at the child's level of understanding.
	• Be prepared to give extra demonstrations of skills and activities.
	• Consider using an FM loop system (microphone worn by the teacher to amplify the voice into the hearing aid worn by the Deaf student).
	• Avoid excess noise in the learning environment.

Difficulties to watch for:

If...	Then...
Children are not standing sideways to the target.	Have the child straddle a line so that the shoulder opposite the throwing hand is facing the target.
Children bring the ball upwards in the preparation to throw.	Have the child make a downward circle and take the object behind the head.
Children are not keeping their eyes on the target.	A partner can hold some flash cards with letters or numbers on them as the thrower goes through the throwing action but does not throw anything.
Children are stepping forward with the foot on the same side as the throwing arm.	A partner can hold the ball behind the thrower so that the thrower has to reach behind them to initiate the throw.
Children are stepping with a small step with the opposite foot.	Place a skipping rope a bit further forward and coach the thrower to step across the rope. Gradually add more distance to increase the length of the step.
Children rotate their trunk and hips as a block.	Instruct the children to get into their final preparation position. Lead them in how to isolate some hip rotation, and then rotate the upper body and shoulders.
Children are ending their throw with their throwing hand pointing at the target.	Ask them to throw the object and then touch the outside of the knee opposite the throwing arm.

To view and analyze video for this skill, and all the skills in this manual online, please visit:

🏹 **www.phecanada.ca**

"what has worked in real life...."

Mary has spastic cerebral palsy and uses a wheelchair full time. She also has limited use of her upper limbs due to her spasticity and persistent reflexes. To include Mary in throwing activities Mary's physical education teacher didn't know what to do. It appeared that Mary wasn't going to be able to grasp a ball, or throw it. Undeterred, Mary's teacher started experimenting with different balls to see if she would be able to throw them. First Mary's teacher gave her smaller and lighter balls to throw. These attempts were not overly successful. Finally, Mary's teacher found a small ball that was heavier than most balls. This heavier ball provided Mary with more success than the smaller balls. Mary's throwing abilities improved drastically once the right balls were found for her!

UNDERARM THROW

Characteristics of the Underarm THROW	Cue Word for Children
Body faces forward	"Belly button facing the wall/target"
Preferred hand swings down and back	"Arm's back"
Steps forward with the foot opposite to the throwing arm	"Opposite (right or left) foot"
Bends knees to lower the body	"Bend knees"
Releases the ball with palm facing up	"Roll off your fingers" or "just like bowling"
Throwing arm follows through	"Arms to the wall/target"

Adaptations of the Underarm THROW for:

Children in wheelchairs	• Allow the child in the wheelchair to experiment to find the most effective way to throw while in the wheelchair based on their own body and the size of their chair.
	• Children with no upper-body limitations should be encouraged to practice all the typical throwing patterns.
	• Explore the use of different size balls and balls of different weights.
	• Children with upper body limitations (especially in the hands such as children with severe spastic cerebral palsy) should experiment throwing weighted scarves, small bean bags, or very soft balls to provide better grip.
	• Children with severe limitations can use a ramp to learn how to participate in games such as Boccia ball which require precision, distance and strategy.
	• The use of suspended balls or balls on a tether attached to the chair that will allow the children in wheelchairs more independence as the ball will return to them without depending on others to retrieve the ball.
	• Some children might have success by pushing the ball off their lap.
Children with mobility aids	• Children with cerebral palsy will likely have motor control difficulties; a heavier, but smaller ball could increase their success in throwing.
	• To allow the child greater opportunities to practice throwing it may be appropriate at certain times to allow the child who uses crutches or a walker to sit down freeing up his or her hands to practice throwing. Alternatively, if the child can try throwing with one hand if he/she is comfortable maintaining his or her balance with only one crutch or one hand on their walker this could be used as well.
	• During the initial stages of learning the child may not be able to keep his or her balance with one hand holding on. Gradually decrease the amount of support when possible.
Children with mobility limitations	• Allow the child with lower limb mobility limitations to experiment throwing with balls of different size and weight. Try using weighted scarves or balls that provide for increased grip (often children with cerebral palsy will have upper body mobility limitations as well).

- The child's throwing pattern may never reach the mature stage of throwing due to his or her mobility limitations; therefore accuracy and function should be emphasized keeping in mind the skill may never "look" perfect.
- For children with a single arm amputation, have the child practice throwing with their dominant arm.
- For children with double arm prosthesis, have the child experiment with the types of balls that are easiest for him or her to grasp and throw.

Children with visual impairments

- Use of a suspended ball (preferably one with a bell in it) will allow the child more opportunities to practice and less time chasing the balls (ensure there is a long enough rope).
- Provide targets that make noise when hit e.g. bowling pins knocked over, or a flat target that makes music when hit.
- Use verbal as well as tactile cues to give instructions.
- Use very brightly coloured balls if possible.

Children who are deaf

- If an interpreter is not available (or necessary) have a cue card at each station (or for each physical education lesson) with the task or plan clearly outlined at the child's level of understanding.
- Be prepared to give extra demonstrations of skills and activities.
- Consider using an FM loop system (microphone worn by the teacher to amplify the voice into the hearing aid worn by the Deaf student).
- Avoid excess noise in the learning environment.

"what has worked in real life...."

Jing is a nine year old girl who has spastic quadriplegic cerebral palsy. She uses a wheelchair full time and often has an education assistant. Jing loves her physical education class and is now the best Boccia ball player in her class. Jing's PE teacher worked with her family to devise a ramp made out of plumbing supplies to be attached to Jing's chair. When playing Boccia ball in class, the PE teacher has Jing's classmates play while sitting in a stationary chair. All the students work on both underarm and overarm throwing accuracy and control, and Jing is able to participate fully and successfully. In fact, when playing Boccia ball in pairs, Jing is often the most in demand as a partner.

Activities for the THROW

Boccia Ball Games

The main objective of Boccia is to place your coloured ball closer than your opponent's ball to the white target (jack) ball. The scoring is similar to that of curling; each ball closer to the jack than your opponents equals one point. At the end of four ends, the player with the most points wins. Players can throw, kick or use a chute to propel the balls onto the court. Boccia can be played in individual (1 vs. 1) pair (2 vs. 2) or team (3 vs. 3) formats. Boccia is played with 13 balls (6 red, 6 blue, 1 white) 6 per competitor and 1 target ball (jack ball). The jack ball (white) is used to start off the game and is thrown by one of the competitors on the court. Once this is done, the object of the game is to come as close to the jack ball as possible to gain points.

Boccia players may play using their hands or feet, with or without assistive devices to throw or direct the ball to the target. It is a strategic game that requires tactical, technical and mental preparation to beat your opponent. It is a game where anything can happen.

Specific Modifications:

- Children with severe spastic cerebral palsy can use ramps to "throw" the ball.
- Have able-bodied children sit in chairs while playing boccia ball with children with disabilities – children with movement limitations and children who use mobility aids should also sit down when playing boccia ball for the success and inclusion of all.
- Provide very detailed feedback for children with visual impairments.

Goal Ball

Goal ball is a Paralympic game for people with visual impairments

Game consists of 2 7-minute periods

3 players on the court per team at a time (for physical education purposes more players may be allowed)

All players wear blind folds to keep the game fair.

Players must respect their play zones – the pitch is 18m long by 9m wide, the goal is the whole width of the end (volleyball courts can be used)

Play begins when the designated team throws the ball to start the game

The ball must touch the floor at least once in the neutral zone as well as in the landing or team areas of the opposite team

Goal ball is the most appropriate game for children with visual impairments and able-bodied classmates but is not recommended for children in wheel-chairs.

When playing Goal Ball as a class, have all the children wear blindfolds to even the playing field.

Ball's eye

Skill: Underarm throw for accuracy.

Children: Pairs

Equipment: One large cone and one large ball that can rest on the cone. Organize the cones close to the side wall of the gymnasium; one small ball for each child

Area: Gymnasium

Activity: Children stand behind a line that is 10-15 meters from the cone with a ball resting on top. Children throw the small ball at the large ball on the cone to try to knock it off. Children alternate throws and retrieve their own ball.

THROW (Overhand and Underhand):
Propelling the ball towards a given objective or direction.

OVERHAND THROW

Continuum of Prompts for the Overhand THROW

Physical Prompts	Physical prompts should be paired with verbal prompts.
- Complete manipulation	Physically move the child's arms through the motion of the overhand throw — stand behind the child, place one hand over the throwing hand, and move the whole arm.
- Manipulative prompting	Provide assistance only during critical parts of the desired movement (e.g., tactile guidance during the backward windup for the overhand throw).
- Minimal guidance	Make contact with a relevant body part to initiate a movement (e.g., hand or elbow to redirect the thrower's hand).
Visual Prompts	**Visual prompts should be paired with verbal prompts.**
- Complete skill demonstration	Accurately and slowly demonstrate the complete overhand throw including the placement of the feet.
- Partial skill demonstration	Accurately and slowly demonstrate the parts of the overhand throw. (Try demonstrating without the ball to focus attention on the motor pattern). Demonstrate the foot placement, the backswing, the weight shifting and the rotation of the upper body as well as the throwing action with follow-through.
- Gestural prompting	Point to the arm or the foot to remind the child of the important components.
Verbal Prompts	
- Skill cue	Try focusing the child's attention on a key component of the task (e.g., "Step forward," "Bring your arm back," "Rotate," "Release the ball," "Follow through").
- Action command	Give a verbal description of the desired skill (e.g., "Throw the ball").
- Action cue	Make a motivational statement to help the child perform the skill (e.g., "One, two, three").

No Prompts

- Initiation with environmental cue	Placing balls of various sizes and colours out for children to experiment with will facilitate spontaneous throwing.
- Imitative initiation	Child performs the skill after watching other participants performing it.
- Initiation in free play	Child performs the skill at an appropriate time in free play but with no peer demonstration.

Behaviour Management and Pedagogical Considerations for THROWING Overhand

ASD	• If a child uses pic-syms in the classroom, find pic-syms for the overhand throw (baseball, softball, football) and throwing-related activities and tasks, and create a storyboard of activities for the lesson. • Reduce distractions. • Avoid the child's sensitive aversions (e.g., loud noises, certain textures or colours). • Use structure and "sameness" for consistency (e.g., follow the same warm-up routine, the same general lesson structure). • Capitalize on the child's preferences for motivation (e.g., certain colours, textured balls).
DS	• Keep instructions clear and simple. • Encourage positive behaviours. • Visual demonstrations are highly recommended. • Force production, strength and balance may be limited in children with DS, making physical education a critical component of a child's education plan. • Provide a larger target on the wall for the child to aim at. • Peer tutors can be effective for modelling and promoting on-task behaviour.
ADHD	• Reduce distractions: use small groups, keep space smaller. • Keep instructions clear and simple. • Maintain good "timing" — boredom may result in off-task behaviours. • Create an environment of success. • Set clear boundaries, both physical and task related. • Reinforce respect, teamwork and sportsmanship concepts in all aspects of the lesson.

ID	• Use a peer tutor or educational assistant to keep the child on task. • Keep instructions simple and concise. • Repetition may be needed of both instructions and demonstrations. • Start with a simple task and add difficulty as the child progresses. • Allow the child with an ID to choose his or her ball from a variety of sizes, shapes, colours and weights.
DCD	• Create an environment of success to prevent frustration. • Ensure the class rules are consistently enforced and the expectations are very clear. • Allow for and encourage repetition and practice. • Provide a large target on the wall for the child to aim at. • Use self-rehearsal strategies, talk-aloud strategies (e.g., have the child assign words to the parts of the skill and say them aloud during practice — arm down and back, step forward, arm forward, throw ball, follow through). • Discourage off-task behaviours such as excessive water breaks, time outs and "clowning around" by keeping groups small and tasks age- and skill-level appropriate.

Characteristics of the Overhand THROW / Cue Words for Children

Characteristics of the Overhand THROW	Cue Words for Children
Side facing	"Side facing target."
Weight on the back foot	"Lean on your back foot."
Throwing arm circles downward and backward	"Bring your arm back."
Eyes on the target	"Look where you want to throw."
Foot opposite throwing hand steps forward	"Step forward with your opposite foot."
Hips rotate first and then the upper body	"Start to rotate in your legs first."
Weight transferred from back foot to front foot	"Shift your weight from the back to the front."
Ball released just in front of head	"Let go right around your head."
Throwing hand drops down and towards body	"Release your hand across your body."

Difficulties to Watch For

If...	Then...
Child is not standing sideways to the target.	Have the child straddle a line so that the shoulder opposite the throwing hand is facing the target.
Child brings the ball upwards in the preparation to throw.	Have the child make a downward circle and move the object behind the head.
Child is not keeping his or her eyes on the target.	A partner can hold some flash cards with letters or numbers on them as the thrower goes through the throwing action but does not throw anything.
Child is stepping forward with the foot on the same side as the throwing arm.	A partner can hold the ball behind the thrower so that the thrower has to reach back to initiate the throw.
Child is taking a small step with the opposite foot.	Place a skipping rope a bit farther forward, and coach the thrower to step across the rope. Gradually add more distance to increase the length of the step.
Child rotates his or her trunk and hips as a block.	Instruct the child to get into the final preparation position. Lead him or her through hip rotation and then rotate the upper body and shoulders.
Child is ending the throw with the throwing hand pointing at the target.	Ask the child to throw the object and then touch the outside of the knee opposite the throwing arm.

To view and analyze video for this skill, and all the skills in this manual online, please visit:
www.phecanada.ca

What Has Worked in Real Life

Julio is five years old and has been diagnosed with a generalized developmental delay. He is a delightful little boy who is very friendly, but he is developmentally delayed in both his motor skills and his language. To engage Julio in throwing activities, I always bring out a large variety of balls and let the children choose which ball they would like to use. Julio is often attracted to the balls that make noises (bells inside) or the balls that have a textured surface. By allowing choice and providing balls that motivate him, Julio's throwing has definitely improved this semester.

UNDERHAND THROW

Continuum of Prompts for the Underhand THROW

Physical Prompts	Physical prompts should be paired with verbal prompts.
- Complete manipulation	Stand behind the child, hold the child's hand, and move the child's arm through the action of throwing.
- Manipulative prompting	Provide assistance only during critical parts of the underhand throw (e.g., tactile guidance during the backward windup for the underhand throw).
- Minimal guidance	Make contact with a relevant body part to initiate or direct a movement (e.g., hand or elbow to redirect the thrower's hand).
Visual Prompts	**Visual prompts should be paired with verbal prompts.**
- Complete skill demonstration	Accurately and slowly demonstrate the underhand throw in its entirety.
- Partial skill demonstration	Accurately demonstrate the components of the underhand throw — the backward windup, the step forward. Try demonstrating without the ball to focus the child's attention.
- Gestural prompting	Gesture to remind participant of key component (e.g., point at a wall or target, point at the hand or ball).
Verbal Prompts	
- Skill cue	Try focusing the child's attention on a key component of the task (e.g., "Step forward," "swing your arm back," "Release the ball").
- Action command	Give a verbal description of the desired skill (e.g., "Throw me the ball").
- Action cue	Make a motivational statement to help the child perform the skill (e.g., "One, two, three").

No Prompts

- Initiation with environmental cue	Placing balls of various sizes and colours around the gym may encourage children to engage in throwing — having targets on the walls for children to throw at can also facilitate throwing.
- Imitative initiation	Child performs the skill after watching other participants performing it.
- Initiation in free play	Child performs the skill at an appropriate time in free play but with no peer demonstration.

Behaviour Management and Pedagogical Considerations for THROWING Underhand

ASD	• If a child uses pic-syms in the classroom, find pic-syms for the underhand throw (bowling, Boccia) and throwing-related activities and tasks, and create a storyboard of activities for the lesson. • Reduce distractions. • Avoid the child's sensitive aversions (e.g., loud noises, certain textures or colours). • Use structure and "sameness" for consistency (e.g., follow the same warm-up routine, the same general lesson structure). • Capitalize on the child's preferences for motivation (e.g., certain colours, textured balls).
DS	• Keep instructions clear and simple. • Encourage positive behaviours. • Visual demonstrations are highly recommended. • Force production, strength, and balance may be limited in children with DS, making physical education a critical component of a child's education plan. • Peer tutors can be effective for modelling and promoting on-task behaviour.
ADHD	• Reduce distractions: use small groups, keep space smaller. • Keep instructions clear and simple. • Maintain good "timing" — boredom may result in off-task behaviours. • Create an environment of success. • Set clear boundaries — place a spot on the floor for the child to stand on while throwing. • Reinforce respect, teamwork and sportsmanship concepts in all aspects of the lesson.

ID	• Use a peer tutor or educational assistant to keep the child on task.
	• Keep instructions simple and concise.
	• Repetition may be needed of both instructions and demonstrations.
	• Start with a simple task and add difficulty as the child progresses.
DCD	• Create an environment of success to prevent frustration.
	• Ensure the class rules are consistently enforced and the expectations are very clear.
	• Allow for and encourage repetition and practice.
	• Use self-rehearsal strategies, talk-aloud strategies (e.g., have the child assign words to the parts of the skill and say them aloud during practice).
	• Discourage off-task behaviours such as excessive water breaks, time outs and "clowning around" by keeping groups small and tasks age- and skill-level appropriate.

Characteristics of the Overhand THROW

Characteristics of the Overhand THROW	Cue Words for Children
Body faces forward	"Face your target." "Your body should be facing the wall."
Preferred hand swings down and back	"Bring your arm back behind you."
Steps forward with the foot opposite to the throwing arm	"Step with the opposite foot to the hand with the ball."
Bends knees to lower the body	"Bend your knees."
Releases the ball with palm facing up	"Let the ball roll out of your fingers — just like bowling."
Throwing arm follows through	"Make sure your arm follows your throw straight to the wall."

Difficulties to Watch For

If...	Then...
Child brings the ball upwards in the preparation to throw.	Have the child make a downward circle before bringing the ball forward for the release.
Child does not keep his or her eyes on the target.	Give the child a target that is attractive or motivating to that individual child.

Child releases the ball too late (e.g. the ball goes straight up in the air).	Provide a verbal cue as to when the ball should be released or hold an object (e.g. a hoola-hoop or pool noodle) in front of a child at the height the child should release the ball. Tell the child to release the ball before their hands hit the hoola-hoop.
Child steps forward with the foot on the same side as the throwing arm.	A peer tutor can hold the ball behind the thrower so that the thrower has to reach behind them to initiate the throw.
Child uses a very small step with the opposite foot.	Place a skipping rope a bit further forward and coach the thrower to step across the rope. Gradually add more distance to increase the length of the step.

To view and analyze video for this skill, and all the skills in this manual online, please visit:
ᐳ www.phecanada.ca

What Has Worked in Real Life

Tyrell is a 14-year-old boy, wheelchair bound, non-verbal. Only one arm has mobility, and someone needs to push his chair during physical education.

Cooperative activity: *"Doctor, Doctor," or we also call it "Guard Your Captain."*

Organization: *Divide the class into two large groups; each group uses half the gym.*

Objective: *Hit the doctor (captain) by throwing soft balls.*

Rules: *Select the doctor (captain) for each team in secret; using three soft balls, players attempt to find and hit the doctor (captain); if a regular player is hit, he or she must sit down. The doctor (captain) can free his or her players with a touch.*

Story: *Our class chose Tyrell to be the doctor (captain). The other students cooperatively guarded him and wheeled him around to heal (or free) their teammates who were sitting because they had been hit with the ball. The students came up with great strategies to include Tyrell and make the game work on their own, and Tyrell felt part of class — he was animated and excited and showed his team and all involved lots of smiles.*

Activities for the THROW

Let's Roll That Ball!

* *Suitable for young children with developmental delays.*

Skills: Rolling a ball along the ground, at a target, in different pathways and directions; catching; relationships with others

Children: In pairs, threes or fives

Equipment: Small and large balls, cones, hoops, skittles, ropes, chairs, one ball per pair or group

Area: Smooth, hard surface

Activity: Ask the children in pairs to try to . . .
- Roll the ball to your partner through a target or obstacle (e.g., between two cones, through a hoop, at a skittle, at another ball, along a line, under a chain, between ropes).
- Take turns at rolling the ball to a wall target.
- Roll the ball to your partner, varying the distance between 3 and 10 metres.
- Roll the ball to your partner, then change places.
- Roll the ball as many times as you can in 30 seconds.

Ask the children in fives to try to . . .
- Roll the ball around/across a circle towards your partner or other players.
- Roll the ball to hit a skittle in the centre of a circle.
- Place one player in the centre who rolls the ball to others in turn.

Chocolate Chip Cookies

* *Suitable for very young children with developmental delays.*

Skills: Throwing (overhand and underhand)

Children: Whole class

Equipment: Beanbags and one hoop per child

Area: Classroom or outside

Activity: Place the children an appropriate distance from their hoops based on ability level (i.e., the more skilled, the farther away the child should be). Have the children toss beanbags (underhand or overhand) into the hoop. Tell the children you're making chocolate chip cookies.

10 Pin

Skills: Rolling a ball to a stationary target, accuracy

Children: Pairs or groups

Equipment: A set of 10 pins (milk containers filled with sand, drink cans or skittles) and a ball per pair or group

Area: Smooth, hard surface

Activity: Arrange the pins in the 10-pin formation. One player rolls at the pins, another replaces them as they are knocked over and calls the score. Players change roles after each turn.

Variations:
- Decrease or increase the number of pins.
- Decrease or increase the distance of the pins from the player.

Mini Golf

Skill: Throwing (underhand)

Children: Individual

Equipment: Hoops designating the holes; one badminton bird or beanbag per child

Area: Large open outdoor area to accommodate 24 holes (or the number of children in your class); hoops must be spread apart far enough to necessitate overhand throws for force

Activity: Each child starts at a different hole and proceeds to throw the badminton bird or beanbag into the hoop. Children cannot go onto the next hole until the child in front of them has moved onto his or her next hole

Unders

Skill: Throwing (underhand) for accuracy

Children: Groups of two or three

Equipment: Small balls, bucket/bin/box, targets on wall, ground targets (such as hoops, rope circles, bases, discs), markers

Area: walls of gymnasium

Activity 1: Underhand darts

Each player has a ball and stands in front of a wall target (numbers in a square, or a circle with several rings, like a dartboard). The players throw underhand five times and count their score.

Activity 2: Underhand golf

Ground targets (holes) are arranged as a "golf" course, positioned at varying distances from one another and with a marker (tee) near each one. Players throw from the starting tee until they can land the ball on the first target. They continue in this way around the remainder of the course, following the correct sequence.

Variations:
- Bean bags can be used for children with greater challenges, alternatively, lighter or heavier balls can also be used based on the needs of the individual child.
- Increase difficulty: Increase the distance between tee and target.
- Play with a partner: Have a competition to see who can score the most points with a limited number of throws.

KICK: *Striking an object with the foot*

A. Characteristics of the mature KICK   Cue Words for Children

GET READY:	
Stand behind the ball	
Step forward with kicking foot	Step forward
Plant support foot beside ball	Plant foot
KICKING ACTION:	
Kicking leg with knee bent swings freely from the hip through an arc toward the ball	
Backward body lean for initial balance	Balanced
Knee is quickly extended as the foot contacts ball	Lean into kick
Aim for midline slightly below centre of ball	Aim
Contact on tops of toes and instep inside of foot	
Left arm (right kick) extends toward direction of kick	
FOLLOW THROUGH:	
Backward lean of trunk	
Kicking leg continues its movement forward across the body	Kick/swing through the ball
Use arms to maintain balance	

B. Teaching Tips

(i) Developmental changes to watch for prior to mature kick:

- Increase in angle of forward lean in back swing and backward lean in follow-through.
- Increase in range of motion in kicking motion (back swing through to follow-through).

(ii) Difficulties to watch for:

If...	Then...
Child uses limited back swing of kicking leg.	Without using a ball, the child should stand on non-kicking foot and practice full-range leg swing with kicking leg.
Non-kicking foot is not planted beside the ball.	Place a mark where the child should plant the non-kicking foot. Child repeats kicks using this mark until able to plant the foot accurately without the mark.
Instep of foot does not contact ball below the centre.	Make a mark (e.g., piece of tape) on the ball to show child the point of contact.
Kicking foot does not follow through in direction of the kick.	Without using a ball, coach the child to swing through with kicking leg to touch fingers of outstretched opposite arm. Repeat same action as above with ball.

(iii) Practice kicking a stationary ball before practicing with a moving ball.

(iv) Inside of foot kick is best for controlling the height of ball.

(v) Focus on kick for distance (promotes mature pattern), then add accuracy.

(vi) Practice using both right and left foot.

(vii) Give each child a ball, and provide balls of various sizes and weights.

(viii) Space children far enough apart to allow for errant kicks.

(ix) Use exploration activities in early stages of practice.

To view and analyze video for this skill, and all the skills in this manual online, please visit:

www.phecanada.ca

C. Activities for KICKING

This section provides a selection of activities that focus on development of the kick. Activities are for individuals, pairs, small groups, or large groups. (Note: in some instances the activities may be adapted and used to practice throwing skills.)

Exploration Activities

Skill: Kicking

Children: Individual

Equipment: One ball per child, range of target-making equipment (cones, hoops, wooden pins, etc.)

Area: Outdoor field space

Activity: Try to…
- Kick the ball with different parts of your foot: instep, inside of foot, outside of foot
- Kick the ball at a target: hit the wall, between two cones, into a goal
- Kick the ball in different directions: forward, backward, diagonal
- Kick the ball when it is stationary, rolling toward you, rolling away from you
- Kick the ball to a partner who is stationary, moving
- Kick the ball high in the air or along the ground
- Kick the ball with a running approach
- Kick at a moving target
- Kick the ball to the wall and trap the rebound; move closer to the wall, move away
- Kick the ball as hard as possible

Target Challenges

Skill: Kicking

Children: Groups of 3-4

Equipment: One ball per child, range of target making equipment (cones, hoops, wooden pins, etc.)

Area: Outdoor field space

Activity: Using assigned equipment, each group makes up a "kicking to a target" challenge for the other groups (e.g., How may kicks does it take your group to kick the ball off the cone, from 3 meters away?) Groups rotate through each challenge.

Pin in the Middle

Skill: Kicking

Children: Pairs

Equipment: One ball per child, one wooden pin per pair or pylon/cone/empty milk bottle

Area: Gymnasium or outdoor field space

Activity: Partners stand about 20 meters apart with the pin midway between them. On the count of three, both players kick their ball toward the pin/pylon/cone. A point is scored for each knock down. Players must kick at the same time.

Players take one giant step away from the pin with each successful knock down.

Goccer (golf/soccer)

Skill: Kicking

Children: Groups of four

Equipment: One soccer ball or playground ball per player, hoops, cones

Area: Large outdoor field space

Activity: Using existing obstacles (cones, hoops) design an eight-hole "goccer" course (modified golf course). Consider having each group design one of the "holes" on the course. Holes may be set up to involve hitting a target such as a cone or kicking a ball through a hoop, or hitting an existing object such as a soccer goal post. Using the same scoring as in the game of golf, children use a number of kicks to get their ball in the target in order to complete each hole.

Clean Up

Skill: Kicking

Children: Groups of 8-12

Equipment: As many kickable balls as possible

Area: Outdoor field space

Activity: Two teams (any number) scattered on either half of large play area (soccer field). All balls start on one team's side of the field. On the signal, the kicking team starts kicking the balls as quickly as possible over the centre line. The receiving team kicks the balls back as quickly as possible.

Play for a predetermined time (e.g., two minutes).

Count the number of balls on each side. The team with the least number of balls wins the round.

Kick-away

Skills: Kicking, trapping

Children: Groups of 8-12

Equipment: 2-3 soccer balls/playground balls per group

Area: Gymnasium or outdoor field space

Activity: In circle formation, one child kicks the ball across the circle, keeping the ball low. The receiving child traps the ball and kicks it quickly to another and so on. Add a second ball, then a third. Try to keep all the balls in the circle for as long as possible.

Free Ball

Skills: Kicking, trapping

Children: Groups of 5-8

Equipment: One soccer ball or playground ball per group

Area: Outdoor field space

Activity: One player (the kicker) has the ball, while other players scatter behind a line about 10 meters away. Standing with the ball, the kicker faces the other players, calls another player's name and kicks the ball toward the line. The player named tries to trap the ball before it goes over the line and kick it back. The activity continues until the kicker has kicked it at least once to each player. The kicker then calls "Free ball" and kicks the ball toward the line. The player who traps the ball becomes the new kicker.

Kick the Pin

Skills: Kicking, trapping

Children: Groups of 6-8

Equipment: One wooden club/pin/cone/ pylon (or anything else found in the equipment bag), one soccer ball or play-ground ball per group

Area: Gymnasium or outdoor field space

Activity: Groups form a circle and place a pin in the middle. Players stand approximately two meters apart and try to knock down the centre pin by kicking the ball. All kicking must be done from the circle. On the signal, groups begin kicking, and the first one to knock down the pin scores a point. First group to reach 10 points wins.

Kick and Go

Skill: Kicking

Children: Groups of 4-5

Equipment: One soccer ball or playground ball per group

Area: Outdoor field space

Activity: Each group stands in a single file line. On the start signal, the first player in line in every group kicks the ball once, straight ahead, as far as possible. The player then runs and retrieves any ball other than his/her own and brings it back to the start line. The first runner back scores a point for their team.

Kick it Out

Skills: Kicking, trapping

Children: Two teams of 10-12

Equipment: 10-12 soccer balls or playground balls

Area: Large outdoor field space

Activity: One team is scattered inside a large circle, the other team is spaced on the perimeter of the circle (each with a ball). On the signal, the players on the outside roll the balls to the inside players; they trap the balls and kick them out of the circle. Outside players retrieve the balls and roll them back in. Change groups every one or two minutes.

Wall Target Challenges

Skill: Kicking

Children: Pairs or small groups

Equipment: One ball per child, range of targets different shapes and sizes) on the wall (e.g., paper shapes, balloons)

Area: Gymnasium (or outdoor wall space)

Activity: Groups rotate through each target station and keep track of how many tries they used (as a team) to hit the target.

KICK
- Plant support foot
- Lean backward into the kick
- Kicking leg swings freely
- Contact on tops of toes and instep
- Follow through across body
- Use arms for balance

KICK: *Imparting force to an object with the foot*

Characteristics of the KICK	Cue Words for Children
Stand behind the ball	"Behind ball"
Step forward with kicking foot	"Step forward"
Plant support foot beside ball	"Foot beside ball"
Kicking leg with knee bent swings freely from the hip through an arc toward the ball	"Foot back and through"
Backward body lean for initial balance	"Balanced"
Knee is quickly extended as the foot contacts ball	"Lean into kick"
Contact on tops of toes or instep	"Kick with the inside of your foot"
Left arm (right kick) extends toward direction of kick	"Press opposite hand"
Kicking leg continues its movement forward across the body	"Kick/swing through the ball"
Use arms to maintain balance	"Spread your arms out a little bit"

Adaptations of the KICK for:

Children in wheelchairs

- Children in manual chairs who have some function in their lower limbs (e.g. muscular dystrophy, cerebral palsy) can be encouraged to sit forward in their chair with the foot braces put away to attempt kicking the ball.

- Experiment with different size and weight to ensure success – even balloons could be used for children with severe mobility limitations.

- Allow a child in a wheelchair to throw or roll the ball instead of kicking it.

- For children with significantly limited movement, a soft ball can be held by the teacher or education assistant near the child's head and he or she can practice hitting the ball with their head (use a soft ball).

- A peer tutor or an education assistant will be a great help in positioning the ball for the child to kick.

	• For children with little or no movement capabilities in their legs, a long stick or pole or a floor hockey stick, even a badminton racquet, could be used to hit the ball instead of the foot. In other words – as the other children practice kicking, the child in a wheelchair uses an implement to move the ball in the same games or exercises.
	• It is not recommended that children in wheelchairs hit the ball with their chair; this could result in breaking the chair or injury.
Children with mobility aids	• Encourage children who use mobility aids to approach the ball much the same as an able-bodied peer with the opposite foot first and then kicking through the ball.
	• Ensure to teach the child how to position their mobility aid to allow for the ball to be kicked and not hit the aid.
	• Experiment with balls of different sizes and weights to ensure the child has success kicking.
	• Be aware that some children with cerebral palsy will be wearing braces on the lower leg limiting ankle flexibility and control.
Children with mobility limitations	• Children with mobility limitations may have balance difficulties – especially during kicking as it requires a degree of dynamic balance on one foot.
	• Due to balance difficulties there may be a very short follow through on the kick. Have the child practice the follow through while holding onto something for balance.
	• Encourage the child to bend their knees and use their arms for stability.
	• Using a variety of balls, varying in both size and weight. Encourage the children to practice – softer balls are suggested for safety.
	• Use balls suspended on a tether or attached to a rope to allow the child to retrieve his or her own ball. This will increase practice time and independence.
Children with visual impairments	• Balls that make sounds (e.g. a beep ball) should be used when practicing kicking with children with visual impairments.
	• Provide very detailed instructions using both verbal and tactile cues.
	• Use targets that make a noise when hit.

Children who are deaf

- If an interpreter is not available (or necessary) have a cue card at each station (or for each physical education lesson) with the task or plan clearly outlined at the child's level of understanding.
- Be prepared to give extra demonstrations of skills and activities.
- Consider using an FM loop system (microphone worn by the teacher to amplify the voice into the hearing aid worn by the Deaf student).
- Avoid excess noise in the learning environment.

Difficulties to watch for:

If...	Then...
Child uses limited back swing of kicking leg.	Without using a ball, the child should stand on non-kicking foot and practice full-range leg swing with kicking leg.
Non- kicking foot is not planted beside the ball.	Place a mark where the child should plant the non-kicking foot. Child repeats kicks using this mark until able to plant accurately without the mark.
Tendency to lose balance.	Have the child practice the kick slowly.
Instep of foot does not contact ball below the centre.	Make a mark (e.g., piece of tape) on the ball to show child the point of contact.
Kicking foot does not follow through in direction of the kick.	Without using a ball, coach the child to swing through with kicking leg to touch fingers of outstretched opposite arm. Repeat same action as above with ball.

To view and analyze video for this skill, and all the skills in this manual online, please visit:
➤ **www.phecanada.ca**

"what has worked in real life...."

Mrs. Jones is an elementary physical education teacher who has a little girl named Janelle in grade two who is deaf and uses sign language to communicate. Mrs. Jones made sure she had picture descriptions of each lesson and clear explanations at all the stations in her class. She flashed the lights on and off once to signal when she wanted the children to stop and look at her. When giving instructions, Mrs. Jones made sure the class was seated in a semi-circle and used a lot of demonstrations, checking along the way for understanding. Mrs. Jones felt that Janelle was learning everything she was teaching, but she did not feel as if she knew Janelle very well. Mrs. Jones decided that before each class she would learn the basic signs for the lesson. For example, on a kicking lesson she would learn the signs for kick, kick hard, kick soft, far, short, stop, start, good job, more and try again. Over time Mrs. Jones and Janelle began to communicate better and better and Mrs. Jones noticed that Janelle appeared to be trying harder in physical education class and soon became one of the most skilled, all-round students in the class.

Activities for the KICK

Kicking Exploration

Skill: Kicking

Children: Individual

Equipment: One ball per child, range of target making equipment (cones, hoops, wooden pins, etc.)

Area: Outdoor field space

Activity: Try to...

- Kick the ball with different parts of your foot – instep, inside of foot, outside of foot.
- Kick the ball at a target – hit the wall, between two cones, into a goal.
- Kick the ball in different directions – forward, backward, diagonal.
- Kick the ball when it is stationary, rolling toward you, rolling away from you.
- Kick the ball to a partner who is stationary, moving.
- Kick the ball high in the air, along the ground.
- Kick the ball with a running approach.
- Kick at a moving target.
- Kick the ball to the wall and trap the rebound, move closer to the wall, move away.
- Kick the ball as hard as possible.

Specific Modifications:

- For children who use wheelchairs, crutches and walkers, use balls that are attached to a tether with one end attached to their chair or walker. To allow the student increased independence in retrieving the ball – this is also a viable option for children with visual impairments where the tether is attached to the child's ankle.

Seated Circle Soccer

Skill: Kicking

Children: groups of 6-12

Equipment: Chairs for all who are not in wheelchairs, soccer ball

Activity: Set chairs in a circle about 1m between each chair. Participants sit in the chairs with the ball in the middle. While they remain seated, they try to kick the ball out of the circle. When a child kicks the ball out of the circle he or she gets a point, retrieves the ball and then returns to his or her seat for the next round. For extra challenges add more balls

Specific Modifications:

- For children with visual impairments use a ball with a bell – to make the game even more inclusive have all the children wear blindfolds.

Boccia Ball Game

Paralympic boccia ball is most often played by throwing the ball, however it is perfectly legal at all levels of competition for players to kick the ball. This is a great activity for children with and without disabilities. Have able-bodied children sit in chairs to play this game. Some children with no lower body mobility (e.g. spinal cord injury, spina bifida, cerebral palsy- may still have to throw the ball).

The main objective of Boccia is to place your coloured ball closer than your opponent's ball to the white target (jack) ball. The scoring is similar to that of curling where each ball closer to the jack than your opponents equals one point. At the end of four ends, the player with the most points wins. Players can throw, **kick** or use a chute to propel the balls onto the court. Boccia can be played in individual (1 vs. 1) pair (2 vs. 2) or team (3 vs. 3) formats. Boccia is played with 13 balls (6 red, 6 blue, 1 white) 6 per competitor and 1 target ball (jack ball). The jack ball (white) is used to start off the game and

is thrown by one of the competitors on the court. Once this is done, the object of the game is to come as close to the jack ball as possible to gain points.

Boccia players may play using their hands or feet, with or without assistive devices to throw or direct the ball to the target. It is a strategic game that requires tactical, technical and mental preparation to beat your opponent. It is a game where anything can happen.

Specific Modifications:

- Children who use crutches or walkers can be allowed to sit in regular chairs to participate in Boccia.
- Have all able-bodied children sit in chairs to 'even the playing field'.
- For children with visual impairments, have an education assistant give very specific feedback regarding the location of the balls on the playing field.

KICK: *Imparting force to an object with the foot (involves standing on one foot while the other foot kicks).*

Continuum of Prompts for the KICK

Physical Prompts	**Physical prompts should be paired with verbal prompts.**
- Complete manipulation	Physically move the child's leg to make contact with the ball.
- Manipulative prompting	Provide assistance only during critical parts of the desired movement (e.g., holding a hand while the one foot is off the ground to make contact with the ball).
- Minimal guidance	Make contact with a relevant body part to initiate a movement (e.g., tap foot to initiate kick).
Visual Prompts	**Visual prompts should be paired with verbal prompts.**
- Complete skill demonstration	Slowly demonstrate the step forward with the non-kicking foot, then the backswing of the kicking foot and the contact with the ball.
- Partial skill demonstration	Accurately demonstrate the step forward, the backswing of the leg, the moving of the leg forward to make contact with the ball and the follow-through.
- Gestural prompting	Gesture to remind participant of key component (e.g., point at the ball to signal kicking).
Verbal Prompts	
- Skill cue	Try focusing the child's attention on a key component of the task (e.g., "Step forward," "Bring your foot back," "Kick the ball as hard as you can").
- Action command	Give a verbal description of the desired skill (e.g., "Kick the ball").
- Action cue	Make a motivational statement to help the child perform the skill (e.g., "One, two, three, kick").

No Prompts

- Initiation with environmental cue	Placing balls throughout the space may entice the children to kick them; having strategically placed low targets may also help.
- Imitative initiation	Child performs the skill after watching other participants performing it.
- Initiation in free play	Child performs the skill at an appropriate time in free play but with no peer demonstration.

Behaviour Management and Pedagogical Considerations for KICKING

ASD	• If a child uses pic-syms in the classroom, find pic-syms for kicking and kicking-related activities (e.g., soccer) and tasks, and create a storyboard of activities for the lesson.
	• Reduce distractions.
	• Avoid the child's sensitive aversions (e.g., loud noises, certain textures or colours).
	• Use structure and "sameness" for consistency (e.g., follow the same warm-up routine, the same general lesson structure).
	• Capitalize on the child's preferences for motivation (e.g., certain colours, textured balls, balls that make noises).
DS	• Keep instructions clear and simple.
	• Encourage positive behaviours.
	• Visual demonstrations are highly recommended.
	• Force production, strength and balance may be limited in children with DS, making physical education a critical component of a child's education plan.
	• Peer tutors can be effective for modelling and promoting on-task behaviour.
ADHD	• Reduce distractions: use small groups, keep space smaller.
	• Keep instructions clear and simple.
	• Maintain good "timing" — boredom may result in off-task behaviours.
	• Create an environment of success.
	• Set clear boundaries — set clear targets for kicking the ball at.
	• Reinforce respect, teamwork and sportsmanship concepts in all aspects of the lesson.

ID	• Use a peer tutor or educational assistant to keep the child on task. • Keep instructions simple and concise. • Repetition may be needed of both instructions and demonstrations. • Start with a simple task and add difficulty as the child progresses. • Try using a ball on a tether (attached to something nearby) to decrease the amount of time spent chasing balls.
DCD	• Create an environment of success to prevent frustration. • Ensure the class rules are consistently enforced and the expectations are very clear. • Allow for and encourage repetition and practice. • Use self-rehearsal strategies, talk-aloud strategies (e.g., have the child assign words to the parts of the skill and say them aloud during practice). • Discourage off-task behaviours such as excessive water breaks, time outs and "clowning around" by keeping groups small and tasks age- and skill-level appropriate.

Characteristics of the KICK	*Cue Words for Children*
Standing behind the ball	"Stand behind the ball."
Stepping forward with kicking foot	"Step forward."
Planting support foot beside ball	"Plant the foot on your standing leg."
Kicking leg with knee bent swings freely from the hip through an arc towards the ball	"Bring your kicking foot back, and then move it through towards the ball."
Backward body lean for initial balance	"Balance on your foot."
Knee quickly extends as the foot contacts ball	"Lean into kick."
Contact on tops of toes or instep	"Kick with the inside of your foot."
Left arm (right kick) extends towards direction of kick	"Hold out your opposite hand while you kick."
Kicking leg continues its movement forward across the body	"Kick/swing through the ball."
Arms maintain balance	"Spread your arms out a little bit."

Difficulties to Watch For

If...	Then...
Child uses limited backswing of kicking leg.	Without using a ball, the child should stand on non-kicking foot and practise full-range leg swing with kicking leg.
Child "walks" into the ball.	The child should practise planting the support leg and the backswing of the kicking leg. The child may need support in balance for kicking.
Non-kicking foot is not planted beside the ball.	Place a mark where the child should plant the non-kicking foot. The child repeats kick using this mark until able to plant accurately without the mark.
Child has a tendency to lose balance.	Have the child practise the kick slowly.
The instep of the child's foot does not contact ball below the centre.	Make a mark (e.g., piece of tape) on the ball to show the child the point of contact.
Kicking foot does not follow through in direction of the kick.	Without using a ball, coach the child to swing through with kicking leg to touch fingers of outstretched opposite arm. Repeat same action with the ball.

To view and analyze video for this skill, and all the skills in this manual online, please visit:
www.phecanada.ca

What Has Worked in Real Life

Samir is 10 years old with high-functioning autism spectrum disorder; he is socially awkward, he does not have a lot of friends, and his motor skills are awkward at best. The best personal physical education story I can think of for Samir is when he was playing a soccer relay game. The game consisted of two teams, each dribbling around the pylons and then shooting at the soccer net until they got a goal. Samir was on the team with the most overly competitive boys in the entire class. He was the last person on his team, and he was going up against the other team's last player. Samir dribbled the best he could, then took a shot and missed. He took another one — missed again. The third shot . . . went in! His entire team had a look of bewilderment on their faces, but suddenly the gym exploded in cheers for Samir because he scored the winning goal for his team. Samir had a proud smile on his face for the rest of that day, and he truly felt as if he was part of his class. It also demonstrated to his classmates that he is capable.

Activities for the KICK

Exploring the Kick

Skill: Kicking

Children: Individual

Equipment: One ball per child, range of targets (cones, hoops, wooden pins, and so on)

Area: Outdoor field space

Activity: Ask the children to try to . . .

- Kick the ball with different parts of your foot — instep, inside of foot, outside of foot.
- Kick the ball at a target — hit the wall, between two cones, into a goal.
- Kick the ball in different directions — forward, backward, diagonally.
- Kick the ball when it is stationary, rolling towards you, rolling away from you.
- Kick the ball to a partner who is stationary, moving.
- Kick the ball high in the air, along the ground.
- Kick the ball with a running approach.
- Kick the ball at a moving target.
- Kick the ball to the wall and trap the rebound, varying your distance from the wall.
- Kick the ball as hard as possible.

Target Challenges

Skill: Kicking

Children: Groups of three or four

Equipment: One ball per child, range of targets (cones, hoops, wooden pins, and so on)

Area: Outdoor field space

Activity: Using assigned equipment, each group makes up a "kicking to a target" challenge for the other groups (e.g., how many kicks does it take your group to kick the ball off the cone, from 3 metres away?). Groups rotate through each challenge.

Boccia Ball

Skills: Kicking, throwing

Children: Pairs or in groups

Equipment: Boccia Ball set

The main objective of Boccia is to place your coloured ball closer than your opponent's ball to the white target (jack) ball. The scoring is similar to that of curling; each ball closer to the jack than your opponent's equals one point. At the end of four ends, the player with the most points wins. Players can throw, kick or use a ramp to propel the balls onto the court. Boccia can be played in individual (one versus one), pair (two versus two) or team (three versus three) formats. Boccia is played with 13 balls (six red, six blue, one white) — six per competitor and one target ball (jack ball). The jack ball (white) is used to start off the game and is thrown by one of the competitors on the court. Once this is done, the objective of the game is to come as close to the jack ball as possible to gain points.

Boccia players may play using their hands or feet, with or without assistive devices to throw or direct the ball to the target. It is a strategic game that requires tactical, technical and mental preparation to beat your opponent. It is a game where anything can happen.

Pin in the Middle

Skill: Kicking

Children: Pairs

Equipment: One ball per child, one wooden pin/pylon/cone per pair

Area: Gymnasium or outdoor field space

Activity: Partners stand about 20 metres apart with the pin midway between them. On the count of three, both players kick their ball towards the pin/pylon/cone. A point is scored for each knockdown. Players must kick at the same time. Players take one giant step away from the pin with each successful knockdown.

Wall Target Challenges

Skill: Kicking

Children: Pairs or small groups

Equipment: One ball per child, range of targets (different shapes and sizes) on the wall (e.g., paper shapes, balloons)

Area: Gymnasium or outdoor wall space

Activity: Groups rotate through each target station and keep track of how many tries they took (as a team) to hit the target.

Cleanup

Skills: Kicking, running

Children: Groups of eight to 12

Equipment: As many kickable balls as possible

Area: Outdoor field space

Activity: Two teams (8 to 12 players per team is ideal, however, the number of players can be adjusted based on availability) scatter on either half of a large play area (e.g., soccer field). All balls start on one team's side of the field. On the signal, the kicking team starts kicking the balls as quickly as possible over the centre line. The receiving team chases down the balls and kicks them back as quickly as possible. Play for a predetermined time (e.g., 2 minutes). Count the number of balls on each side. The team with the lowest number wins the round.

Seated Circle Soccer

Skill: Kicking

Children: Groups of six to 12

Equipment: Chairs for all who are not in wheelchairs, soccer ball

Area: Gymnasium

Activity: Set chairs in a circle, with about 1 metre between each chair. Participants sit in the chairs with the ball in the middle. While they remain seated, they try to kick the ball out of the circle. When a child kicks the ball out of the circle, he or she gets a point, retrieves the ball and then returns to his or her seat for the next round. For extra challenges, add more balls.

PASSING: *Throwing or kicking an object to another person*

A. *Characteristics of the PASS*

Cue Words for Children

Overhand Pass

GET READY:

Turn sideways so the side of the body opposite the throwing arm faces the target	Face sideways to target
Feet are shoulder width apart with the front foot being opposite to the dominant hand	Opposite foot forward
Knees are slightly bent and the weight is on the rear foot	Weight on back foot
Hold the ball at chest height in the spread fingers and thumb of the dominant hand (behind the ball) while using the other arm to provide support (stabilize) the ball	Hold the ball at the chest
Focus on the target (if the target is moving, focus on the point at which you want the thrown object to meet with the moving target)	Focus on the target point
Imagine a successful throw	Imagine success

B. *Teaching Tips*

(i) *Children can initially practice the passing movment pattern against a wall, progress to a stationary partner— close, then father away— and then finally to a moving partner so the child learns to predict where the object should be sent to.*

SIDE ARM STRIKE: *Propelling an object using the hand or an implement using a side arm action*

A. Characteristics of the mature SIDEARM STRIKE

Characteristics of the mature SIDEARM STRIKE	Cue Words for Children
PREPARATION:	
Stand facing the incoming object to be struck	Front face
Legs bent with hands out in front	
Watch the object to be struck all the time	Watch
STRIKING ACTION:	
Turn so that the shoulder opposite the striking hand is facing the object to be struck	
Take striking hand back and point to the incoming object with the non-striking hand to make a "W" shape with the arms and body	Back, "W"
Contact the object in front of the foot, opposite the striking hand (foot closest to the incoming object)	Hitting zone
Transfer weight from back foot to front foot	Back to front
Strike through the object	
Striking hand follows through high to the opposite shoulder	Follow high
Return to front facing	

B. Teaching Tips

(i) Developmental changes to watch for prior to the mature sidearm strike:

- As the striking pattern develops, there is an increase in the forward weight shift to initiate the strike.
- There is a greater range of motion throughout the strike which causes the 'opening up' in preparation to increase.
- The hips and trunk begin to rotate before the arms and the wrist goes from a stiff action to more of a cock and uncock action.

(ii) Difficulties to watch for:

If...	Then...
Children are not watching the incoming object.	Ask them to watch an X marked on an incoming ball.
Children are not opening up when getting prepared to strike.	They should get in the ready position facing the incoming object and then turn sideways with their arms apart; this sideways turning action can be done with a ball tossed to the striker, let it bounce and turn sideways at the bounce.
Children are striking the object outside the hitting zone (out front of the foot closest the target).	Place a ball on a large cone or batting tee and hit the ball in the hitting zone; the children open up and strike the ball off the cone/batting T; this can be done with a moving object by attaching a string to a plastic ball with holes in it and attaching the string to a rope suspended between volleyball poles. The height of the ball can be set to the hitting zone of the striker and then you have the ball on a pendulum.
Children are not transferring their weight from the back foot to the front foot.	Practice opening up with weight on the back foot and as the striking action is made step onto the front foot; children can repeat out loud as they open up "back" and as they strike "front."
Children are having trouble striking an object continuously in the air.	Add a bounce to give the striker more time to get ready.
Children are having difficulty striking small objects.	Try practicing with balloons.
Children are having an easy time striking with their hands.	Let them practice striking with a paddle bat instead; start with popping the object up and letting it bounce between each strike.

To view and analyze video for this skill, and all the skills in this manual online, please visit:
↘ **www.phecanada.ca**

C. Activities for STRIKING

Pop Up

Skill: Striking
Children: Individual
Equipment: One balloon per child
Area: Gymnasium
Activity: Children strike their balloons straight up in the air and count how many strikes can be made before loosing control.

Pairs Keep It Up

Skill: Striking
Children: Pairs
Equipment: One balloon for each pair
Area: Gymnasium
Activity: Working with their partner, children work to strike the balloons and keep them up in the air, alternating strikes.

Back Up

Skill: Striking
Children: Individual
Equipment: One ball per child
Area: Wall space for each child
Activity: The child drops the ball and strikes it against the wall. If on the return the child can catch the ball, after letting it bounce, he/she takes one step back and repeats the activity. With each successful attempt the child takes another step back.

Line Ball

Skills: Striking, running
Children: Pairs
Equipment: One ball and two markers per pair
Area: Large gymnasium
Activity: Spreading out around the gym, partners place markers halfway between them to designate a 'net.' The game starts when one partner drops the ball and then strikes it across the line; the other partner lets the ball bounce before striking it back over the line. Keep the ball going for as long as possible. Restart if the partner loses control.

STRIKE
- Face forward
- Legs bent – hands in front
- Eyes on object
- Face body to the side, pullstriking hand back
- Contact in front of front foot
- Transfer weight – back to front
- Follow through – hand to opposite shoulder
- Return to face the front

T Strike

Skills: Striking, catching

Children: Groups of three

Equipment: Batting T's or large cones and balls

Area: Playing field outside

Activity: In each group, one person strikes the ball from the T or the cone to the two fielders who try to catch the ball after it bounces. Rotate positions every few strikes so everyone gets a turn.

West African Hand Tennis

Skills: Striking, running

Children: Pairs

Equipment: Two cones and one ball per pair

Area: Each pair will work in a space the size of a table tennis (ping-pong) table.

Activity: Place two cones as the net. The game is played just like table tennis (ping-pong) – the child drops the ball and strikes it over the 'net.' The receiver lets it bounce before striking it over the net. Continue until the ball is not returned into the opposite court. The server gets five serves before the other partner serves. Score a point on every serve.

One At a Time

Skill: Striking

Children: Groups of four

Equipment: One ball per group

Area: Each group has their own space in the gymnasium

Activity: In each group, one child takes a position out in front of the other three who are standing in a line beside each other. The child in front drops the ball and strikes it to the first child in line who strikes the ball back to the child in front. This continues as the child out front strikes to each successive child in the line and then works back to where he/she started. Switch the child out front. Continue until all children have had a turn standing in front.

SIDEARM STRIKE: *Propelling an incoming object using the hand or an implement using a side arm action.*

Characteristics of the SIDEARM STRIKE

Characteristics of the SIDEARM STRIKE	Cue Words for Children
Stand facing the incoming object to be struck	"Face object(ball)"
Watch the object to be struck all the time	"Watch the ball"
Rotate so that the shoulder opposite the striking hand is facing the object to be struck	"Rotate"
Transfer weight from back foot to front foot	"Step forward" or "Back to Front"
Strike through the object	"Hit the ball"
Striking hand follows through high to the opposite shoulder	"Follow through"
Return to front facing	"Return to face forward"

Adaptations of the SIDE STRIKE for:

Children in wheelchairs	• For children in wheelchairs, use a ball on a tether to allow the child more chances to practice without chasing the ball constantly.
	• Some children in wheelchairs become very proficient at the side strike and enjoy playing tennis. As a simple rule change to enhance participation is to allow two bounces of the ball before the student in the wheelchair strikes the ball to allow enough time for the student to wheel to the necessary court position.
	• Use larger, lighter balls (or smaller balls) and a striking implement with a larger striking surface and a shorter handle.
	• Position the child closer to the net.
	• Allow the child to strike the ball off a tee.
	• Try using a badminton racquet because it is very light.
	• Start with having the child practice striking a balloon to work on eye-hand coordination.

Children with mobility aids	• Use larger, lighter balls, a striking implement with a larger striking surface and a shorter handle. • Allow the child to strike the ball off a tee. • Position the child closer to the net. • Start with having the child practice striking a balloon to work on eye-hand coordination. • Try using a badminton racquet because it is very light.
Children with mobility limitations	• Use larger, lighter balls, a striking implement with a larger striking surface and a shorter handle. • Allow the child to strike the ball off a tee. • Position the child closer to the net. • Start with having the child practice striking a balloon to work on eye-hand coordination. • Try using a badminton racquet because it is very light.
Children with visual impairments	• Allow the child to strike the ball off a tee. • Try using a badminton racquet because it is very light. • Position the child closer to the net. • Use balls that make sounds. • Have a peer tutor or educational assistant give constant verbal instructions about which way to face and where to hit the ball. • If possible, put a radio or a cd player playing near the net to provide an auditory cue for the child as to where the net is. • Allow the student to self toss and then hit the ball. • When practicing, use a ball that is tethered to the child's ankle (long enough rope) to allow the child to retrieve the ball without difficulty.
Children who are deaf	• If an interpreter is not available (or necessary) have a cue card at each station (or for each physical education lesson) with the task or plan clearly outlined at the child's level of understanding. • Be prepared to give extra demonstrations of skills and activities. • Consider using an FM loop system (microphone worn by the teacher to amplify the voice into the hearing aid worn by the Deaf student). • Avoid excess noise in the learning environment.

Difficulties to watch for:

If...	Then...
Children are not watching the incoming object.	Ask them to watch an X marked on an incoming ball.
	Use a brightly coloured ball – have the child call out the ball's colour.
Children are not opening up when getting prepared to strike.	They should get in the ready position facing the incoming object and then turn sideways with their arms apart. This sideways turning action can be done with a ball tossed to the striker. Let it bounce and turn sideways at the bounce.
Children are striking the object outside the hitting zone (out front of the foot closest to the target).	Place a ball on a large cone or batting Tee and place the ball in the hitting zone; the children open up and strike the ball off the cone/batting Tee. This can be done with a moving object by attaching a string to a plastic ball with holes in it and attaching the string to a rope suspended between volleyball poles. The height of the ball can be set to the hitting zone of the striker and then you have the ball on a pendulum.
Children are not transferring their weight from the back foot to the front foot.	Practice opening up with weight on the back foot and as the striking action is made step onto the front foot. Children can repeat out loud as they open up "back" and as they strike "front."
Children are having trouble striking an object continuously in the air.	Add a bounce to give the striker more time to get ready.
Children are having difficulty striking small objects.	Try practicing with balloons.
Children are having an easy time striking with their hands.	Let them practice striking with a paddle bat instead. Start with hitting the object up and letting it bounce between each strike.

To view and analyze video for this skill, and all the skills in this manual online, please visit:

➤ **www.phecanada.ca**

"what has worked in real life…."

Jake is a 12 year old student who has a spinal cord injury and uses a manual wheelchair. Jake's favourite game in physical education is baseball. Because Jake is proficient at striking a pitched ball, he asks a teammate to be his "runner" for him. When it is Jake's turn at bat he directs his "runner" where to stand in order to be ready to run to first base. When Jake's team is out in the outfield, his responsibility, in addition to having his own glove for catching, is to direct his teammates for the best defensive position based on who is at bat and whether there are runners on base. These small adaptations allow Jake to participate in the game to the best of his ability and the game is not significantly altered for his other teammates.

Activities for STRIKING

Pop up
Skill: Striking
Children: Individual
Equipment: One balloon per child
Area: Gymnasium
Activity: Children strike their balloons straight up in the air and count how many strikes can be made before losing control

Pairs keep it up
Skill: Striking
Children: Pairs
Equipment: One balloon for each pair
Area: Gymnasium
Activity: Working with their partner, children work to strike the balloons and keep them up in the air, alternating strikes.

Back up
Skills: Striking and catching
Children: Individual
Equipment: One ball per child
Area: Wall space for each child
Activity: The child drops the ball and strikes it against the wall. If after letting it bounce the child can catch the ball, he/she takes one step back and repeats the activity. With each successful attempt the child takes another step back.

Beat me
Skill: Striking
Children: Pairs
Equipment: One ball per pair
Area: Walls inside or outside the gymnasium
Activity: Children alternately strike the ball against the wall with a bounce in between. They count the number of times they strike the ball without losing control. Once they lose control they start again and try to beat their score.

Line ball

Skill: Striking

Children: Pairs

Equipment: One ball and two markers per pair

Area: Large gymnasium

Activity: Spreading out around the gym, partners place markers half way between them to designate a 'net.' The game starts when one partner drops the ball and then strikes it across the line. The other partner lets the ball bounce before striking it back over the line. Keep the ball going for as along as possible. Restart if the partner loses control.

Circle strike

Skill: Striking

Children: Groups of five

Equipment: One ball per group

Area: Groups in a large circle.

Activity: One child drops the ball and strikes it to another child (not beside them). This child catches the ball and then repeats the drop and strike.

Tee strike

Skills: Striking and catching

Children: Groups of three

Equipment: Batting Tee's or large cones and balls

Area: Playing field outside

Activity: In each group, one person strikes the ball from the Tee or the cone to the two fielders who try to catch the ball after it bounces. Rotate positions every few strikes so everyone gets a turn.

West African hand tennis

Skill: Striking

Children: Pairs

Equipment: Two cones and one ball per pair

Area: Each pair will work in a space the size of a table tennis (ping-pong) table.

Activity: Place two cones as the net. The game is played just like table tennis (ping-pong) and each child drops the ball and strikes it over the 'net.' The receiver lets it bounce before striking it over the net. Continue until the ball is not returned into the opposite court. The server gets five serves before the other partner serves. Score a point on every serve.

One at a time

Skill: Striking

Children: Groups of four

Equipment: One ball per group

Area: Each group has their own space in the gymnasium

Activity: In each group, one child takes a position out in front of the other three who are stand in a line beside each other; the child out front drops the ball and strikes to the first child in line who strikes the ball back to the child out front; this continues as the child out front strikes to each successive child in the line and then works back to where he/she started. Switch the child out front.

Target strike

Skill: Striking

Children: Pairs

Equipment: One hula hoop and a ball per pair

Area: Gymnasium

Activity: Children stand about five meters apart with a hula hoop in between. One child drops the ball and strikes it trying to get into the hoop. After five tries the other partner attempts to strike the ball into the hoop.

SIDEARM STRIKE: *Propelling an incoming object using the hand or an implement using a sidearm action.*

Continuum of Prompts for the SIDEARM STRIKE

Physical Prompts	**Physical prompts should be paired with verbal prompts.**
- Complete manipulation	Stand behind the participant with your hand over the child's hand as he or she grips the bat or racquet. When the appropriate time comes, move the child's arm through the striking motion to strike the ball or birdie.
- Manipulative prompting	Provide assistance only as the ball or birdie hits the bat or racquet (e.g., hand over hand to provide support for the grip).
- Minimal guidance	Make contact with a relevant body part to initiate a movement (e.g., tap the hand or the elbow to signal the child should prepare to strike the incoming object).
Visual Prompts	**Visual prompts should be paired with verbal prompts.**
- Complete skill demonstration	Accurately and slowly demonstrate the entire striking action with an actual birdie or ball.
- Partial skill demonstration	Accurately demonstrate only the backswing, only the point of contact, only the follow-through. For more advanced children, demonstrate the weight transfer. Try demonstrating without having a ball or birdie to strike.
- Gestural prompting	Gesture to remind participant of key component (e.g., point at the racquet, point at the incoming object).
Verbal Prompts	
- Skill cue	Try focusing the child's attention on a key component of the task (e.g., "Bring your racquet back").
- Action command	Give a verbal description of the desired skill (e.g., "Strike the ball," "Hit the ball").
- Action cue	Make a motivational statement to help the child perform the skill (e.g., "One, two, three").

No Prompts

- Initiation with environmental cue	Place racquets and balls out for participants to use. Additionally, T-ball tees and bats will encourage the children.
- Imitative initiation	Child performs the skill after watching other participants performing it.
- Initiation in free play	Child performs the skill at an appropriate time in free play but with no peer demonstration.

Behaviour Management and Pedagogical Considerations for STRIKING

ASD	• If a child uses pic-syms in the classroom, find pic-syms for striking and striking-related activities (e.g., tennis, badminton), and create a storyboard of activities for each day. • Reduce distractions — have the children practise striking towards a wall for safety. • Avoid the child's sensitive aversions (e.g., loud noises, certain textures or colours). • Use structure and "sameness" for consistency (e.g., follow the same warm-up routine, the same general lesson structure). • Capitalize on the child's preferences for motivation (e.g., certain colours, textured balls).
DS	• Keep instructions clear and simple. • Encourage positive behaviours. • Visual demonstrations are highly recommended. • Force production, strength and balance may be limited in children with DS, making physical education a critical component of a child's education plan. • Peer tutors can be effective for modelling and promoting on-task behaviour.
ADHD	• Reduce distractions: use small groups, keep space smaller. • Keep instructions clear and simple. • Maintain good "timing" — boredom may result in off-task behaviours. • Create an environment of success. • Set clear boundaries, both physical and task related. • Reinforce respect, teamwork and sportsmanship concepts in all aspects of the lesson.

ID	• Use a peer tutor or educational assistant to keep the child on task. • Keep instructions simple and concise. • Repetition may be needed of both instructions and demonstrations. • Start with a simple task and add difficulty as the child progresses. • Use larger balls, a larger bat or racquet, or both to facilitate success for children with severe disabilities.
DCD	• Create an environment of success to prevent frustration. • Ensure the class rules are consistently enforced and the expectations are very clear. • Allow for and encourage repetition and practice. • Use self-rehearsal strategies, talk-aloud strategies (e.g., have the child assign words to the parts of the skill and say them aloud during practice). • Discourage off-task behaviours such as excessive water breaks, time outs and "clowning around" by keeping groups small and tasks age- and skill-level appropriate. • Try increasing the size of the bat or racquet or shortening the handle to increase success.

Characteristics of the SIDEARM STRIKE   Cue Words for Children

Characteristics of the SIDEARM STRIKE	Cue Words for Children
Faces incoming object to be struck	"Face the target."
Watches object to be struck at all times	"Watch the ball."
Rotates shoulder opposite the striking hand to face object to be struck	"Rotate your shoulder."
Transfers weight from back foot to front foot	"Step forward." "Back to front."
Strikes through the object	"Hit the ball."
Striking hand follows through high to the opposite shoulder	"Follow through."
Returns to front facing	"Face forward after you've hit the ball."

Difficulties to Watch For

If...	Then...
Child is not watching the incoming object.	Ask the child to watch an X marked on an incoming ball.
	Use a brightly coloured ball and have the child call out the ball's colour.
Child is not opening up when getting prepared to strike.	The child should get in the ready position, facing the incoming object, and then turn sideways with the arms apart. This sideways turning action can be done with a ball tossed to the striker — the child lets the ball bounce and turns sideways at the bounce.
Child is striking the object outside the hitting zone (out front of the foot closest to the target).	Place a ball on a large cone or batting tee in the child's hitting zone; the child opens up and strikes the ball off the cone or batting tee. This can be done with a moving object by attaching a string to a plastic ball with holes in it and attaching the string to a rope suspended between volleyball poles. The height of the ball can be set to the hitting zone of the striker.
Child is not transferring his or her weight from the back foot to the front foot.	The child practises opening up with weight on the back foot, and as the striking action is made, steps onto the front foot; the child can say "back" out loud as he or she opens up and "front" as he or she strikes the object.
Child is having trouble striking an object consistently in the air.	Add a bounce to give the striker more time to get ready.
Child is having difficulty striking small objects.	The child can try practising with balloons.
Child is having an easy time striking with his or her hands.	Let the child practise striking with a paddle bat instead; the child can start with popping the object up and letting it bounce between each strike.

To view and analyze video for this skill, and all the skills in this manual online, please visit:

↘ **www.phecanada.ca**

What Has Worked in Real Life

Jin is a 10-year-old girl who has cerebral palsy and a moderate to severe intellectual disability. She has very limited range of motion with her arms and hands and no mobility in her legs; her spine is not straight, so she is not able to sit upright in her wheelchair. When we were working on hand-eye coordination —specifically striking — I had stations set up around the gymnasium. All the students moved from station to station to practise indoor modified tennis against a partner. Jin stayed at the Wii station and played "tennis" against different students using the Wii tennis program. I have found that the Wii has increased Jin's interest in some of the physical education units. It allows her to practice the skills and have success.

Activities for the SIDEARM STRIKE

Pop Up
Skill: Striking
Children: Individual
Equipment: One balloon per child
Area: Gymnasium
Activity: Children strike their balloons straight up in the air and count how many strikes they can make before losing control.

Pairs Keep It Up
Skill: Striking
Children: Pairs
Equipment: One balloon per pair
Area: Gymnasium
Activity: Working with their partners, children strike the balloons and keep them up in the air, alternating strikes.

Back Up
Skills: Striking, catching
Children: Individual
Equipment: One ball per child
Area: Wall space for each child
Activity: Each child drops his or her ball and strikes it against the wall. If the child can catch the ball after it bounces, he or she takes one step back and repeats the activity. With each successful attempt, the child takes another step back.

Pop That Bubble

** Suitable for very young children with
developmental delays.*

Skills: Striking, running

Children: Individual

Equipment: Bubble machine (if available) or blowing wands and bubble juice; foam paddles; scooters (optional)

Area: Outside field (to prevent a wet gym floor)

Activity: The participants are spread out (either sitting on scooters or not) around the field. The teacher starts blowing bubbles, preferably with a bubble machine, which is inexpensive and excellent for use with children with developmental delays (similar experiences have revealed that young children with ASD love bubbles). Participants must run around and pop the bubbles using their foam paddles. You could also adapt this game by having the children jump up when they are about to pop the bubble. If you use scooters, participants must remain seated on the scooters. To add an extra challenge, you can have the children hold the foam paddles with their non-dominant hands and still try to pop the bubbles.

Beat My Score

Skill: Striking

Children: Pairs

Equipment: One ball per pair

Area: Walls inside or outside the gymnasium

Activity: Children alternately strike the ball against the wall, with a bounce in between. They count the number of times they strike the ball without losing control. Once they lose control, they start again and try to beat their score.

Line Ball

Skill: Striking

Children: Pairs

Equipment: One ball and two markers per pair

Area: Large gymnasium

Activity: Spreading out around the gym, partners place markers halfway between them to designate a net. The game starts when one partner drops the ball and then strikes it across the line; the other partner lets the ball bounce before striking it back over the line. Players keep the ball going for as long as possible and restart if they lose control.

Circle Strike

Skills: Striking, catching

Children: Groups of five

Equipment: One ball per group

Area: Large gymnasium

Activity: The groups stand in circles. One child drops the ball and strikes it to another child (not beside him or her). This child catches the ball and then repeats the drop and strike.

Tee Strike

Skills: Striking, catching

Children: Groups of three

Equipment: Batting tees or large cones and balls

Area: Playing field outside

Activity: In each group, one person strikes the ball from the tee or the cone to the two fielders, who try to catch the ball after it bounces. Rotate positions every few strikes so everyone gets a turn.

West African Hand Tennis

Skill: Striking

Children: Pairs

Equipment: Two cones and one ball per pair

Area: Gymnasium

Activity: Each group works in a space the size of a table tennis (Ping-Pong) table. Place two cones as the net. The game is played just like table tennis (Ping-Pong). Each child drops the ball and strikes it over the "net," and the receiver lets it bounce before striking it back. Players continue until the ball is not returned into the opposite court. The server gets five serves before the other partner serves. A point is scored on every serve.

One at a Time

Skill: Striking

Children: Groups of four

Equipment: One ball per group

Area: Gymnasium

Activity: The groups spread out around the gym. In each group, one child takes a position out in front of the other three, who are standing in a line beside each other. The child out front drops the ball and strikes it to the first child in line, who strikes the ball back to the child out front; this continues as the child out front strikes to each successive child in the line and then works back to where he or she started. Switch the child out front.

Target Strike

Skill: Striking

Children: Pairs

Equipment: One hoop and one ball per pair

Area: Gymnasium

Activity: Children stand about 5 metres apart with a hoop in between. One child drops the ball and strikes it, trying to get it into the hoop. After five tries, the other partner attempts to strike the ball into the hoop.

STRIKING Sideways, Overhand, and Underhand:

Propelling an object using an implement, arm, or hand and either a side-arm, underhand, or overhead swinging action

Note: Has application to striking-fielding games such as cricket, rounders, softball, and baseball as well as net-wall games such as tennis, volleyball, squash, badminton, and handball.

A. Characteristics of the mature STRIKE
Sideways, Overhand and Underhand   Cue Words for Children

Sideways Strike (Forehand)

GET READY:	
Hand-shake grip (generally)	Handshake grip
Stand in the ready position (legs bent with hands and implement out in front) facing the incoming object to be struck	Face the incoming object
Maintain visual focus on the object to be struck	Focus
Imagine a successful sidearm swing and strike	Imagine
Anticipate the position and movement of the approaching object to be in an optimal position to sideways strike the object	Anticipate
ACTION:	
Turn so that the shoulder opposite the striking hand is facing the object to be struck. The waist is turned sideways to the target	Shoulder towards object; waist sideways from target
Take striking hand back early	Implement back early
Point to the incoming object with the non-striking hand to make a W shape with the arms and body	"W" ready position
Step into the swing. Transfer weight from back foot to front foot	Transfer weight forward
Rotate the hips and shoulders to face the target	Rotate bellybutton towards target

Contact the object in front of the foot and hip opposite the striking hand (foot closes object)	Strike ball in the "zone"
Strike level through the object while maintaining visual focus, extended arm(s), and firm wrist(s)	Strike solid
Striking hand(s) and wrist(s) follow-through high to target and then on to the opposite the shoulder	Follow to target and then high
The foot on the swinging arm side rotates so the shoelaces face the target	Rotate the shoelaces on the back foot
Return to ready position facing the next target	
Alter the swing (e.g., force, angle, length of swing) for various objectives (e.g., bunting, slicing, top-spin, lob, striking to various locations)	Alter the swing to meet a specific goal

B. Teaching Tips

Important Variations to the Characteristics for the One (Right) Handed Backhand Sideways Strike

(e.g., tennis, squash, badminton)
- Grip is altered slightly. The racquet is rotated slightly (1/8) clockwise (opposite for a left-handed striker) so that the racquet is perpendicular to the ground when contacting the object.
- Rather than sideways to the target as in the forehand, the hips (and shoulders) are turned more away from the target prior to contact (about 135 degrees) and during contact (90 degrees).

Important Variations to the Characteristics for the One (Right) Handed Underhand Strike

GET READY:
- Feet should be shoulder width apart in a stride position (with the left slightly in front of the right.
- Bend forward slightly from the waist.
- Hold the ball in the palm of the left hand at waist height and directly below the chin.
- Focus your eyes on the target to which you would like to strike the ball.
- Change your focus so your eyes view the ball.
- Alter the shape and tone of your striking (right) hand so it is rigid and slightly cupped.

STRIKING ACTION:

- Move your striking arm back to shoulder height and place your weight on the back foot.
- Swing forward with a straight arm so the ball is struck on the back side and slightly below the center with the cupped (mainly the heel) right hand. While swinging, step forward with the left foot.
- The striking arm should follow-through towards the target.

Important Variations to the Characteristics for the One (Right) Handed Overhead Strike

GET READY:

- Feet should be shoulder-width apart in a stride position (with the left slightly in front of the right.
- Hold the ball in the palm of the left hand at waist height and with a straight arm in front of the body.
- Focus your eyes on the target to which you would like to strike the ball.
- Change your focus so your eyes view the ball.
- Alter the shape and tone of your striking (right) hand so it is rigid and slightly cupped.

STRIKING ACTION:

- In the backswing, place your striking arm elbow out 90° and level with your hand (palm should face away from the body and thumb downwards towards the ground). Rotate your body (shoulders and waist, not the feet) partially to the right and shift most of your weight to the back foot.
- Toss the ball up in front of the body, in-between the target and striking arm, and about one to two feet above the outstretched tossing hand.
- Swing forward forcefully with a slightly bent arm so the ball is struck slightly in front of the striking shoulder and on the backside and slightly below the center of the ball with the cupped (mainly the heel) right hand.
- While swinging, step forward with the left foot so the body weight is transferred forward, straighten the legs, and rotate the waist and shoulders to face forward.
- The striking arm should follow-through towards the target.

C. *Sample Activities for STRIKING Sideways, Underhand, or Overhead*

Sample Guided Discovery Activities

1. Can you model the technically correct sidearm, underhand, or overhead strike?
2. Mirror the model or instructor in slow motion and then in regular or full speed.
3. Can you correctly strike a ball hanging from a suspended rope? Off of a stricking tee? Can you do it so the ball goes to a particular location? How?
4. Can you sideways, underhand, or overhead strike the ball 20 times against the wall and above the net line (with a racquet) allowing only one bounce before each swing?

5. Can you toss an object up to yourself and sideways, underhand, or overhead strike it to a specified location against the wall?
6. Partner activities:
   a. Can you volley back and forth with a partner?
   b. Can you strike the object to your partner so they do not have to move to catch it? Can you do the same if there is a net between you and your partner over which you must strike it?
   c. Partner stands to the side of the striker with ten objects to be struck (e.g., tennis or whiffle balls) and slightly ahead of the striker. They toss (3-4 feet) one to-be-struck object at a time so the striker can approach and strike it to the intended target (90 degrees) from the thrower. If necessary, allow the ball to bounce once after the toss. Alter the activity so the ball is thrown from a safe distance in front of the striker.
   d. Stand on opposite sides of the net or cone from one another. Sideways, underhand, or overhand strike the object back and forth to each other trying to land it in the legal landing zone each time.

D. Activities for STRIKING Sideways, Overhand and Underhand

West African Hand Tennis
Participants: Students in pairs
Equipment: Cones, Volleyballs
Area: Each pair takes will work in a space the size of a table tennis (ping-pong) table.
Description: Place two cones as the net. The game is played just like table tennis (ping-pong); the child drops the ball and strikes it over the 'net.' The receiver lets it bounce before striking it over the net. Continue until the ball is not returned into the opposite court. The server gets five serves before the other partner serves. Score a point on every serve

One at a Time
Participants: In groups of four
Equipment: Volleyballs
Area: Each group has their own space in the gymnasium.
Description: In each group, one child takes a position out in front of the other three who are standing in a line beside each other; the child out front drops the ball and strikes to the first child in line who strikes the ball back to the child out front; this continues as the child out front strikes to each successive child in the line and then works back to where he/she started. Switch the child out front.

Sideways Striking a Stationary Ball for Distance

Participants: All students

Equipment: Volleyball, Stationary Softball Striking Tee

Area: 100 -200 foot square area arranged in four concentric circles each 10-20 feet apart.

Description: 4-6 strikers stand safely apart along the line of the innermost circle, each with one ball and a stationary softball striking tee. 2-3 fielders stand outside the line of the outermost circle. When the teacher yells "strike" the striker strikes the ball to their respective group of fielders. The fielders take turns or compete to field the ball and toss it underhand (rolling) back to the striker to repeat.

Modifications: Play 500 up by having the teacher yell out a certain point value that each struck ball is worth if fielded correctly by a fielder. Once a fielder earns 500 points, they become the striker (or win that series and the next striker in the order goes to strike). Instead of using a stationary ball off of a tee, allow students to self-toss it.

Safety Tip (if applicable): Be sure that the circles are large enough so that each striker and group of fielders are spread far enough apart. Make sure that they do not leave the inner circle to retrieve a thrown ball from the fielders and get hit by a struck ball from another striker. Perhaps make all strikers wait until the teacher signals it is safe to strike by calling out "hit" whenever all of the strikers can hit. Place cones to mark distinct boundaries (or, for example, a large hoola-hoop for the striker) wherein each striker and/or fielding group must stay.

Wall Ball (from *www.playsport.net*)

Purpose: Striking with the Hand; Tactical placement; Return to neutral court position.

Participants: In pairs or triples.

Equipment: Volleyballs

Area: 10 foot square area with a wall on one end.

Description: One individual begins play from a service line by dropping the ball to let it bounce once and striking it so it bounces against the wall over the height line and lands in the playing court. The next player must to strike after it bounces once so that it again contacts the wall over the height line and lands in the playing court. Repeat until one player fails to do so. Use rally point scoring (1 point per rally.

Modifications: Allow students to modify the size of the playing area, some rules (e.g., underhand throw and catch may be easier for some than sidearm striking with the hand), and the type of ball that is used.

RECIEVING SKILLS

CATCH: *receiving an object with the hands*

A. Characteristics of the mature CATCH

Characteristics of the mature CATCH	Cue Words for Children
PREPARATION:	
Eyes on object to catch	Look
Align body with incoming object	Get behind
Arms at rest at side of body or slightly in front	Ready
CATCHING:	
Move hands to meet the object	Soft hands
Elbows are bent and bend as object is brought down and towards the body	
Object is brought down and toward the body	Bring to body
Hands adjust to flight and size of object; if object is below the waist little fingers are close together	Pinkies together
If object is above the waist the thumbs are close together	Thumbs together

B. Teaching Tips

(i) Developmental changes to watch for prior to the mature catch:

- Initially, catching is very passive with the catcher simply holding the arms out toward the direction of the incoming object with little or no attempt to adjust the body or arms to the flight of the object.
- Next, there is a negative response to the object in that as contact is made the object is cradled into the chest and the head is turned to the side to avoid the object.

- Finally, the catcher makes deliberate adjustments of the body and arms to the flight of the object and absorbs the incoming object by giving with the finger, hands and arms as the object is brought closer to the body.
- Large, sponge balls should be used when the child is 'afraid' of the ball.
- Children should catch first from a helpful adult, later a ball thrown against a wall as its pathway is predictable, and finally, from a peer.
- Children should be encouraged to receive the ball when it is thrown short and long as well as to the right and left of the receiver.

(ii) Difficulties to watch for:

If...	Then...
Children are not watching the object to be caught.	A partner has two different coloured balls behind their back; on a count, one of the balls is tossed in the air and the catcher has to call out the colour of the ball. Or, tape an X on the ball and ask the catcher to watch for the X.
Children are not able to catch an object thrown by a partner.	They can start with catching a ball that is rolled to them. Then try having the child who is catching the ball simply drop it in front of himself/herself and catch it.
Children are having trouble trying to catch an object that is thrown to them by a partner.	Choose a ball that will bounce before the catch is made; this will give the catcher more time to get in position to catch.
Children are cradling the ball against their chest and turning their head away from the object being caught.	Select a large, light object to be caught and have the child reach for the object to catch it but not let it touch his/her chest.
While working in partners, the catcher is having to move to catch and is being unsuccessful.	The thrower should toss the ball underhand into the catcher's 'catching zone' so the catcher does not have to move.
Children are having difficulty catching small objects.	Increase the size of the object to be caught. This may make it more difficult to throw but it will make catching easier.

To view and analyze video for this skill, and all the skills in this manual online, please visit:
- **www.phecanada.ca**

C. Activities for CATCHING

Roll Ball

Skills: Catching, rolling

Children: Pairs

Equipment: Medium-sized balls

Area: Children spread out in gymnasium, with one ball per pair

Activity: One child rolls the ball to his/her partner who is sitting down with legs apart; the partner reaches to catch the incoming ball; children switch places after a few tries.

Balloon Toss and Catch

Skills: Catching, throwing

Children: Individual

Equipment: One large balloon for each child

Area: Children spread out in gymnasium

Activity: Children toss the balloon up in the air and reach with their hands to catch. Focus on thumbs close together to catch above their heads; little fingers close together if catching below the waist.

Catch Up

Skills: Catching, throwing

Children: Groups of five

Equipment: Two balls of different sizes per group

Area: Each group forms a circle. Groups spread out in the gymnasium or on an outdoor field.

Activity: Groups begin by tossing one of the balls to the person on the right; the second ball is then tossed with the goal of trying to catch up to the first ball.

Trick Catch

Skills: Catching, throwing

Children: Pairs

Equipment: Balls of various sizes; one per child

Area: Children spread out in the gymnasium

Activity: One child begins with a simple toss and catch and the partner attempts to replicate the toss and catch. The first partner then tosses the ball and does a trick (e.g., a half turn) before catching the ball; the partner tries to replicate the trick.

CATCH

- Eyes on ball
- Position yourself behind ball
- Arms in ready position
- Soft hands — meet the ball
- Elbows bent
- Bring ball to body
- Ball below the waist — pinkies together
- Ball above the waist — thumbs together

Line Ball

Skills: Catching, throwing

Children: Groups of five

Equipment: One ball per group

Area: Groups are spread out in the gymnasium

Activity: One member stands out in front of the other four who are in a straight line, side by side. The leader throws the ball to the first person in line who then throws it back to the leader. This pattern is repeated down the line until at the end the last person becomes the new leader. Move the leader further away as the skill level increases.

Call Ball

Skills: Catching, throwing

Children: Groups of four

Equipment: One ball per group

Area: Groups spread out in the gymnasium

Activity: Groups are in a circle with one person in the middle holding the ball. The middle person tosses the ball high in the air and calls out the name of another person in the circle. This child must catch the ball after one bounce and then becomes the middle person to call another name. Remove the bounce to make the catch more difficult.

Back Up

Skills: Catching, throwing

Children: Pairs

Equipment: One ball per pair

Area: Pairs take positions around the gymnasium with their own wall space.

Activity: One partner tosses the ball against the wall; the other partner lets the ball bounce once and then catches it. If successful, the partner takes one step back and repeats the sequence gradually moving farther and farther away from the wall. If the ball is not caught, the pair must start from their beginning position.

Star Catch

Skills: Catching, throwing

Children: Groups of five

Equipment: Five balls per group

Area: Gymnasium or playing field

Activity: Each group forms a circle. The children number themselves off but consecutive numbers cannot be standing immediately beside each other. Start with person 1 tossing the ball to person 2 who catches it and then tosses it to person 3; 3 tosses to 4 and 4 tosses it to 5 who tosses it back to 1. Once the pattern is repeated, add another ball. As soon as 1 tosses the first ball to 2, 1 picks up another ball and tosses the second ball as 2 tosses the first ball to 3. Once the sequence is being performed successfully with two balls, add a third ball, and so on until four or five balls can be tossed simultaneously.

CATCH: *Receiving a ball with the hands*

INCLUSION & ADAPTATIONS

Characteristics of the mature CATCH	Cue Words for children
Eyes on object to catch	"Look at the ball"
Align body with incoming object	"Body behind the ball"
Arms at rest at side of body or slightly in front	"Hands ready"
Elbows are bent	"Elbows bent"
Object is brought down and toward the body	"Soft hands" or, "absorb the ball"
Catch ball with hands only. Hands adjust to size of object.	"Make your hands fit the ball"
If object is above the waist the thumbs are close together	"Thumbs together"

Adaptations of the CATCH for:

Children in wheelchairs	• Some children in wheelchairs may choose to use a large glove to assist with catching.
	• Velcro glove with matching ball may be used to facilitate catching.
	• Using a ball on a string or a tether will allow the child to practice catching without having to chase the ball during the learning process.
	• Allow children with upper body limitations to trap the ball against his or her chest or in his or her lap.
	• Using a balloon to catch will significantly slow down the speed of the "ball" for children with severe limitations in the upper body.
Children with mobility aids	• Children who use a mobility aid for locomotion will likely have decreased balance if asked to let go of their crutches or their walker. Try using a Velcro glove with a matching ball to facilitate catching.
	• Using a balloon to catch will significantly slow down the speed of the "ball" for children with severe limitations in the upper body.

- Soft or deflated balls can also be used to facilitate catching during the early learning stages.
- Allow the child to sit down during some of the early stages of learning. This will allow the child to concentrate on the catching component without fear of falling when letting go of the mobility aid.

Children with mobility limitations	- Even though children with mobility limitations have their hands free, they may still have movement restrictions in their upper limbs. - Try using a Velcro glove with a matching ball to facilitate catching. - Try using large balls that are very light to make the task easier. - Try using deflated or soft balls could also be used. - For children with a single arm amputation or a congenital birth condition impacting the upper limbs, allow the child to experiment with his or her own capabilities to figure out the best way to catch. - If the student has a prosthetic arm, that arm can be used as the stabilizing arm while the dominant arm traps the ball. - For children with amputations above the elbow who do not uses prosthesis, catching might be a difficult task – depending on the child's ability to bring their arms together, larger, lighter balls can be used and the child can trap the ball against his or her body using their upper arms. - For children with double amputations or missing limbs at the shoulder level, it might be possible to teach the child to catch with his or her feet.
Children with visual impairments	- Ensure that the thrower verbally communicates with the child with a visual impairment. - Use larger balls that are brightly coloured for children with partial vision. - Soft or deflated balls are also useful in facilitating catching. - Try having the student with a visual impairment catch the ball following a bounce pass. The bounce makes a noise and gives the child an auditory cue about timing the ball's arrival. - Balls that make sounds can be a powerful tool for children with visual impairments.

Children who are deaf

- If an interpreter is not available (or necessary) have a cue card at each station (or for each PE lesson) with the task or plan clearly outlined at the child's level of understanding.
- Be prepared to give extra demonstrations of skills and activities.
- Consider using an FM loop system (microphone worn by the teacher to amplify the voice into the hearing aid worn by the Deaf student).
- Avoid excess noise in the learning environment.

Difficulties to watch for:

If...	Then...
Children are not watching the object to be caught.	A partner has two different coloured balls behind their back. On a count, one of the balls is tossed in the air and the catcher has to call out the colour of the ball. Or, try taping an X on the ball and ask the catcher to watch for the X.
Children are not able to catch an object thrown by a partner.	They can start with catching a ball that is rolled to them. Then try having the child who is catching the ball simply drop it in front of himself/herself and catch it.
Children are having trouble trying to catch an object that is thrown to them by a partner.	Choose a ball that will bounce before the catch is made. This will give the catcher more time to get in position to catch.
Children are cradling the ball against their chest and turning their head away from the object being caught.	Select a large, light object to be caught and have the child reach for the object to catch it but not let it touch his/her chest.
While working in partners, the catcher is having to move to catch and is being unsuccessful.	The thrower should toss the ball underarm into the catcher's 'catching zone' so the catcher does not have to move.
Children are having difficulty catching small objects.	Increase the size of the object to be caught. This may make it more difficult to throw but it will make catching easier.

To view and analyze video for this skill, and all the skills in this manual online, please visit:
www.phecanada.ca

"what has worked in real life...."

This year I have had the pleasure of working with a young boy with several physical and learning challenges. He has limited use of his arms and hands and uses a wheelchair unless lifted out by assistants. He also found it difficult to keep his head up for sustained periods. When the other students worked with beach balls or balloons we tied his balloon or beach ball to a high jump standard or hung it from the basketball net so he could maintain contact with it and cause it to move in a new direction without someone having to chase after stray balls.

Activities for CATCHING

Roll ball

Skill: Catching

Children: Pairs

Equipment: Medium-sized balls

Area: Children spread out in gymnasium, with one ball per pair

Activity: One child rolls the ball to his/her partner who is sitting down with legs apart; the partner reaches to catch the incoming ball; they switch places after a few tries.

Specific Modifications:

- For Deaf children, use flashcards, with the instructions on them, or a Sign Language interpreter to ensure the instructions/changes are communicated.
- For children in wheelchairs have the balls tossed into the child's lap.
- For children with mobility limitations in their upper body, allow the child to wear a Velcro glove and use a Velcro ball to facilitate catching.

Balloon toss and catch

Skill: Catching (specific hand technique)

Children: Individual

Equipment: One large balloon for each child

Area: Children spread out in gymnasium

Activity: Children toss the balloon up in the air and reach with their hands to catch. Focus on thumbs close together to catch above their heads; little fingers close together if catching below the waist.

Specific Modifications:

- For children with visual impairments, instead of balloons use light balls that make noise.
- For children with visual impairments use a buddy/peer tutor system, or use an educational assistant to facilitate inclusion.

Catch up

Skills: Catching and throwing

Children: Groups of five

Equipment: Two balls of different sizes per group

Area: Each group forms a circle. Groups spread out in the gymnasium or on an outdoor field.

Activity: Groups begin by tossing one of the balls to the person on the right; the second ball is then tossed with the goal of trying to catch up to the first ball.

Specific Modifications:

- For children with mobility limitations in
  their upper body, allow the child to wear a Velcro glove and use a Velcro ball to facilitate catching.

Trick catch

Skills: Catching and throwing in movement transition

Children: Pairs

Equipment: Balls of various sizes; one per child

Area: Children spread out in the gymnasium

Activity: One child begins with a simple toss and catch and the partner attempts to replicate the toss and catch. The first partner then tosses the ball and does a trick (e.g., a half turn) before catching the ball; the partner tries to replicate the trick.

Specific Modifications:

- For children with mobility limitations in
  their upper body, allow the child to wear a Velcro glove and use a Velcro ball to facilitate catching.

High, low and to the side

Skills: Catching and throwing

Children: Pairs

Equipment: One ball for each pair

Area: Children spread around the gymnasium

Activity: One partner is designated the catcher, the other the tosser. The tosser throws the ball to various places around the catcher; the catcher must track the ball and adjust the catching position to catch the ball.

Specific Modifications:

- For children with mobility limitations in
  their upper body, allow the child to wear a Velcro glove and use a Velcro ball to facilitate catching.

CATCH: *Receiving a ball with the hands.*

Continuum of Prompts for the CATCH

Physical Prompts	**Physical prompts should be paired with verbal prompts.**
- Complete manipulation	Stand behind the child with both hands on the child's hands. When the ball is tossed, execute the actions using the child's hands.
- Manipulative prompting	Provide assistance only during critical parts of the catch (e.g., helping to contain the ball within the child's hands to provide "success" in catching).
- Minimal guidance	Make contact with a relevant body part to initiate a movement (e.g., tap hands to signal the child to get them ready in front of the body).

Visual Prompts	**Visual prompts should be paired with verbal prompts.**
- Complete skill demonstration	Accurately and slowly demonstrate the entire catch.
- Partial skill demonstration	Accurately demonstrate getting the hands ready in front of the body; demonstrate how to catch without trapping the ball on the body. Use a big ball to exaggerate the catching motion.
- Gestural prompting	Gesture to remind participant of key component (e.g., point at the child's hands, or point at the person throwing the ball).

Verbal Prompts	
- Skill cue	Try focusing the child's attention on a key component of the task (e.g., "Hands up," "Close your hands on the ball").
- Action command	Give a verbal description of the desired skill (e.g., "Catch this").
- Action cue	Make a motivational statement to help the child perform the skill (e.g., "One, two, three").

No Prompts

- Initiation with environmental cue	Placing balls around the gymnasium might lead some children to play a game of catch; placing baseball mitts could do this as well. Catching usually involves having someone throw the ball, meaning interactions with other children may be necessary.
- Imitative initiation	Child performs the skill after watching other participants performing it.
- Initiation in free play	Child performs the skill at an appropriate time in free play but with no peer demonstration.

Behaviour Management and Pedagogical Considerations for CATCHING

ASD	• If a child uses pic-syms in the classroom, find pic-syms for catching-related activities (e.g., baseball) and tasks, and create a storyboard of activities for the lesson. • Reduce distractions. • Avoid the child's sensitive aversions (e.g., loud noises, certain textures or colours). • Use structure and "sameness" for consistency (e.g., follow the same warm-up routine, the same general lesson structure). • Capitalize on the child's preferences for motivation (e.g., certain colours, textured balls).
DS	• Keep instructions clear and simple. • Encourage positive behaviours. • Visual demonstrations are highly recommended. • Force production, strength and balance may be limited in children with DS, making physical education a critical component of a child's education plan. • Peer tutors can be effective for modelling and promoting on-task behaviour.
ADHD	• Reduce distractions: use small groups, keep space smaller. • Keep instructions clear and simple. • Maintain good "timing" — boredom may result in off-task behaviours. • Create an environment of success. • Set clear boundaries, both physical and task related. • Reinforce respect, teamwork and sportsmanship concepts in all aspects of the lesson.

ID	• Use a peer tutor or educational assistant to keep the child on task. • Keep instructions simple and concise. • Repetition may be needed of both instructions and demonstrations. • Start with a simple task and add difficulty as the child progresses. • For children with severe and profound disabilities, use a Velcro mitt to facilitate the catching action.
DCD	• Create an environment of success to prevent frustration — vary the size and weight of the balls to be caught. • Ensure the class rules are consistently enforced and the expectations are very clear. • Allow for and encourage repetition and practice. • Use self-rehearsal strategies, talk-aloud strategies (e.g., have the child assign words to the parts of the skill and say them aloud during practice). • Discourage off-task behaviours such as excessive water breaks, time outs and "clowning around" by keeping groups small and tasks age- and skill-level appropriate.

Characteristics of the CATCH	Cue Words for Children
Eyes on object to catch	"Look at the ball."
Body aligned with incoming object	"Move your body to where the ball is."
Arms at rest at sides of body or slightly in front	"Get your hands ready in front."
Elbows bent	"Bend your elbows."
Object brought down and towards the body	"Have soft hands." "Absorb the ball."
Ball caught with hands only Hands adjust to size of object	"Make your hands fit the ball."
Object caught above waist: thumbs close together	"Keep your thumbs together."

Difficulties to Watch For

If...	Then...
Child is not watching the object to be caught.	A partner has two different-coloured balls behind his or her back; on a count, the partner tosses one of the balls in the air, and the catcher has to call out the colour of the ball. Or tape an X on the ball and ask the catcher to watch for the X.
Child is not able to catch an object thrown by a partner.	The child can start by catching a ball that is rolled to him or her. Then try having the child simply drop the ball in front of himself or herself and catch it.
Child is having trouble trying to catch an object that is thrown by a partner.	Choose a ball that will bounce before the catch is made; this will give the catcher more time to get in position to catch.
Child is cradling the ball against the chest and turning his or her head away from the object being caught.	Select a large, light object to be caught, and have the child reach for the object and catch it without letting it touch his or her chest.
While working in partners, the catcher is having to move to catch and is being unsuccessful.	The thrower should toss the ball underhand into the catcher's "catching zone" so the catcher does not have to move.
Child is having difficulty catching small objects.	Increase the size of the object to be caught. This may make it more difficult to throw, but it will make catching easier.

To view and analyze video for this skill, and all the skills in this manual online, please visit:

↘ **www.phecanada.ca**

What Has Worked in Real Life

Melanie is an 8-year-old girl with a limited vocabulary who has PDD-NOS. She prefers it when her teachers stick to a strict routine, and one of her restricted interests is "glittery things." For example, Melanie loves jewellery; she loves anything that is shiny or glittery. For the first two years I had Melanie in my physical education class, I was not able to effectively engage her with our equipment or the tasks at hand. Then last summer, I received a catalogue with all sorts of adapted physical education equipment. I ordered some new equipment with Melanie in mind. I ordered three different sizes of balls, all of which "glittered"; I ordered a hoop that was shiny and glittery and two skipping ropes that were silver and gold. In September when Melanie first came to class, I established a routine that we follow every class, and I slowly introduced the new equipment when appropriate based on the lesson. The look on Melanie's face the first day she was able to use a glittery ball was priceless. I have found this simple modification to be very effective in motivating Melanie to engage more fully in physical education class.

Activities for the CATCH

Roll Ball

* Suitable for very young children with developmental delays.

Skills: Rolling, catching a rolling ball

Children: Pairs

Equipment: One medium-sized ball per pair

Area: Gymnasium

Activity: The children are spread out in the gymnasium. One child rolls the ball to his or her partner, who is sitting down with legs apart; the partner reaches to catch the incoming ball; they switch places after a few tries.

Variations:

For children with great difficulty catching (e.g., DCD or DS or severe cognitive impairment), allow them to wear a Velcro glove and use a Velcro ball to facilitate catching.

Call Ball

Skills: Tossing, catching

Children: Groups of four

Equipment: One ball per group

Area: Gymnasium

Activity: Groups form circles around the gymnasium, with one person in the middle holding the ball. The middle person tosses the ball high in the air and calls out the name of another person in the circle. This child must catch the ball after one bounce before becoming the middle person and calling another name. Remove the bounce to make the catch more difficult.

Sticky Marshmallow

* Suitable for very young children with developmental delays.

Skills: Rolling, catching

Children: Four to eight

Equipment: A large deflated beach ball

Area: Classroom or gymnasium

Activity: The children lie on their stomachs in a circle, with their heads facing the centre (ensure there is enough room in the centre for the ball to move). Each player must push the beach ball away and towards someone else in the circle. Instruct participants to use one or two hands depending on their objective. Each child tries to ensure the "sticky marshmallow" doesn't touch the top of his or her head or face to avoid being covered with a sticky mess.

Variations:
- Have more than one ball at a time in play (use different-sized balls).
- Have the participants catch the ball with two hands (a complete catch instead of just hitting the ball away) and then roll it away
- Decrease or increase the distance between the players and the size of the circle.

TRAP: *a player strategically stops the flight of the object to bring it under control*

Note: Trapping can involve the use of various body parts such as the sole of the foot, inside or outside of the foot, thigh, chest, or head.

A. Characteristics of a mature TRAP   Cue Words for Children

(This could apply to trapping with the feet, thighs, chest, or forehead)

Characteristics of a mature TRAP	Cue Words for Children
Place yourself in the ready position	Ready position
Anticipate a successful trap	Imagine success
Move quickly to intercept the approaching ball while deciding which part of the body to best initiate the trap	Move to intercept Decide on the type of trap
In a balanced position, present the trapping surface to the ball and block it with that surface (e.g., inside of the foot or thigh, upper chest, forehead)	Present the trapping surface to the ball and block the ball using that surface
As the ball contacts that body part, absorb the impact (soften, cushion) by slightly and slowly moving that body part in the direction of the ball flight	Cushion the ball like you are "catching an egg"
If the ball is still not in control, use an applicable body part to further "trap" the ball	Continue to execute a trap until the object (ball) is under control

B. Activities for TRAPPING

Sample Guided Discovery Activities

Trapping:

Can you:

1. Trap a low self-tossed ball? With the sole of your foot? In-step? Thigh and then foot? Chest and then foot? Can you do the same with a higher tossed ball?
2. Throw the ball against the wall five times and use a different trap to control the ball on each one?
3. Trap the ball using those various traps when the ball is rolled, tossed, or kicked from a partner? When should you use a certain body part to trap the ball?
4. Kick the ball back and forth with a partner at various heights and see how quickly you can trap and control the ball?

RETAINING SKILLS

DRIBBLE: *bouncing the ball with the hands or controlling it with the feet, usually while travelling*

A. Characteristics of the mature DRIBBLE with hands

Characteristics of the mature DRIBBLE with hands	Cue Words for Children
EYES:	
Eyes looking forward	Look ahead
BODY POSITION:	
Feet in forward stride	Opposite foot forward to dribbling hand
Body flexed at knees, hips, waist with slight forward lean	
Fingers and thumbs spread; five finger pads touching ball	Cup the ball
HAND ACTION:	
With wave (yo-yo) action with hand on ball, push ball to the floor	Wave to the ball
Control the bounce with fingers and wrist	
Contact ball at about waist level	
Ball bounces back to waist level	

B. Teaching Tips

(i) Developmental changes to watch for prior to mature dribbling action:

- Gradual improvement in ability to push the ball toward the ground.
- Improved smooth, rhythmical arm action.

(ii) Difficulties to watch for:

If...	Then...
Child uses a slapping motion with hand with limited force production.	Ask the child to imitate waving good-bye to the ball.
Child looks toward the ball while dribbling.	While dribbling, have child follow a partner (follow the leader).
Child uses palm instead of finger pads to contact ball.	While a partner holds the ball from the bottom, child pushes the ball with finger pads

(iii) Give each child a ball, and provide balls of different sizes and weights.

(iv) Use right and left hands equally with practicing.

To view and analyze video for this skill, and all the skills in this manual online, please visit:
www.phecanada.ca

C. Activities for controlled DRIBBLING (hands)

The following section provides a selection of individual, partner, small group, and large group activities that focus on development of the controlled dribble with the hands. (Note: many of the activities may also be adapted and used to practice controlled dribbling with the feet.)

Exploratory Activities

Skill: Dribbling

Children: Individual

Equipment: One basketball or bouncing playground ball per child

Area: Gymnasium

Activity: Can you dribble the ball...

- With your right hand, left hand?
- While moving forward, backward, sideways, and diagonal?
- With one hand, then the other?
- In place?
- With your eyes closed?
- Around your body?
- With a really high bounce?
- Close to the floor?
- Across your body?
- Around your body?
- In a zigzag pattern?-
  With one hand and touch the floor with the other?
- Walk/jog around the ball while you bounce it in place?
- With your left hand, high five other players?
- With your right hand, high five other players?
- Switch dribbling hand?
- In a circle around your body without moving your feet (clockwise, counterclockwise)?
- Standing in a forward stride position, dribble the ball around the front leg, under the front leg?
- Using a yo-yo motion?
- Standing in a straddle position, dribble the ball in a figure eight through your legs?
- In time to music?
- One ball with each hand?
- With the hand you write with?

More Challenging Activities

1. Can you dribble (in a confined area respecting personal space) fast and far? Around others in a small space? With the outside of foot? Inside of foot? Toe, instep, head, chest or torso?

2. How fast can you dribble around each of the four outside cones but return around the center cone between dribbling around each outer cone?

3. Can you dribble fast but under control around this large circle of cones? Can you dribble in a zig-zag pattern inside and outside of each as you dribble around? Dribble across the circle around a cone and back again continuously (to a different cone each time)?

4. In a small group, can you design a "dribble-dance" to music?

5. As you can see, there are about 10-12 pairs of cones around (3' between cones) called "gates." Try to:
   a. Jog through as many as possible or give a specific number. Side shuffle though one, run backward through another.
   b. Dribble through 9 and go back to where you started.
   c. Dribble around and through each of 9.
   d. Shadow (Follow) the leader and do what they do.
   e. Follow the leader who tries to lose you.
   f. Catch the leader (run around a circle so players do not collide).

6. In Pairs, can you?
   a. Toss (or kick) high, low, hard, soft... to each practice trapping.
   b. In 3's, play 500 up with one tosser and two trappers (first in control of ball gets the points).
   c. Face each other with two cones in between. Must kick between the cones to get a goal (and off the ground).
   d. One versus one with cones as goals.
   e. One on knees with hands behind the ball on the ground; other comes up and kicks it (50-60%) to show correct form. Can also do with one standing and having foot behind the ball.
   f. Ball between two cones. One has back to ball and legs spread out. Other kicks ball through the legs so the one with spread legs runs after and retains it, dribbles back. Switch. Can do continuously.
   g. One person rolls the ball at another and the other kicks it back so they can catch it like a goalie. Continuous.
   h. Face each other in pairs (10 ft apart). One runs backwards while the other runs and dribbles forward before passing to the partner who traps in and leaves it there for the partner to retrieve, dribble, and pass again. Do the length of the field.

Stationary Dribble

Skills: Dribbling
Children: Individual
Equipment: One basketball or bouncing playground ball per child
Area: Gymnasium
Activity: Children start dribbling in place from double-kneeling position, to single-knee, to standing position.

Cross the Line

Skills: Dribbling, walking, running, changing direction
Children: Individual
Equipment: One basketball or bouncing playground ball per child
Area: Gymnasium
Activity: Using existing lines on the gymnasium floor, children dribble throughout the gym, changing dribbling hands each time they cross over a line.

Watch Me

Skills: Dribbling, changing direction, side-stepping
Children: Individual
Equipment: One basketball or bouncing playground ball per child
Area: Gymnasium
Activity: Children practice dribbling while looking forward at the teacher/leader. Teacher holds up signals (e.g., directional arrows, numbers) to encourage dribbling without looking down at the ball.

On My Signal

Skills: Dribbling, changing direction, running, dodging
Children: Individual
Equipment: One basketball or bouncing playground ball per child, whistle
Area: Gymnasium
Activity: Children start dribbling with their right hand throughout the gym. On a whistle signal, the teacher/coach will call out a task (e.g., switch hands, dribble right, criss-cross, circle ball around your waist). On the next whistle, children start dribbling again. When the teacher/coach calls out "Switch," it's the signal to drop the ball, pick up another one, and start dribbling again.

Musical Hoops

Skills: Dribbling, dodging, running, changing direction

Children: Individual

Equipment: One basketball or bouncing playground ball per child, 12-15 hoops, music, CD player

Area: Gymnasium

Activity: Hoops are scattered on the gym floor. Children dribble throughout the gymnasium while the music is playing. When the music stops, players must find a hoop (1-2 players per hoop to start); place one foot in the hoop and pivot in place while dribbling. When music starts, players leave hoop and dribble throughout the gymnasium. Gradually remove the number of hoops and increase the number of players at each hoop. Do not eliminate players.

Dribble and Weave

Skills: Dribbling, running, changing direction

Children: Individual

Equipment: One basketball or bouncing playground ball per child, large cones or chairs

Area: Gymnasium

Activity: Set up several lines of cones or chairs.

While dribbling, children weave through the straight lines of chairs or cones. Emphasize switching hands and keeping the body between ball and chair/cone.

Dribble Tag

Skills: Dribbling, running, changing direction, dodging

Children: Individual

Equipment: One basketball or bouncing playground ball per child

Area: Gymnasium

Activity: While dribbling within the court, each player must keep control of his/her own dribble while attempting to cause other players to lose control of their dribble. If a player loses control of their ball or goes out of bounds, he/she must perform a task (e.g., 20 speed dribbles) before returning to the game. Gradually decrease the area of play.

Capture the Tail

Skills: Dribbling, dodging, changing direction, running

Children: Individual

Equipment: One basketball or bouncing playground ball per child; tails

Area: Gymnasium

Activity: While dribbling within the basketball court, each player must keep control of his own dribble while at the same time attempting to catch "tails" (flags, scarves, or pinnies tucked in waist band) from other players. If a player loses control of the ball, he/she must leave the game area, and make one basket at a designated hoop before returning to the game. Players attempt to collect as many tails as possible.

Follow the leader

Skills: Dribbling, dodging, changing direction, running, walking

Children: Partners (in file)

Equipment: One basketball or bouncing playground ball per child

Area: Gymnasium

Activity: Lead partner starts dribbling. The follower must stay within one meter of leader and perform the dribbling actions the leader performs (e.g., switching hands, dribble high, low, change direction).

The leader must allow the follower to stay one meter behind. Switch leaders.

Mirror Dribbling

Skills: Dribbling, dodging, changing direction, walking, faking

Children: Partners facing each other

Equipment: One basketball or bouncing playground ball per child

Area: Gymnasium

Activity: The lead partner starts dribbling. Facing the lead partner, the follower tries to mirror all the lead partner's dribble movements. On the signal, switch lead partner.

Partner Dribble and Pass

Skills: Dribbling, passing, catching

Children: Partners facing each other.

Equipment: One basketball or bouncing playground ball per child

Area: Gymnasium

Activity: Facing each other, partners start dribbling in unison. On a signal, they bounce their ball toward their partner, and try to continue dribbling in place with the new ball. Try to develop a sequence to repeat (e.g., 10 dribbles then pass).

DRIBBLE
- Look ahead
- Stride stand
- Lean forward slightly
- Five fingers spread — cup the ball
- Make a wave action with wrists/fingers
- Control the ball
- Contact the ball at waist level

Incredible Shrinking Space

Skills: Dribbling, changing direction, walking, running

Children: Large group

Equipment: Each child with a basketball or playground ball

Area: Gymnasium

Activity: On the signal, dribblers must dribble anywhere within the basketball court without making contact with other dribblers. Gradually shrink the dribbling space (e.g., half court, three point area, key area). As the dribble space shrinks, dribblers must maintain control while avoiding contact with other dribblers.

Control and Protect

Skills: Dribbling, dodging, faking

Children: Pairs

Equipment: One basketball or bouncing playground ball per child, four cones per pair

Area: Gymnasium

Activity: Each pair plays in a two-meter square marked with cones. Within their square, players must keep control of their own dribble while attempting to cause their partner to lose control of the dribble. If a player loses control of the ball or goes out of bounds, his or her partner scores a point.

Dribble Routine

Skills: Dribbling, passing, catching

Children: Groups of 4-6

Equipment: One basketball or bouncing playground ball per child

Area: Gymnasium

Activity: Each group puts together a series of coordinated dribbling moves and passes (routine). Include a floor pattern, different dribbles (e.g., right hand, left hand), pathways, directions, traveling skills. Perform the routine.

DRIBBLE: *Bouncing the ball up and down with one hand so that it stays in the dribbler's possession*

PHOTO BY DAVE ARNOLD, COMPLIMENTS OF PARASPORT ONTARIO

Characteristics of DRIBBLING *with hands*

Characteristics	Cue words for Children
Eyes looking forward	"Look ahead"
Feet in forward stride (Opposite foot forward to dribbling hand)	"Opposite foot, opposite arm"
Body flexed slightly at knees, hips, waist, with slight forward lean	"Stay low"
Fingers and thumbs spread, five finger pads touching ball	"Cup the ball" (Reminder: let your finger tips push the ball)
With wave (yo-yo) action with hand on ball, push ball to the floor	"Wave to the ball"
Contact ball at about waist level	"Bounce at waist"
Ball bounces back to waist level	"Controlled bounce"

Adaptations of the DRIBBLE for:

Children in wheelchairs

- Vary the size and weight of the ball to facilitate success.
- For children with typical upper-body strength, have child hold ball on lap and push wheelchair a few rotations and then bounce ball and then push wheelchair again.
- For students with limited upper-body strength, have a peer push the wheelchair while student holds ball on his or her lap. Have peer physically assist student in bouncing the ball.
- For children with severe upper-body limitations, use a small light ball and have the child bounce the ball on his or her lap or tray attached to the wheelchair.
- While being pushed in the wheelchair, have the student repeatedly hit the ball as it sits on the lap tray.

Children with mobility aids	• If the student uses two crutches (requiring both hands), ask child if he or she feels comfortable using one crutch to try dribbling with the other hand. Be aware the child will have poor balance while only using one crutch for support.
	• A peer tutor can be used to help retrieve the basketball when the ball inevitably gets away from the child who uses mobility aids.
	• Children who use walkers can be encouraged to stand outside the walker on one side holding onto the side of the walker to facilitate the dribbling of the ball – this may not work for all children.
	• Children who use walkers can also be encouraged to practice dribbling the ball while sitting down or while using a wheelchair.
Children with mobility limitations	• Children with mobility limitations may or may not have limitations in their upper limbs.
	• Encourage children who have limited movement in their hands to try to control the ball as best they can.
	• Use a lighter ball to allow the child to dribble in one place
	• Allow the use of two hands.
Children with visual impairments	• Have the student with a visual impairment stand in the corner of the gym while dribbling to help reduce the chances of the ball getting away from the student – use a ball with a bell or sound so the student can retrieve the ball when it does roll away.
	• Allow the child to dribble with two hands at first – as the student becomes more proficient encourage one-handed dribbling.
	• Allow the student to dribble in one place (not while running or walking).
	• When adding forward movement, allow the student to bounce and catch while walking.
	• At the initial learning stages, allow the child to drop the ball and catch it while walking forward.
	• Have a peer tutor or an educational assistant work alongside the child with a visual impairment to provide verbal directions and to retrieve the ball when it gets away from the student.

Children who are deaf	• If an interpreter is not available (or necessary) have a cue card at each station (or for each physical education lesson) with the task or plan clearly outlined at the child's level of understanding.
	• Be prepared to give extra demonstrations of skills and activities.
	• Consider using an FM loop system (microphone worn by the teacher to amplify the voice into the hearing aid worn by the Deaf student).
	• Avoid excess noise in the learning environment.

Difficulties to watch for:

If...	Then...
Child uses a hand slapping motion with limited force production.	Ask the child to imitate waving good-bye to the ball.
Child looks toward the ball while dribbling rather than looking forward.	While dribbling, have child follow a partner (follow the leader).
Ball controls the child, not the child controlling the ball (i.e. child follows the ball erratically).	Have the child ease up on the force pushing the ball down – tell him or her to have soft hands.
Inconsistent and/or inappropriate force applied to the ball.	Vary the weight of the ball to allow the child to experiment with force production.
Child uses palm instead of finger pads to contact ball.	While a partner holds the ball from the bottom, child pushes with finger pads on the ball.

To view and analyze video for this skill, and all the skills in this manual online, please visit:
✎ **www.phecanada.ca**

"what has worked in real life...."

Liam is a 10 year old boy who loves basketball. When Liam was five years old he was in a car accident that left him with a spinal cord injury in his lower lumbar region. Liam has full use of his arms but uses a manual wheelchair for locomotion. When Liam first returned to school his physical education teacher found it very difficult to engage Liam in class. Liam's mother told the teacher one day that Liam really enjoyed watching NBA Basketball on television because his father enjoyed it too. Liam's physical education teacher found some video of the Canadian National Wheelchair Basketball Team and showed them to Liam. She told him that if he put his mind to it, and practiced very hard there was no reason he couldn't try out for the national team one day. In consultation with Liam's parents, basketball was written into Liam's IEP. Although Liam participates in all aspects of his physical education class now, he is particularly motivated when his teacher can relate the skill back to the game of basketball. For example, when practicing "dodging" she makes sure he realizes how the skill translates to the game, the same for dribbling, throwing and catching. Liam's teacher has found that making the skills the class is learning relevant has helped increase Liam's motivation.

Activities for the controlled DRIBBLE (hands)

Dribbling Exploration

Skill: Dribbling

Children: Individual

Equipment: One basketball or bouncing playground ball per child

Area: Gymnasium

Activity: Can you dribble the ball…

- With your right hand, left hand.
- While moving forward, backward, sideways and diagonal.
- With one hand then the other.
- In one place.
- With your eyes closed.
- Around your body.
- With a really high bounce.
- Close to the floor.
- Across your body.
- Around your body.
- In a zigzag pattern.
- With one hand and touch the floor with the other.
- Walking or jogging around the ball while you bounce it in place.
- With your left hand, high five other players with your right hand.
- Switch dribbling hand.
- In a circle around your body without moving your feet (clockwise, counterclockwise).
- Standing in a forward stride position; and dribble the ball around the front leg, under the front leg.
- Using a yo-yo motion.
- Standing in a straddle position and dribble the ball in a figure eight through your legs.
- In time to the music.
- With one ball with each hand.
- With the hand you write with.
- With the hand you don't write with.

Specific Modifications:

- Allow children with visual impairments to experiment with dribbling in one place and allow the child to catch the ball between bounces as necessary.

DRIBBLE:
Bouncing the ball up and down with one hand so that it stays in the dribbler's possession.

Continuum of Prompts for DRIBBLING

Physical Prompts	**Physical prompts should be paired with verbal prompts.**
- Complete manipulation	Stand behind the participant and hold his or her wrist, facilitating the dribbling motion with the ball.
- Manipulative prompting	Provide assistance only when contact with the ball is made (i.e., lightly rest hand on top of child's hand to facilitate the dribbling action).
- Minimal guidance	Make contact with a relevant body part to initiate a movement (e.g., tap the hand lightly to initiate the dribbling movement).
Visual Prompts	**Visual prompts should be paired with verbal prompts.**
- Complete skill demonstration	Accurately demonstrate the dribble slowly (knees bent, controlled dribble).
- Partial skill demonstration	Demonstrate the dribble without the ball to allow the child to focus on the hand movement and not on the ball.
- Gestural prompting	Make a gesture towards the ball to signal the child should start dribbling, or make a short up and down action to cue the child.
Verbal Prompts	
- Skill cue	Try focusing the child's attention on a key component of the task (e.g., "Gentle push on the ball," "No slapping the ball," "Bounce to your waist").
- Action command	Give a verbal description of the desired skill (e.g., "Dribble 10 times" or "Bounce the ball 10 times").
- Action cue	Make a motivational statement to help the child perform the skill (e.g., "One, two, three").

No Prompts

- Initiation with environmental cue	Place basketballs out for participants to use. For more advanced dribblers, having obstacles such as cones could also facilitate dribbling.
- Imitative initiation	Child performs the skill after watching other participants performing it.
- Initiation in free play	Child performs the skill at an appropriate time in free play but with no peer demonstration.

Behaviour Management and Pedagogical Considerations for DRIBBLING

ASD	• If a child uses pic-syms in the classroom, find pic-syms for dribbling- and basketball-related activities and tasks, and create a storyboard of activities for the lesson.
	• Avoid the child's sensitive aversions (e.g., loud noises, certain textures or colours — many basketballs bouncing at once could be too loud for some children).
	• Use structure and "sameness" for consistency (e.g., follow the same warm-up routine, the same general lesson structure).
	• Capitalize on the child's preferences for motivation (e.g., certain colours, textured balls).
	• Physical activity and exercise can have a positive impact on repetitive and stereotyped movements common in children with ASD; therefore, starting a lesson with vigorous physical activity may be effective at increasing on-task behaviours for the rest of the lesson or practice.
DS	• Keep instructions clear and simple.
	• Encourage positive behaviours.
	• Visual demonstrations are highly recommended.
	• Force production, strength and balance may be limited in children with DS, making physical education a critical component of a child's education plan.
	• Peer tutors can be effective for modelling and promoting on-task behaviour.
ADHD	• Reduce distractions: use small groups, keep space smaller.
	• Keep instructions clear and simple.
	• Maintain good "timing" — boredom may result in off-task behaviours.
	• Create an environment of success.
	• Set clear boundaries — set out a geographic space on the floor, and instruct the child to dribble the ball within it.
	• Reinforce respect, teamwork and sportsmanship concepts in all aspects of the lesson.

ID	• Use a peer tutor or educational assistant to keep the child on task. • Keep instructions simple and concise. • Repetition may be needed of both instructions and demonstrations. • Start with a simple task and add difficulty as the child progresses.
DCD	• Create an environment of success to prevent frustration. • Ensure the class rules are consistently enforced and the expectations are clear. • Allow for and encourage repetition and practice. • Use self-rehearsal strategies, talk-aloud strategies (e.g., have the child assign words to the parts of the skill and say them aloud during practice). • Discourage off-task behaviours such as excessive water breaks, time outs and "clowning around" by keeping groups small and tasks age- and skill-level appropriate.

Characteristics of the DRIBBLE (With Hands)

Characteristics of the DRIBBLE (With Hands)	Cue Words for Children
Eyes looking forward	"Look ahead."
Feet in forward stride	"Keep your opposite foot forward to your dribbling hand."
Body flexed slightly at knees, hips, waist, with slight forward lean	"Stay low."
Fingers and thumbs spread, five finger pads touching ball	"Cup the ball — let your fingertips push the ball."
Wave (yo-yo) action with hand on ball used to push ball to the floor	"Wave to the ball."
Contact with ball at about waist level	"Contact the ball around your waist."
Ball bounces back to waist level	"Give the ball enough power that it comes back up to your waist, but not too much power."

Difficulties to Watch For

If...	Then...
Child uses a hand-slapping motion with limited force production.	Ask the child to imitate waving goodbye to the ball.
Child looks at the ball while dribbling rather than looking forward.	While dribbling, have the child follow a partner (follow the leader).
Ball controls the child, not the other way around (i.e., the child follows the ball erratically).	Have the child ease up on the force pushing the ball down — tell him or her to have soft hands.
Child applies inconsistent or inappropriate force to the ball.	Vary the weight of the ball to allow the child to experiment with force production.
Child uses palm instead of finger pads to contact ball.	While a partner holds the ball from the bottom, the child pushes with finger pads on the ball.

To view and analyze video for this skill, and all the skills in this manual online, please visit:
➤ **www.phecanada.ca**

What Has Worked in Real Life

When I first met Bradley he was in grade one, so he had to be about six years old. He had an older brother who was in grade three. I worked with Bradley because he was identified as having a developmental delay. When Bradley's brother joined the basketball team in grade five, Bradley came to all the practices. He sat on the bench as our "good luck" charm. He knew all the players. He would high-five the players as they came off the court. Bradley was a part of our team. The next year, Bradley, again, joined the bench. He wasn't on the team (he needed to be in grade five), but he faithfully came to every game. In the meantime, he practised his dribbling and shooting in anticipation of trying out. When Bradley finally tried out in grade five, he had "paid his dues" — he made the team. He never missed a practice. Bradley wasn't the fastest player, and he wasn't the best shot. But he was a member of our basketball team. When we played, everyone knew Bradley. He would encourage his teammates. He could remember scores from game to game, so he told me when the team was doing well and also when the team was not doing so well. One tournament, Bradley got the ball. He dribbled down the court as the players guarded him, and he scored. Bradley came off the court with the biggest smile, shouting, "I scored!" The crowd went crazy! That same tournament, Bradley had a huge fan group that started shouting, "Bradley! Bradley!" He smiled, even blushed, at the fact that these people were cheering for him. It was quite a moment.

Activities for the Controlled DRIBBLE (Hands)

Exploring the Dribble

Skill: Dribbling
Children: Individual
Equipment: One basketball or bouncing playground ball per child
Area: Gymnasium
Activity: Ask the children if they can dribble the ball . . .

- with your right hand?
- with your left hand?
- while moving forward, backward, sideways and diagonally?
- with one hand and then the other?
- in one place?
- with your eyes closed?
- with a really high bounce?
- close to the floor?
- across your body?
- around your body?
- in a zigzag pattern?
- with one hand while touching the floor with the other?
- while walking or jogging around the ball, keeping it in one place?
- with your left hand while high-fiving other players with your right hand?
- while switching dribbling hands?
- in a circle around your body without moving your feet (clockwise, counterclockwise)?
- while standing in a forward stride position, moving the ball around and under the front leg?
- using a yo-yo motion?
- while standing in a straddle position, moving the ball in a figure eight through your legs?
- in time to the music?
- with one ball in each hand?
- with the hand you write with?
- with the hand you don't write with?

Stationary Dribble

Skill: Dribbling
Children: Individual
Equipment: One basketball or bouncing playground ball per child
Area: Gymnasium
Activity: Children start dribbling in place from double-kneeling position, to single-kneeling position, to standing position.

Cross the Line

Skills: Dribbling, walking, running, changing direction
Children: Individual
Equipment: One basketball or bouncing playground ball per child
Area: Gymnasium
Activity: Using existing lines on the gymnasium floor, children dribble throughout the gym, changing dribbling hands each time they cross over a line. For a greater challenge have the children run while dribbling.

COMBINATIONS OF GAMES SKILLS

COVER (guard), DODGE and INTERCEPT

Cover or Guard: *a defensive skill in which a player(s) strategically travels alongside an opponent(s) so that player(s) is less likely to retain an object or gain an advantage.*

Dodge *is an offensive skill wherein a player attempts to free themselves from the opposition.*

Intercept: *an offensive skill in which a player takes control of the ball or object away from the opposition..*

A *Characteristics of
the mature COVER or GUARD*

Characteristics of the mature COVER or GUARD	Cue Words for Children
(Touch or Flag)	
Maintain slightly bent knees and elbows, head up, back straight, weight on balls of both feet	Ready for action
Generally, keep on the goal side of your opponent	Self between opponent and own goal
Consistently travel near or alongside the person you are assigned to cover in order to fulfill your specific objective (e.g., to prevent them from shooting, delay their forward progress, or channel them towards the sideline)	Stay as near or alongside as necessary
Use walking, shuffles, jogs, backwards and/or forward runs to maintain coverage	Effectively move in a variety of ways to maintain coverage.
React and adjust your coverage position based on the moves (e.g., speed, directions) of your opponent	React and adjust to your coverage
Maintain balance and appropriate use of quickness and speed to apply the desired level of coverage	Be balanced and quick
Alter the level of coverage (proximity) according to circumstances. For example, cover more closely if your opponent is close to your goal or	Adjust coverage to the need

basket with or without the ball and if you are trying to preventthem from gaining possession of the ball

Maintain visual focus on both the person whom you are covering and the other important features of the game (e.g., the location of the ball and other players)

Focus on both your opponent and the important elements of the action

Contribute to team coverage by moving with your teammates in the mid-field area to minimize your opponent's forward progress

Contribute to your team's coverage

B. Sample Lead-Up Games for COVER, DODGE

Gold Rush

Purpose: Cover, dodge, and tag

Equipment: Beanbags (20-30), 30 cones for marking boundaries and "jail".

Participants: All

Area: Large field space

Description:

- Participants are in two equal teams
- Mark an end line and place beanbags behind the end line on each side
- Teams are to try and get the beanbags from the opponents' side, but once they cross the center line, they are able to be tagged by opponents and then they are sent to a restricted area ("jail") that is on the right side of the gym or field. Every 2-3 minutes a whistle is blown signaling that those in "jail" are free and can return to the playing area.
- Once a player has passed their opponents end line, they are able to either grab some beanbags or tag a prisoner to get out of jail, but they cannot do both.
- If they grab beanbags, they must try to make their way back on their side. And when they cross the safety zone (end line) they can get tagged again.

Modifications: Play a similar version called "Energy" in which a player who leaves their end line after an opponent has more "energy" and therefore can tag that player (who must then go to the "jail") – but be careful, others might have more energy than you!

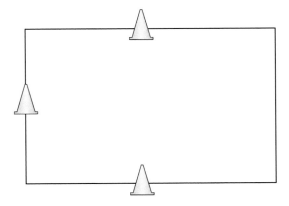

Triangle Soup

Source: *www.playsport.net*

Purpose: Cover, pass, catch (or trap), and dodge

Equipment: Ball or implement for passing, 3 cones per group, and pinnies.

Area: Large field space with ample space for each group.

Description:
- One group of four per grid as above (Three players on offense and one on defense). The person on offense puts on a pinnie.
- Offensive players work on "give-and-go" by attempting to complete a successful pass to the offensive player with the pinnie and then receive a successful pass back. After this, the player with the pinnie must then run to a different pylon.
- Change defenders if and when the offensive players have thrown to the player with the pinnie and received a pass back at all 3 cones.
- Once a defensive player gets possession they become offense and the person with pinnie becomes the defender
- Discuss the role of movement "off-the-ball" to create space and how to protect space as a defender.

Modifications:
- Play passive defense to start then change roles if defender can intercept a pass (no tackling).
- Play using hands, then feet, and then alternate between hands and feet (for example, if player with pinnie received the ball from a throw, they must send it away with a kick and vice versa).

Four Lines Pass and Go

Purpose: Cover, pass, catch (or trap), and dodge

Equipment: Ball or implement for passing and 4 cones per group to mark the square.

Participants: In groups of 4, each in a square playing area (about 5m2).

Area: Large field space with ample space for each group.

Description:
- To begin the game, one player is chosen to remain inside the square while the other three players must choose a corner of the square from which to begin. Players cannot dribble the ball; they can only control the ball and then pass it to an open teammate. Essentially, the player in the middle of the square is free to move anywhere he/she thinks would be an effective place to intercept the ball. The remaining three players are only allowed to move from corner to corner along the lines of the square.
- In order to initiate game play, one player on the outside of the square begins with the ball. This player must pass the ball from his/her corner to another teammate who is moving along the edges of the square trying to get open for a pass.
- If the player in the middle of the square intercepts another player's pass, these two players must switch places.
- If a player kicks the ball outside of the square then he/she must switch places with the middle person.

Hoopster

Purpose: Cover, Pass, Catch (or Trap), and Dodge

Equipment: Ball or implement for passing, 2 large hula-hoops, and 4 cones per group to mark the square.

Participants: In teams of 3-6 participants playing another team.

Area: Large field space with ample space for each game (about 15m x 7m).

Description:
- One game consists of two teams with four players on each.
- One player (the hoopster) from each team stands in a hoop (or in the end zone).
Regularly switch hoopsters.
- Players advance the ball by passing to each other but must pass within five seconds and may only take a maximum of two steps with the ball.
- The player with the ball tries to pass to another teammate with the ultimate goal of earning a point by passing to the hoopster standing in the hoop or end zone.

Modifications:
- Play 3v3, 5v5, or 6v6
- Do not have a designated hoopster. Allow any one player to enter the hoop (or end zone) whenever they feel it is necessary. Consider requiring a minimum number of passes before a pass to the hoopster can be attempted.
- After playing for a while, have participants in each game "modify" the game based on the restrictions placed on them by rolling the "dice." For example, the game could be modified in the following way based on the number rolled by the "dice."
- Can not use hands
- Divide into 3 teams and play 3-team soccer
- Play inside a circle
- Have at least 2 ways to score
- Add a bonus point rule
- Everyone must touch object to score

Such modifications made by students demonstrates how students can "apply" their knowledge of invasion games by using the modification to come up with a new invasion game.

Can't Touch This

Source: *www.playsport.net*

Purpose: Cover, pass, catch (or trap), and dodge

Equipment: Object to safely throw (e.g., ball or Frisbee), cones for marking boundaries, and pinnies to identify teams.

Participants: Teams of 3-5

Area: Play within a space approximately 20m x 10m.

Description: Each team has an end. The offensive team is trying to pass the object 5 times in a row. The defensive team is trying to block and gain possession of the Frisbee. Players cannot move when they have the Frisbee. If a team gets 5 passes in a row they score 1 point. If after 5 passes, you can throw the Frisbee to a partner and he/she catches it in the end zone, than the team gets a bonus 1 point. The teams do not have to immediately score the bonus point; they can keep passing between teammates. After point is gained, possession of the Frisbee goes to the other team. Players cannot grab or knock the Frisbee from someone's hands.

Modifications: Add a pin to one of the each of the sides. Teams can now score a point by hitting over either of other team's pins.

One-Line-of-Scrimmage Touch Football

Purpose: Cover, pass, catch, dodge, and tackle (tag or flag)

Equipment: Object to safely throw (e.g., football or Frisbee), cones for marking boundaries, and pinnies to identify teams.

Participants: Teams of 4

Area: Mark out one playing area for each group of 8 (in teams of 4) about 10m wide and 10 m long (that includes a 5 m long end zone).

Description: For every play, the ball is placed at the 10 yard (3 m) line. Positions will be a quarterback (who self-snaps), two receivers, and one running back. Alternate positions (including quarterback) every play (or series of 3 plays). Each team meets a maximum of 20 seconds to call their next play. When the quarterback yells hike and self-snaps the ball, they carry out their planned play. The defense (person to person defense) tries to prevent the offensive team from running or throwing successfully into the end zone for a score. The offensive team gets 3 plays (downs) to score a touchdown. The two sides then switch from offense to defense (and vice versa). After this game, play another team.

Modifications: Add another player per team. Make the end zone larger or smaller. Allow the line of scrimmage to change according to where the play ends.

Four versus Four Touch and Pass Only Rugby

Purpose: Pass (underhand), catch, dodge, and tackle (tag or flag)

Participants: Teams of 3-6

Equipment: Object to safely throw (e.g., football or Frisbee), cones for marking boundaries, and pinnies to identify teams.

Area: Mark out one playing area for each group of 8 (in teams of 4) about 10m wide and 10m long (that includes a 5m long end zone).

Description:

- Play two-hand touch above the waist rugby in which players can only run and pass underhand and backward (lateral) from the ball. Remember that in rugby, there is no blocking as in football. In fact, all players on the ball carrying team must be behind the line of the ball.

- Once the ball carrier is tagged by a defensive player the ball is dead. All defensive players must quickly move on their side of the ball at least 1 m away from the ball. The tagged team gets to begin play from that point (when the ball is lifted from the ground) after a maximum of 5 seconds as a dead ball

- If a player runs out of bounds, it is the other team's ball.

- After being tagged 5 times without crossing the goal line, the defensive team takes over on offense.

- If a player advances (runs) the ball over the opponent's goal line without being tackled (touched), their team earns 6 points (a try) and the other team takes over from their 20m line.

- When passing, remember to lead the player to whom you are throwing so they can catch the pass in stride. When passing, try to point the nose of the ball and spin it to a teammate for the most speedy and accurate results.

Modification: Allow the ball carrier to run a maximum of 5 steps before passing. Use more or less players and alter the field size. Play without goal lines and instead simply require 6 passes in a row with no tackles to score a try (6 points).

RECEIVE (Trap or Catch) and DRIBBLE

Refer to page 90 for the mature catch and page 95 for characteristics of the mature trap or catch

A. Sample Activities for TRAPPING and DRIBBLING

Trapping:

Can you:

- Trap a low self-tossed ball? With the sole of your foot? In-step? Thigh and then foot? Chest and then foot? Can you do the same with a higher tossed ball?
- Throw the ball against the wall five times and use a different trap to control the ball on each one?
- Trap the ball using those various traps when the ball is rolled, tossed, or kicked from a partner? When should you use a certain body part to trap the ball?
- Kick the ball back and forth with a partner at various heights and see how quickly you can trap and control the ball?

B. Activities for TRAPPING and DRIBBLING

Dribble Tag Games

A. **Clap Tag:** In a prescribed area, everyone dribbles a ball except 2-3 who are the taggers. Once tagged, a player stands with their ball placed on the floor and between their legs and begins clapping to indicate they need someone to "free" them. To be "freed," a dribbling (untagged) player must pass their ball up to a tagged player so they can catch it and toss it back to the kicker. They are then free to continue dribbling. Focus on communication, change of pace, lead passing, and changing directions.

B. **Everybody's It:** All players dribble a ball within a prescribed playing area. As they each dribble they try to tag others gently on the back while avoiding being tagged. Each time they tag another they earn a point and each time they are tagged they lose one point (without going below 0).

C. **Knock-On:** Each player dribbles in a confined group area and tries to knock the ball of the others out of the prescribed playing area while maintaining possession of their own. Once knocked out, the player must dribble around the prescribed playing area once before coming back in.

D. **Pirates:** Two individuals are taggers (without a ball) and can only skip, hop, or side shuffle. Everyone else has a ball and dribbles it in the prescribed playing area. If a person is tagged they become the pirate and the pirate takes their ball and continues dribbling.

Facing Lines (Foot Shooting)

Purpose: Shooting and Trapping (and catching/goal-keeping if desired)

Equipment: One ball per person and cones for marking goals or targets.

Participants: Two groups of 10-15 on opposite sides.

Area: about 40m²

Description:

A. Arrange two lines of students facing each other with approximately 10m between them. Between the two lines place 10 pylons (about 3m apart) in a parallel line to serve as goals. Have one line of students start with a ball.

B. Students shoot their ball through the goals (pylons) from a safe distance. They then trap or retrieve balls

Modified Territorial Game

(e.g., soccer, lacrosse, basketball, hockey)

Purpose: Shooting, dribbling, rebounding, kicking, passing, and catching

Equipment: 1 ball/game and cones for marking boundaries and goals

Participants: Teams of 2-6

Area: about 15-20m wide and 20-40m long

Description: Play a small-sided territorial game with fewer players and with modified rules and objectives. For example:

a. It is highly recommended to play most territorial games in small-sided teams of 2-6 depending on the game.

b. Score only by either striking a cone, dribbling across the goal line to score, or by having the ball roll across the goal line.

c. Modify the size of the goal, field, or ball.

d. Use fewer defenders or do not use any goalies (e.g., 3 attackers versus 2 defenders and a goalie). Rotate.

e. Limit to only a certain number of touches on the ball or time with the ball.

f. Play an invasion game like soccer with several (e.g., none) zones and restrict how many players from each team may be in a zone at once (e.g., other than in goalie box, only 1 player per team can be in a zone).

g. Play with 1 – 2 sideline players to teach the idea of spread or width.

h. Add another ball or more teams and goals to a game. For example, in a four-goal territorial game four nets are set up at four corners to form a square. There needs to be 4 equal teams of 5 or more. Of the 5 players, one is a defender and one is a goalie; the rest of the team are attackers or defenders (as they choose). Each team starts with a ball and using soccer skills, attempt to score on any of the other 3 nets while preventing the other teams from scoring on their net. Teams should keep track of their goal total; once the balls are in play they are all live.

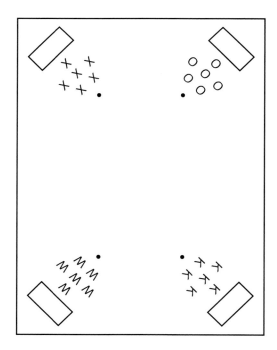

RECEIVE (Catch, Trap) and PASS

A. Activities for RECEIVING and PASSING

Sample Guided Discovery Activities

Can you pass:

1. At different targets and distances? At a moving target? High? Low? Soft? Hard? Slow? Fast?
2. Without using your legs? When leading with the foot/leg on the same side of the body as the passing arm? Without using your hips or shoulders? Why is leading with the opposite foot and transferring weight forward so important?
3. Another object (e.g., disc, whiffleball, football, baseball)?
4. To a partner? As far as your partner? The same way as your partner?
5. When combining the pass with other skills? After catching or fielding a ground ball? While jumping? While walking this way? That way? While running and/or twisting? Why is this difficult? How does such movement while throwing influence the flight of the ball? Why is it so important to have your body stable and shoulders parallel to the target when you release the ball?

Important Variations for Fielding (Relocating and Catching) a Fly Ball

- Instead of the "gorilla stance," begin in the "ready position."
- Move quickly to position the body square to the ball and slightly behind the anticipated meeting (fielding) point.
- Raise the glove towards the ball so the fingers face upwards while keeping the other hand nearby in order to trap the ball in as it enters the glove.

Can you catch or field:

1. With your arms in different positions (e.g., straight, bent)? Without making any sound? Without moving your   legs or feet? While seated, lying down, jumping, walking, or jogging?
2. With one hand, with two hands? With only the arms, chest, or both?
3. From overhead? Underhand? From your side?
4. High, low, hard, soft, and other angles?
5. From a self-toss? From a ball rebounding off the wall? From a partner toss or throw? The same way as your partner? While holding hands with a partner?
6. Another object (e.g., disc, whiffleball, football, baseball) or ball size?

Throwing and Fielding with Back-Up

Purpose: Throwing, fielding, and backing-up the fielder.

Equipment: Balls (1-2 per group) to throw, ball gloves (if a hard ball is used).

Participants: Groups of 7.

Area: Large field space with ample space for each group.

Description: Have one thrower (or striker), two fielders (spread out) and one back-up fielder behind each fielder (in the following formation). The thrower throws (or strikes) a ball in a variety of flight paths (high, low, line drives, rolling, bouncing) in the vicinity of the first fielder. This is then repeated for the other fielder (alternate throws to fielders 1 and 2). Once the ball is fielded and controlled, it is thrown overhead to the catcher who then rolls the ball underhand back to the thrower. If the ball gets past the fielder, the back-up fielder fields and controls the ball and throws it to their catcher. Throw ten at each fielder before each player rotates to a new position within their sub-group (X1 or X2).

Modifications: Use a variety of balls and striking implements. Have X1 and X2 co-operate to see how many of the 20 ground balls they can field, control, and safely throw to their catcher.

Safety Tip (if applicable): Ensure that there is a safe distance from the thrower and fielders and between fielders (X1 and X2). Remind all players to be attentive and the thrower to throw (or strike) only when the fielders are clearly ready.

Five Hundred

Purpose: Throwing (and striking if desired) and fielding

Equipment: 1-2 balls appropriate for throwing and fielding (and a bat if desired) per group.

Participants: In groups of 4-5

Area: Large field space with ample space for each group.

Description: In groups of 4-5 in a large playing area (each group must begin each play from a central position and proceed outwards). One person throws (or strikes) to the others (every 2nd throw must be along the ground) who compete with one another to field the ball. Once legally fielded and controlled, the ball is rolled back to the thrower/striker. If a player fields (catches) a ball in the air, he/she receives 100 points. If a player fields a ball travelling along the ground, he/she receives 50 points. Points are not deducted if the fielder misplays the ball. The first participant to 500 becomes the thrower (or striker).

Modifications: To minimize competition, each fielder can be designated a certain zone from which to field. Various striking implements or ball types can be used. Eliminate the rule requiring a ground ball on alternating throws.

Safety Tip (if applicable): Ensure that each group stays within their playing area and that balls being rolled back to the thrower (or striker) are not thrown high and overhead.

Two Versus Four Throw-and-Field Softball

Purpose: Throwing (and striking if desired) and fielding

Equipment: Four bases and 1-2 balls appropriate for throwing and fielding per group.

Participants: In groups of 6

Area: Large field space with ample space for each group.

Description: Four bases (e.g., cones) are set-up in a diamond formation. Two individuals will go up to throw (or bat). The other four players will take positions in the "field". The first thrower steps on home base and performs a throw of the ball so it lands legally in the field of play. The fielders must field (retrieve) the ball and pass it successfully (along the ground so it can be fielded from the ground) to each member of the fielding team. During this time the batter is running around the "bases", with the goal of getting home. If the batter successfully gets "home" before each fielder has caught the ball then a run is scored. Each thrower (e.g., batter) has two opportunities to throw (or bat) before two new throwers become the throwing (batting) team.

Modifications: Instead of throwing to begin each play, have the thrower at the plate bat off of a stationary tee, strike with the hand, or strike a ball underhand tossed from a safe distance by a peer.

Instead of using four bases, use two bases (or wickets as in cricket) with one thrower (or batter) at each. On each throw or strike, each "thrower" must exchange spots (from one base to the other) as many times as possible before all of the fielders have fielded the ball.

Safety Tips (if applicable):

- If more than one of these activities is performed at once, pylons should be arranged so that the different "home plates" (up to four) are in the center; therefore, throwing (or batting) will occur outwards.
- "Heads" must be yelled if a ball is hit foul and could be dangerous. If students hear this, they must put their hands over their head.
- If batting instead of throwing the initial ball, consider having students just "meet the ball" in more of a bunting approach instead of taking a full swing.
- In order to foster greater mastery (intrinsic motivation), do not keep score and just encourage teammates to provide positive and constructive feedback to their peers.

In-Coming

(Retrieved from *www.ophea/Ophea.net/activityideain-coming.cfm* on May 8, 2009; cited from *www.playsport.net*)

Purpose: Throwing (and striking if desired) and fielding

Equipment: 4 hula hoops, 4 racquets, 4 bins of balls

Participants: In groups of 6

Area: Large field space with ample space for each group.

Description: In this game, students learn tactical awareness and how to throw (or hit) and field for control and accuracy. Variations of the game can incorporate catching or modifying the type of throw or strike. To play:

- Divide students into 4-6 teams with 4-5 players per team. Each group occupies a corner of the large square playing area.
- Create four zones in the center of the square, each marked with a bin of balls and a hula hoop.
- The first player runs toward his/her designated bin. As she/he collect a ball, this player steps in the hoop, and attempts to return one ball to his/her corner by striking it with his/her hand.
- Team members field the ball and then pass it along the ground to each other before placing it in a hoop located in their corner.
- The batter (hand-striker) then runs to the back of his/her line and tags the next player on the team to go.
- Time each team to find out how long it takes them to put all the balls in the hoop and encourage them to beat their time on consecutive trials.

Modifications:
- Fielders in the corner attempt to catch the ball using only pylons and cannot use their hands to place the balls in the hoops.
- Modify the object being struck, the type of implement using to throw or strike (e.g., bat or racquet), or size of the playing field.

Safety Tip (if applicable): Ensure that there is ample space if playing several games of this at the same time. Require that the ball remain in their respective playing area to be a legal throw or strike.

Chapter 7: *Planning and Assessment Strategies*

Traditional theoretic models of the instructional process presents assessment and planning within a linear relationship (see Figure 3). In such a model, planning is followed by teaching, which is in turn followed by assessment (Rink, 2010). Within such dated models, assessment was entirely summative in nature, usually implemented for strictly evaluative purposes.

Figure 3: Traditional Model of Instructional Process.

Today, assessment is more easily visualized as an ever-present element within a planning and teaching cycle (see Figure 4). Within such a cycle, pre-assessments allow teachers and students to have a better initial understanding about students' learning needs. For example, assessing students before instruction allows teachers to have a surer understanding of their students' pre-existing knowledge – an essential piece of information in constructivist educational paradigms (Crotty, 2005). With or without this initial information, physical education teachers should select outcomes to teach (rather than particular movement activities) and then select the most appropriate movement experiences to address those outcomes. When planning to teach these outcomes, it is especially important that teachers answer the question, "How will I know that students learned the outcomes I set out to teach them?" In doing so, teachers can set standards and criteria and make decisions about the best ways to collect this important information. While students are then engaged in teaching and learning activities, teachers must endeavor to provide students with feedback that satisfies the "Four C's of Assessment" (see Figure 5). Only after students have been given ample opportunity to develop an understanding of the outcomes, whether they are psychomotor, cognitive, or affective, should teachers introduce summative assessments. With the results of the summative assessments, teachers are then able to evaluate students and set a direction for the teaching and learning of future outcomes.

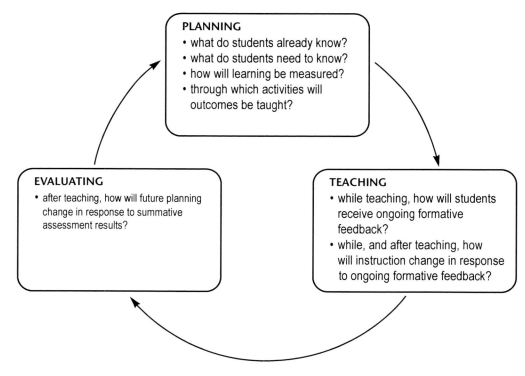

Figure 4: "Modern" Model of Instructional Process

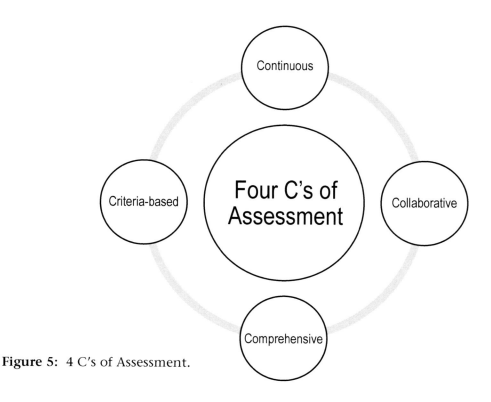

Figure 5: 4 C's of Assessment.

Planning to Teach Fundamental Movement Skills

The teaching and learning of fundamental movement skills ought to occur within physical education for the entirety of students' educational years. While this is especially true for students in the elementary years, as mentioned in Chapters One and Two, various fundamental and specialized movement skills should be focused on during the Long Term Athlete Development's (LTAD; Canadian Sport Centres, 2005) Active Start (females and males ages 0-6), FUNdamentals (females ages 6-8 and males ages 6-9), and Learning to Train (females ages 8-11 and males ages 8-11) stages. These fundamental movements skills, as they are clearly aligned with provincial curricular outcomes, should be taught and learned throughout the school year. Consequently, teachers must adequately consider fundamental movement skills when they plan. A sample lesson plan template is included in Table 6.

Individualized Education Plans (IEPs)

All children with disabilities should have an individualized education plan (IEP) in an educational context. An IEP is:

- a written plan describing the special education program and/or services required by a student participant, based on a thorough assessment of the participant's strengths and needs — that is, the strengths and needs that affect the student's ability to learn and to demonstrate learning;

- a record of the particular accommodations needed to help the student achieve his or her learning expectations, given the student's identified learning strengths and needs;

- a working document that identifies learning expectations that are modified from the expectations for the age-appropriate grade level in a particular subject or course, as outlined in the Ministry of Education's curriculum policy documents;

- a working document that identifies alternative expectations, if required, in program areas not represented in the curriculum;

- a record of the specific knowledge and skills to be assessed and evaluated for the purpose of reporting student achievement of modified or alternative expectations; and

- an accountability tool for the student, the student's parents and everyone who has responsibilities under the plan for helping the student meet the stated goals and learning expectations as the student progresses through the curriculum.

Physical education is an integral part of every child's education and should be included (by law) in every IEP, although lack of resources may prohibit this in reality. It is important for planning and evaluation purposes that each lesson plan and task relate back to the child's IEP goals. Continual assessment against the IEP goals is necessary.

In the sporting context, a formal individualized plan is less common. The principles are the same, with the child's family, coaches and instructors setting goals and parameters that guide the delivery of instruction and achievement for that season.

* *It is important to note that some children (e.g., children with DCD or ADHD) may not have been diagnosed by a physician yet or are waiting to be assessed by a psychologist; however, they are included in physical education and have varying educational and social needs. As a result, an IEP may not exist for some children.*

Name:		Date:	Grade:	Movement Category:
Specific Curriculum Outcomes(s):			Fundamental Movement Skill(s):	

Class Context (class size, skill level, students with special needs, prior learning, etc.):

Equipment:

psychomotor, cognitive, and/or affective

e.g., dance, basic movement

Safety Considerations:

from safety guidelines document

References and Resources:

Time:	Learning Experiences: (e.g., activities, strategies)	Teaching Points: (e.g., cues, questions)	Modifications: (e.g., extensions, challenges)
	Introduction/Warm-up		
		Is active, informs students of learning outcomes and relevance of lesson, and is directly related to learning outcomes.	
	Learning Activities/Teaching Strategies		
		allow for exploration, refinement, and application of learning content	
	Closure/Cool Down		
		review key learnings from lesson	
Assessment:		How will you know students learned what you taught?	

Post Lesson Reflections:

Strengths of Lesson	*Weaknesses of Lesson*

Table 6: Sample Lesson Plan Template.

Defining Assessment

It is important that physical education teachers have a strong understanding of assessment, especially with respect to the introduction and implementation of sound assessment practices. Such an understanding necessitates knowledge of various 'types' of assessment. For example, some more commonly and recently recognized assessment labels include formative assessment, summative assessment, and authentic assessment (Black, Harrison, Lee, Marshall, & Wiliam, 2000; Black & Wiliam, 2009; Lund & Kirk, 2010). Other commonly employed labels include alternative assessment, criterion-based assessment, standardized assessment, and evaluation (Metzler, 2005; Parkay, Hass, & Anctil, 2010).

Most simply, assessment can be defined as the collection of information about students' performance (Pangrazi & Beighle, 2010). Assessment is one of the most important components of teaching; it is truly the ideal means in which "to determine how much student learning occurs relative to the intended outcomes of instruction" (Metzler, 2000, p. 47). Metzler (2000) further explains that there are three primary purposes to assessment, including:

- To describe how much learning has occurred over a period of instructional time,
- To judge or evaluate the quality of that learning, and
- To make decisions about how to improve learning based on that gathered information.

FORMATIVE ASSESSMENT. Formative assessment is often also labeled assessment *for* learning. It generally occurs during a unit or program of instruction. Information gathered during such assessment is used to inform teachers and students about progress relative to learning outcomes achieved up until that moment in time; this information is then, in turn, used to inform future teaching and learning. An example of formative assessment would be when a physical education teacher enables students to use an observation checklist to assess their peers (and provide feedback) for a particular movement task. Formative assessment, among other things, involves students in assessment and goal setting, motivates students to improve their performance, and allows teachers to make judgments about the effectiveness of their own teaching (Rink, 2010).

SUMMATIVE ASSESSMENT. Summative assessment is often also labeled assessment *of* learning. It generally occurs at the conclusion of a unit or program of instruction. Information gathered during such assessment is used to inform teachers so that they may make a judgment (i.e., an evaluation) of students' progress relative to learning outcomes achieved up until that moment in time; this information is then, in turn, shared with students and their parents/guardians and/or submitted as data into school records (Earl, 2003). An example of summative assessment would be when a physical education teacher assigns and grades a written test to assess students' knowledge at the end of a games unit. These assessments and subsequent evaluations are primarily used "to measure achievement and to compare students with others or with a defined standard established by the teacher" (Rink, 2010, p. 242). Evaluating students relative to their peers is called norm-referenced evaluation and evaluating students relative to external stable standards is called criterion-referenced evaluation. Within outcomes-based programs, as those within Canada, evaluation within physical education is typically criterion-referenced.

AUTHENTIC ASSESSMENT. Authentic assessment is often also labeled performance-based assessment or performance assessment (Lund & Kirk, 2010; Metzler, 2005). Authentic assessment requires that students be given authentic (i.e., "real-life" or simulated) opportunities to demonstrate their learning of various outcomes. An example of an authentic assessment would be when a physical education teacher assesses students' ability to create a sport-specific exercise-training program or to apply game skills or strategies within games situations. Authentic assessments can be presented as formative or summative assessment tasks though they are more often utilized as a summative assessment practice.

Principles of Assessment

Assessment practices ought to be continuous, collaborative, comprehensive, and criteria-based. These four principles of assessment, herein labeled as the "4 C's of Assessment" (see Figure 1), are especially important for physical education teachers as they assess with the primary goal of enhancing student learning and the secondary goal of monitoring student achievement (Buck, Harrison, Lund, & Cook, 2007).

CONTINUOUS. Assessment needs to be continuous. It needs to occur throughout units or programs of instruction as an ongoing element. Unlike summative assessment that typically occurs at the end of a unit or program of instruction, the use of formative assessment practices during a unit or program of instruction allows students (and their teachers) to be made constantly aware of students' level of understanding. When students are not afforded continuous assessment practices by their physical education teachers, they are effectively only given feedback "after the fact" – when it is "too late" to improve. Similarly, when assessment is not continuous, physical education teachers are also not afforded opportunities to change, continue, or revisit instruction based on their students' revealed level of understanding. When assessment is continuous, summative assessments typically present no "surprises" to teachers and their students.

COLLABORATIVE. Assessment needs to be collaborative. While traditional assessments have relied mostly-to-completely on physical education teachers themselves (Lund & Tannehill, 2010), more recent "alternative" assessment practices recognize the importance of including students, their peers, and their parents/guardians in the assessment process. Again, this is especially relevant to formative assessment practices. Recognizing that the primary purpose of assessment is to provide students with information so that they can enhance their own learning (Graham, Holt/Hale, & Parker, 2007), people other than physical education teachers can contribute. For example, physical education teachers might engage students (e.g., through welcoming students' input into defining assessment tasks and standards), their peers (e.g., through encouraging, modeling, and scaffolding peer assessment procedures), and their parents/guardians (e.g., through two-way dissemination of students' progress).

COMPREHENSIVE. Assessment needs to be comprehensive. Comprehensive assessment requires that multiple methods of assessment be used to assess students' learning. Physical education teachers should use a broad range of assessment strategies so as to allow students multiple opportunities to demonstrate their knowledge of curricular outcomes. Traditional assessment strategies might include informal teacher observations, standardized skill tests, fitness tests, and written tests (Metzler, 2005) while more-recent assessment strategies might include the use of student journals, exit/entrance slips, authentic assessments, and self assessments (Graham et al., 2007). Furthermore, in order to be comprehensive, assessment practices must address all the curricular outcomes, rather than a select few.

CRITERIA-BASED. Assessment needs to be criteria-based. Given that students are typically assessed and evaluated against criterion-based standards drawn from provincial curricular outcomes, it is especially important that they be made aware of the criteria from which they are to be judged. Furthermore, when assessing students for evaluative purposes, it is also especially important that students be given criteria *before* they complete an assessment task. Such assessment criteria are often presented as rubrics or checklists with differing descriptors to signify different levels of understanding.

Assessing Outcomes

Physical education teachers are responsible for teaching students the outcomes as detailed within their provincial physical education curricula. Teachers are also required to assess students' understanding of these same outcomes. Within all provinces and territories, these curricular outcomes generally fall under one of three categories. They are related to the things students need to be able to do (i.e., psychomotor), be able to know (i.e., cognitive), and be able to value (i.e., affective). An example of a psychomotor outcome is "demonstrate motor skills in all movement categories using efficient and effective body mechanics," an example of a cognitive outcome is, "demonstrate a knowledge of the components and processes needed to develop and maintain a personal level of functional fitness," and an example of an affective outcome is, "demonstrate positive personal and social behaviours and interpersonal relationships" (Nova Scotia Education, 2010, p. 60).

FUNDAMENTAL MOVEMENT SKILLS AND CURRICULAR OUTCOMES. Though fundamental movement skills are, in many respects, the foundational "building blocks" for developing students' physical literacy, physical education teachers are nonetheless required to teach outcomes from their physical education curricula. That is, physical education teachers who teach fundamental movement skills should do so in accordance with the curricula to which they are bound. However, it is certainly not by accident that all provinces and territories have physical education programs (particularly those for elementary grades) that include psychomotor outcomes that are very clearly aligned with the teaching and learning of fundamental movement skills. For example, the fundamental movement skills from the Active Start and FUNdamentals stages are aligned with curricular outcomes from all provinces' and territories' curricula. Table 7 details sample outcomes, from most provinces and territories, aligned with various fundamental movement skills.

	LOCOMOTOR SKILLS (e.g., jump, run)	MANIPULATIVE SKILLS (e.g., kick, dribble)	STABILITY SKILLS (e.g., dodge, stand on one foot)
BC YK	Demonstrate proper ready position for locomotor movement skills	Demonstrate proper technique for performing specific manipulative movement skills including but not limited to the following…	Demonstrate proper technique for performing specific non-locomotor movement skills including but not limited to the following…
AB NWT NU	Perform locomotor skills through a variety of activities	Demonstrate ways to receive, retain and send an object, using a variety of body parts and implements, individually and with others	Perform nonlocomotor skills through a variety of activities
SK	Locomotor skills – Explore, express, and apply, a variety of ways to skillfully move the body through space while participating in movement activities…	Non-locomotor skills – Explore, express, and apply, with guidance, a variety of ways to skillfully move the body on the spot while participating in movement activities…	Manipulative skills – Explore, express, and apply, with guidance, a variety of ways to skillfully move objects while participating in movement activities…
MN	Demonstrate competency in basic transport skills in a variety of movement experiences	Demonstrate balancing in different ways at different levels and/or heights	Demonstrate competency in basic manipulative skills
ON	Perform a variety of locomotor movements, travelling in different directions and using different body parts	Perform a variety of static balances, using different body parts at different levels	Send objects of different shapes and sizes at different levels and in different ways, using different body parts
NB	Students will be expected to demonstrate running, jumping and throwing in a variety of ways	Students will be expected to select and perform locomotor and non locomotor skills in simple sequences, individually, and with a partner	Students will be expected to demonstrate ways to send and receive a variety of objects with and without equipment…
NS	Students will be expected to experience a variety of ways of moving in relation to a stationary partner or object	Students will be expected to demonstrate the use of movement sentences to explore balances and shapes	Students will be expected to demonstrate using the inside of the foot to send and collect a ball
NL	Demonstrate the mechanics of various locomotor skills	Demonstrate a variety and combinations of non-locomotor skills using a range of body joints and positions	Project a small object in a variety of ways

Table 7: Fundamental Movement Skills and Curricular Outcomes.

Assessing Fundamental Movement Skills

Physical education teachers can assess students' fundamental movement skills using the checklists available within this resource. For example, following are three separate sample checklists that might be utilized to assess students' locomotor (jump), manipulative (kick), and stability (balance on one foot) skills (Table 8). These checklists could be used by the teacher as an initial diagnostic assessment tool, they could be used (as a formative assessment tool) during a unit or program, or they could be used after instruction (as a summative assessment tool) focused on improving these fundamental movement skills.

Children's names	Components of the Jump (Locomotion)					
	Knees bent, shoulders forward, arms swing back	Forceful extension of hips, knees, ankles	Forward and upward arm thrust	Full body extension during flight	Balance landing with feet apart, knees bent, arms out	Arms reach forward in direction of flight
Rachel	✗	✗	✗	✓	✓	✗
Liam	✗	✓	✓	✓	✓	✓
Samantha	✓	✓	✓	✓	✓	✓
Darrell	✓	✗	✓	✓	✓	✓

Children's names	Components of the Kick (Manipulation)					
	Plant support foot beside the ball	Kicking leg swings freely from hip through arc toward the ball	Using instep, foot contacts ball at midline slightly below centre	Quick extension of knee on contact	Follow through with kicking leg toward target	Arms extended to side for balance
Bryce	✓	✗	✗	✓	✓	✓
Jillian	✗	✓	✓	✓	✓	✗
Kelly	✓	✓	✓	✓	✓	✓
Paul	✓	✗	✓	✓	✓	✓

Children's names	Components of the Stork Stand (Stability)					
	Head neutral, looking forward	Back straight	Arms straight and perpendicular to the ground	Weight on one foot	Sole of foot placed against inside of knee and thigh of opposite foot	Position held for three seconds
Eugenia	✓	✓	✓	✓	✓	✓
Mark	✓	✗	✓	✓	✓	✓
Courtney	✗	✗	✗	✓	✓	✗
Erik	✗	✓	✓	✓	✓	✓

Table 8: Sample Fundamental Movement Skills Checklists.

While this resource includes a number of checklists for fundamental movement skills, a number of other assessment tools might prove to be more appropriate for various teaching and learning contexts. For example, other possibilities for assessing students' fundamental movement skills include the use of exit slips, authentic assessments, and self-assessments (see Figures 6, 7, 8).

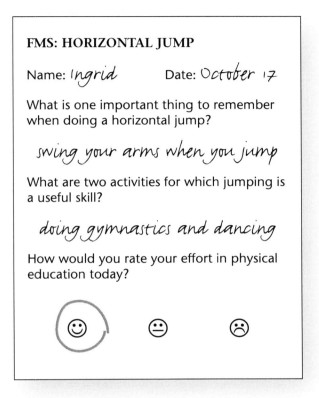

FMS: HORIZONTAL JUMP

Name: *Ingrid*   Date: *October 17*

What is one important thing to remember when doing a horizontal jump?

swing your arms when you jump

What are two activities for which jumping is a useful skill?

doing gymnastics and dancing

How would you rate your effort in physical education today?

☺   😐   ☹

Figure 6: Exit Slip for the Horizontal Jump (Locomotion).

FMS: KICKING	Name: Leah	Date: January 21

SCENARIO:	SET UP: ◈ - target, ⋏ - student, ❶ - ball
In groups of four, students will play Skittles. All students will defend their own target (with their feet) and will attack the other three targets (by kicking a ball).	◈ ⋏ ❶ ❷ ⋏ ◈
Required equipment: four targets and four balls.	◈ ⋏ ❸ ❹ ⋏ ◈

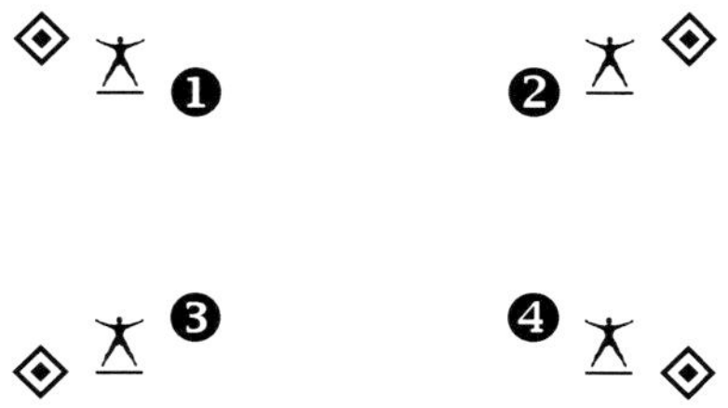

Always kicks with instep of foot, at or below centre of ball, following through towards target	Usually kicks with instep of foot, at or below centre of ball, following through towards target	Sometimes kicks with instep of foot, at or below centre of ball, following through towards target	Rarely kicks with instep of foot, at or below centre of ball, following through towards target

NOTES: Leah, you almost always seem to remember to use the inside of your foot to kick the ball when you have lots of time – good to see. When you get rushed, you seem to kick the ball without aiming for a target. Always remember to follow through towards your target. Great job today – especially with fair play!

Figure 7: Authentic Assessment for Kicking (Manipulation).

FMS: BALANCE ON ONE FOOT	Name: *Tyler*	Date: *March 16*	
Is your head in a neutral position and looking forward?		☑ YES	☐ NO
Is your back upright and straight?		☑ YES	☐ NO
Are your arms straight and perpendicular to the ground?		☑ YES	☐ NO
Is all of your weight on one foot?		☑ YES	☐ NO
Is the sole of your foot placed against the inside of the knee/thigh of the opposite foot?		☐ YES	☑ NO
Can you hold this position for at least three seconds?		☑ YES	☐ NO

Figure 8: Self-assessment for Balance on One foot (Stability).[1]

---

1   Self-assessments of fundamental movement skills can be much more easily facilitated with the employment of assistive technologies such as digital photographs or videos (e.g., through the use of Dartfish media technology). This sample self-assessment can be done in a much more genuine manner if students are afforded such opportunities to capture their own images.

REFERENCES

Allison, P. & Barrett, K. (2000). *Constructing children's physical education experiences: Understanding the content for teaching*. Boston: Allyn & Bacon.

Black, P., Harrison, C., Lee, C., Marshall, B., & Wiliam, D. (2000). *Working inside the black box: Assessment for learning in the classroom*. London: King's College.

Black, P., & Wiliam, D. (2009). Developing the theory of formative assessment. *Educational Assessment, Evaluation and Accountability, 21*(1), 5-31.

Brady, F. (2004). Children's organized sports: A developmental perspective. *Journal of Physical Education, Recreation & Dance, 75*(2), 35-41.

Buck, M., Harrison, J., Lund., J., & Cook, C. B. (2007). *Instructional strategies for secondary school physical education*. New York, NY: McGraw-Hill.

Butcher, J. E., & Eaton, W. O. (1989). Gross and fine motor proficiency in preschoolers: Relationships with free play behavior and activity levels. *Journal of Human Movement Studies, 16*, 27-36.

Canadian Sport Centres. (2005). *Long-Term Athlete Development resource paper V2*. Vancouver, BC: Canadian Sport Centres.

Centre for Inclusive Education. (2008) *http://www.edu.uwo.ca/inclusive_education/*.

Colvin, A. V., Egner-Markos, N. J., & Walker, P. (2000). In Wikgren S., Petit C. E. & Majersky L.W. (Eds.), *Teaching the nuts and bolts of physical education: Building basic movement skills*. Champaign, IL: Human Kinetics.

COPEC (Council of Physical Education for Children). (2000). *Physical activity for children: A statement of guidelines*. Virginia: National Association for Sport and Physical Education, an Association of the American Alliance for Health, Physical Education and Recreation.

Csikszentmihalyi, M. (1990). *Flow: The psychology of optimal experience*. New York, NY: Harper and Row.

Crotty, M. (2005). *The foundations of social research: Meaning and perspective in the research process*. Thousand Oaks, CA: Sage.

Doyle, P. (2001). *Game on*. Champaign, IL: Human Kinetics.

Earl, L. M. (2003). *Assessment as learning: Using classroom assessment to maximize student learning*. Thousand Oaks, CA: Sage.

Eckert, H. M. (1987). Motor development (3rd ed.). Indianapolis, IN: Benchmark Press, Inc.

Fisher, A., Reilly, J. J., Kelly, L. A., Montgomery, C., Williamson, A., Paton, J. Y., et al. (2005). Fundamental movement skills and habitual physical activity in young children. *Medicine & Science in Sports & Exercise, 37*(4), 684-688.

Gabbard, C. (2008). *Lifelong motor development* (5th ed.). San Francisco, CA: Pearson Benjamin Cummings.

Gallahue, D. L. (1989). *Understanding motor development: Infants, children, adolescents*. Indianapolis, IN: Benchmark Press.

Gallahue, D. L., & Donnelly, F. (2003). *Developmental physical education for all children* (4th ed.). Champaign, IL: Human Kinetics.

Goodwin, D.L., Gustafson, P., & Hamilton, B. (2006). The disability experience in physical education. In E. Singleton & A. Varpalotai (Eds.), *Issues, theories, and trends in Canadian secondary school physical education* (pp. 223-255). London, ON: The Althouse Press.

Graham, G., Holt, S. & Parker, M. (2007). *Children moving: A reflective approach to teaching physical education*. New York, NY: McGraw Hill Co. Publishers.

Hands, B. (2002). *How can we best measure fundamental movement skills?* Adelaide, Australia: Australian Council for Health Physical Education and Recreation.

Hart, M. A. (2005). Influence of a physical education methods course on elementary education majors' knowledge of fundamental movement skills. *Physical Educator, 62*(4), 198-204.

Hay, J., & Cote, J. (1998). An interactive model to teach motor skills. *Physical Educator, 55*(1), 50-56.

Haydn-Davies, D. (2005). How does the concept of physical literacy relate to what is and what could be the practice of physical education? *British Journal of Teaching Physical Education, 36*(3), 45-48.

Haywood, K., & Getchell, N. (1995). *Lifespan motor development* (3rd ed.). Champaign, IL: Human Kinetics.

Higgs, C., Balyi, I., Way, R., Cardinal, C., Norris, S., & Bluechardt, M. (2008). *Developing physical literacy: A guide for parent of children ages 0 to 12* (Supplement to Canadian Sport for Life). Vancouver, B.C.: Canadian Sport Centres.

Kentel, J. A., & Dobson, T. M. (2007). Beyond myopic visions of education: Revisiting movement literacy. *Physical Education & Sport Pedagogy, 12*(2), 145-162.

Killingbeck, M., Bowler, M., Golding, D., & Gammon, P. (2007). Physical education and physical literacy. *Physical Education Matters, 2*(2), 20-24.

Knowles, B. (2000). Learning to move: Coaches should learn all they can about how- and when young athletes develop fundamental movement skills. *Ski Racing, 33* (5), 16.

Laban, R. (1971). In Ullmann L. (Ed.), *Modern educational dance* (3rd ed.). London, UK: Macdonald and Evans.

Lacy, A. C., & Douglas, N. H. (2003). *Measurement and evaluation in physical education and exercise science* (4th ed.). San Francisco, CA: Benjamin Cummings.

Langton, T. W. (2007). Applying Laban's movement framework in elementary physical education. *Journal of Physical Education, Recreation & Dance, 78*(1), 17-24.

Lund, J. L., & Kirk, M. F. (2010). *Performance-based assessment for middle and high school physical education* (2nd ed.). Windsor, ON: Human Kinetics.

Lund, J. L., & Tannehill, D. (2010). *Standards-based physical education curriculum development.* Mississauga, ON: Jones and Bartlett.

Magill, R. A., & Anderson, D. I. (1996). Critical periods as optimal readiness for learning sports skills. In F. L. Smoll, & R. E. Smith (Eds.), *Children and youth in sport: A biopsychosocial perspective* (pp. 57-72). Dubuque, IA: Brown and Benchmark.

Malina, R. M., Bouchard, C., & Bar-Or, O. (2004). In Wright J. P., Feld M. (Eds.), *Growth, maturation, and physical activity* (2nd ed.). Champaign, IL: Human Kinetics.

Mandigo, J. L., Francis, N., Lodewyk, K., & Lopez, R. (2009). Physical literacy for educators. *Physical & Health Education Journal, 75*(3), 27-30.

Marsden, E., & Weston, C. (2007). Locating quality physical education in early years pedagogy. *Sport, Education & Society, 12*(4), 383-398.

Matsudo, V. K. R. (1996). Prediction of future athletic excellence. In O. Bar-Or (Ed.), *The child and adolescent athlete* (pp. 92-109). Oxford, UK: Blackwell Science.

Maude, P. (2001). *Physical children, active teaching: Investigating physical literacy.* Buckingham, PA: Open University Press.

McClenaghan, B. (1978). *Personalizing motor development for the elementary child* (No. SPO13522). South Carolina: University of South Carolina.

McKenzie, T. L., Sallis, J. F., Broyoles, S. L., Zive, M. M., Nader, P. R., Berry, C. C., et al. (2004). Childhood movement skills, predictors of physical activity in Anglo American and Mexican American adolescents. *Research Quarterly for Exercise & Sport, 73*, 238-244.

McPherson, B. D., & Brown, B. A. (1988). The structure, processes, and consequences of sport for children. In R. A. Magill, & M. J. Ash (Eds.), *Children in sport* (pp. 265-286). Champaign, IL: Human Kinetics.

Merleau-Ponty, M. (1962). *The primacy of perception* (Arleen Dallery Trans.). NW University Press.

Metzler, M. (2000). *Instructional models for physical education*. Needham Heights, MA: Allyn and Bacon.

Metzler, M. (2005). *Instructional models for physical education* (2nd ed.). Tempe, AZ: Halcomb Hathaway.

National Coaching Certification Program. (2009). In Coaching Association of Canada (Ed.), *NCCP fundamental movement skills: Improving children's lives through physical literacy* (First ed.). Canada: Coaching Association of Canada.

Nova Scotia Education. (2010). *Learning outcomes framework: Grades Primary-Six*. Halifax, NS: Nova Scotia Education.

Okely, A. D., & Booth, M. L. (2004). Mastery of fundamental movement skills among children in New South Wales: Prevalence and sociodemographic distribution. *Journal of Science & Medicine in Sport, 7*(3), 358-372.

Okely, A. D., Booth, M. L., & Chey, T. (2004). Relationships between body composition and fundamental movement skills among children and adolescents. *Research Quarterly for Exercise & Sport, 75*(3), 238-237.

Okely, A. D., Booth, M. L., & Patterson, J. W. (2001). Relationship of physical activity to fundamental movement skills among adolescents. *Medicine & Science in Sports & Exercise, 33*(11), 1899-1904.

Pangrazi, R., & Beighle, A. (2010). *Dynamic physical education for elementary school children* (16th ed.). San Francisco, CA: Benjamin Cummings.

Pangrazi, B., Chomokos, N., & Massoney, D. (1981). From theory to practice: A summary. *Motor development: Theory into practice.* (pp. 65-71) Monograph 3.

Parkay, G., Hass, G.J., & Anctil, E.J. (2010). *Curriculum leadership: Readings for developing quality educational programs* (9th ed.). Upper Saddle River, NJ: Allyn and Bacon.

Patterson, S. B., Anderson, A., & Klavora, P. (1997). Investigating the relationship between physical skill development and active living: A review of the literature. *CAHPERD Journal, 63*(4), 4-9.

Payne, V. G., & Isaacs, L. D. (2002). *Human motor development: A lifespan approach*. Boston, MA: McGraw-Hill.

Penney, D., & Chandler, T. (2000). A curriculum with connections? *British Journal of Teaching Physical Education, 31* (2), 37-40.

Raudsepp, L., & Paasuke, M. (1995). Gender differences in fundamental movement patterns, movement performances, and strength measurements in prepubertal children. *Pediatric Exercise Science, 7*, 294-304.

Raudsepp, L., & Pall, P. (2006). The relationship between fundamental motor skills and outside school physical activity of elementary school children. *Pediatric Exercise Science, 18*, 426-435.

Rink, J. (2010). *Teaching physical education for learning* (6th ed.). New York, NY: McGraw-Hill.

Rowland, T. (1998). Predicting athletic brilliancy or the futility of training till the salchows come home. *Pediatric Exercise Science, 10*, 197-201.

Sage, G. H. (1984). *Motor learning and performance: Principles to practice*. Dubuque, IA: William C. Brown.

Sanders, S., & Stork, S. (2001). What is the best way to teach young children about movement? What really works in the preschool classroom? (editorial) *Teaching Elementary Physical Education, 12*(5), 3-5.

Sartre, J. (1943). *Being and nothingness*. (Hazel Barnes Trans.). London: Methuen Publishers.

Schmidt, R. A. (1991). *Motor learning and performance: Principles to practice*. Champaign, IL: Human Kinetics.

Seefeldt, V. (1980). Developmental motor patterns: Implications for elementary school physical fitness. In C. H. Nadeau, W. R. Halliwell, K. M. Newell, & G. C. Roberts (Eds.), *Psychology of motor behavior and sport* (pp. 314-323). Champaign, IL: Human Kinetics.

Sheehan, D., & Katz, L. (2010). Using interactive fitness and exergames to develop physical literacy. *Physical and Health Education, 76*(1), 12-19.

Siedentop, D. (2001). *Introduction to physical education, fitness and sport*. Mountain View, CA: Mayfield.

Streicher, M. (1970). In Strutt B. E. (Ed.), *Reshaping physical education* (B. E. Strutt Trans.). Manchester, UK: Manchester University Press.

The Council on Physical Education for Children (COPEC, 2000). *http://ewhighered.mcgraw-hill.com/sites/dl/free/0073376450/666639/graham8_sample_ch03.pdf*.

Thomas, J. R., & French, K. E. (1985). Gender differences across age in motor perfomance: A meta-analysis. *Psychological Bulletin, 98*, 260-282.

UK Sports. (2002). *Game plan: A strategy for delivering government's sport and physical activity objectives*. Retrieved 1/3/2010, 2010, from http://www.sportdevelopment.info/index.php?option=com_content&view=article&id61:game-plan-a-strategy-for-delivering-governments-sport-and-physical-activityobjectives&catid=48:policy&Itemid=65 .

United Nations, 2007

van Beurden, E. (2003). Can we teach skill and activate children through primary school physical education lessons? "move it groove it" - a collaborative health promotion intervention. *Preventative Medicine, 36*, 493-503.

Wall, M., & Cote, J. (2007). Developmental activities that lead to drop out and investment in sport. *Physical Education & Sport Pedagogy, 12*(1), 77-87.

Wall, J. & Murray, N. (1994). *Children and movement: Physical education in the elementary school*. Dubuque: Wm.C. Brown Co. Publishers.

Wall, S., Rudsill, M., Goodway, J., & Parish, L. (2004). A comparison opf three movement settings on the development of fundamental motor skills in young children. *Journal of Sport and Exercise Physiology, 26*.

Whitehead, M. (2001). The concept of physical literacy. *European Journal of Physical Education, 6*(2), 127-138.

Whitehead, M. (July, 2005). *Developing physical literacy*. Unpublished manuscript.

Whitehead, M. (2007). Physical literacy: Philosophical considerations in relation to developing a sense of self, universality and propositional knowledge. *Sport, Ethics & Philosophy, 1*(3), 281-298.

Whitehead, M. (Ed.). (2010). *Physical literacy: Through the lifecourse*. New York, NY: Routledge.

Wright, J. & Burrows, L. (2006). Re-conceiving ability in physical education: A social analysis. *Sport, Education & Society, 11* (3), 275-291. 2006.

BIBLIOGRAPHY

Alberta Learning. (2000). *Physical education kindergarten to grade 12, 2000*. Edmonton, AB: Alberta Learning.

Department of Education, Newfoundland and Labrador. (2010). *Physical education, primary and elementary curriculum guide*. St. John's, Newfoundland: Department of Education.

Department of Education, Nova Scotia. (2003). *Learning outcomes framework: Physical education grades primary-6*. Halifax, NS: Department of Education.

Education New Brunswick. (2000). *Elementary physical education curriculum kindergarten – Grade 5*. Fredericton, NB: Education New Brunswick.

Manitoba Education. (2011). *Movement*. Retrieved March 17, 2011 from www.edu.gov.mb/k12/cur/physhlth/framework/movement.pdf

Ministry of Education, Ontario. (2010). *The Ontario curriculum grades 1-8: Health and physical education, interim edition (revised)*. Toronto, ON: Ministry of Education, Ontario.

Ministry of Education, Province of British Columbia. (2006). *Physical education grade 2: integrated resource package*. Vancouver, BC: Ministry of Education, Province of British Columbia.

Ministry of Education, Saskatchewan. (2010). *2010 Saskatchewan curriculum: Physical education 2*. Regina, SK: Ministry of Education, Saskatchewan.

NOTES

NOTES